U.S. HISTORY UNCENSORED

U.S. HISTORY UNCENSORED

What Your High School Textbook
Didn't Tell You

(A Curriculum Abstract For U.S. History,
1865 to the Present)

Carolyn L. Baker

iUniverse, Inc.
New York Lincoln Shanghai

U.S. HISTORY UNCENSORED
What Your High School Textbook Didn't Tell You

Copyright © 2006 by Carolyn L. Baker

All rights reserved. No part of this book may be used or reproduced by any means, graphic, electronic, or mechanical, including photocopying, recording, taping or by any information storage retrieval system without the written permission of the publisher except in the case of brief quotations embodied in critical articles and reviews.

iUniverse books may be ordered through booksellers or by contacting:

iUniverse
2021 Pine Lake Road, Suite 100
Lincoln, NE 68512
www.iuniverse.com
1-800-Authors (1-800-288-4677)

ISBN-13: 978-0-595-39586-6 (pbk)
ISBN-13: 978-0-595-83989-6 (ebk)
ISBN-10: 0-595-39586-4 (pbk)
ISBN-10: 0-595-83989-4 (ebk)

Printed in the United States of America

DEDICATION

To Norman Pollack, professor, mentor, and friend

CONTENTS

FOREWORD ix
INTRODUCTION xiii
PREFACE xxi

1: RECONSTRUCTION (1865-1876) 1
2: WESTWARD EXPANSION 7
3: WORSENING CONDITIONS IN RURAL AMERICA 11
4: URBAN AMERICA AND THE RISE OF THE ROBBER BARONS
   (1865-1914) 17
5: BLACKS IN WHITE AMERICA IN THE "GILDED AGE" 36
6: POLICING THE WORLD: THE DAWN OF IMPERIALISM 37
7: LIBERALISM, PROGRESSIVISM, NEO-LIBERALISM 48
8: WOMEN IN PROGRESSIVE AMERICA 54
9: THE BEGINNINGS OF WORLD DOMINATION 58
10: THE POLITICS OF PROSPERITY AND REACTION:
    THE 1920s 69
11: THE CRASH AND THE GREAT DEPRESSION 79
12: THE RISE OF FASCISM 89
13: WORLD WAR II 92
14: THE DOMESTIC EFFECTS OF U.S. INVOLVEMENT IN WORLD WAR II 95
15: THE BEGINNING OF THE COLD WAR 97
16: THE COLD WAR: THE ENDS JUSTIFY THE MEANS 101
17: FALLING DOMINOES IN SOUTHEAST ASIA 114
18: THE ASSASSINATION OF JOHN F. KENNEDY 119
19: THE CIVIL RIGHTS MOVEMENT: THE SECOND RECONSTRUCTION ...124
20: THE END OF THE VIETNAM WAR AND WATERGATE 131
21: THE CARTER PRESIDENCY 133
22: THE REAGAN-BUSH PRESIDENCY 135
23: HUD, HAMILTON, AND SOLARI: THE STORY OF CATHERINE AUSTIN FITTS 148
24: THE "IRAQGATE" SCANDAL 151
25: THE END OF THE COLD WAR AND THE LOOTING OF THE SOVIET UNION 153
26: CLINTON, MENA, NAFTA, AND THE DISSOLUTION OF THE TWO-PARTY SYSTEM 157
27: PREPARING FOR WORLD DOMINATION 163

28: THE NEW PEARL HARBOR 169
29: PEAK OIL AND GLOBAL RESOURCE WARS 177
30: ELECTIONS IN THE UNITED STATES 200
31: DISSENT IN THE UNITED STATES 207
32: OF NATURE'S WRATH, RACISM, AND RESOURCE WARS 210
33: IS THERE HOPE? 211

CONCLUSION 218
GLOSSARY OF TERMS 223
POSSIBLE OPPORTUNITIES FOR RE-MAKING OUR WORLD 225
A FEW ALTERNATIVE MEDIA LINKS 226

LIVING HISTORY

A Foreword

to

US History Uncensored:
What Your High School Textbook Didn't Tell
by Catherine Austin Fitts

I resisted learning real history for many years. Instead I satisfied my curiosity about the past with the socially acceptable version of history that was taught in school and easily purchased at most bookstores. It seemed to me that the darker side of things was an unpleasant topic. Delving into it ran the risk of attracting the negative. I had precious little time to master the socially acceptable version. Who had time to search out information that was difficult, even dangerous to obtain and depressing if indeed you found it? Why bother looking into the gruesome details of things like narcotics trafficking, money laundering and genocide?

Then, as corruption in the financial markets and in government spread in the 1990's, circumstances forced me to rethink my traditional attitude. Suddenly, I needed to understand the darker side of life. It was a matter of both personal and professional survival.

And so in 1998, I began a process of speed reading over a thousand books and watching hundreds of videos trying to map out the covert cash flows and networks that truly govern resources on our planet. Not satisfied, I networked and published and helped others do the same, hoping to collaborate on building a deeper and richer understanding of how my world really worked.

It was an unpleasant process. A lot of the books and videos were full of anger. The quality of information and writing was all over the map. Various experts were fractured into different specialties or activist interests and overwhelmed from government interference and lack of resources. They could be depressing and draining. There was a huge amount of data to sort through and to integrate. At the same time, the more I learned, the harder I found it to be around people who did not know or care about what was really going on. For a time, I felt alienated from many of the people that I loved.

Then one day, something marvelous happened. Everything I learned clicked into place in a practical way. Suddenly, I had a new framework. I had a new map. My map worked. I could pick up a corporate newspaper that was full of misinformation and omissions and read in between the lines to see what was really going on. I could watch a documentary that only told a story acceptable to the official history, yet intuit what was really happening behind the scenes.

No longer did I feel alienated from people who had not steeped themselves with this knowledge. I felt no urge to share with people information they did not want to know. Rather, I now had a map that could help me help them navigate their risks in a much more timely way. As I moved through the flow of events and people in my day-to-day life, I could see the real opportunities and risks with much more clarity. I started to make better choices. I found a new way to be useful to those I loved.

Something else happened. I started to understand my family and my own past. I could see our histories in the context of the covert activities that had touched our finances, our places and us. For the first time, I started to count up the total cost to my family and me of being naïve about who was in power and how we were being manipulated. It was staggering. It was also staggering that we had simply written it off to bad luck, market forces or fate, and gone back to work to create and build anew. Imagine what could have happened if we instead had an accurate map of how our world worked and the knowledge to navigate the risks in our environment successfully. Suddenly, I appreciated why families that had access to this type of information and quietly handed it down from generation to generation did so much better than those who taught their children to believe the popular explanations of things.

What was happening to me was the process of acquiring an authentic personal power that comes from understanding my history in an intimate way– whether it is the history of my planet, my people or my own family and myself. This is a power many of us desire. We live in dangerous times. Our world is full of predators. We need to be able to see them and evade them. We need to see where our leverage is, and how to use it to withdraw our support from those who would do us harm and invest our time and resources to build support for those who promote the rule of law and the creation of real wealth.

This starts with understanding history—the history of our country, the history of our place, the history of our family and the history of our friends and the organizations with which we interact.

It was about this time that I met a historian and professor of history, Carolyn Baker. Carolyn helped me to understand the strategic importance of building a curriculum that could help teachers ensure that students achieved such power as part of the normal educational process. Inspired by her example and the importance of what she was saying, I wrote a case study along the lines used in business schools called *Dillon, Read & Co. Inc. and the Aristocracy of Prison Profits*. My hope was that it would help Carolyn and other professors teach their students how business and government really work. If enough young people learn this, they will have a much better road map to navigate their careers and their responsibilities as citizens. This type of transparency is essential for a free and economically strong people.

For Carolyn, history is not in the past. History is alive. We study history to understand our world so that we can live our lives integrated into the flow of history. It reveals how the world really works and that we have the power to help shape that world. A people who understand where they came from, their connection to the land, animals and living things in their lives, how the systems and resources around them are governed and where their true opportunities and risks lie— such people understand how to write the history of their time and their future.

The Buddha says, "With our thoughts, we invent our world." Inventing our world is what we do when we live history. That happens when history stops being something separate from our lives—as official history is —and becomes a pathway to connect with the authentic—with what is real. Living history is the way to understand ourselves and those we love within the flow of time, the panorama of events and the age old squabble over resources. When we engage in a living history, we emerge as participants to create and influence the history being created now.

A living history is a history that turns the pupil from student to player. To rise from the level of pupil to player requires looking into our collective shadow, letting go of the official myths and seeing things as they are. It requires unlearning what we have learned. It requires forgiving those who taught us things that turned out to be not true, or failed to tell us what was true. It is not always a pretty picture. It is, however, a real one. When mastered, it starts the student on a journey of taking life with both hands to create something truer and more beautiful. Each of us can say, "I am part of a great story and that story is not over yet—I have something to say about how it goes."

While I am not one to look back and regret the past, what I would not give to have had Carolyn Baker as my history professor in college; it would have saved me a lot of time, but as you can see, I am making up for lost time. You can too.

Catherine Austin Fitts
President
Solari, Inc.

Former Managing Director of Dillon, Read & Co. Inc.
Former Assistant Secretary of Housing and Urban Development (Bush I)
November, 2006

INTRODUCTION

American inventor and entrepreneur, Henry Ford, is famous not only for his astounding success in making the automobile available to nearly every American family in the 1920s, but also for his famous quote: "History is bunk." Many historians, offended by Ford's abrupt dismissal of the subject, defensively retort that history is *not* bunk and set out to prove their "case" regarding the relevance and significance of the study of history.

The reader may be surprised to learn that on one level, I agree with Ford. A few years ago while browsing the titles in the history section of my local bookstore, my eyes fell upon James Loewen's *Lies My Teacher Told Me: Everything Your American History Textbook Got Wrong*. Instantaneously, I snatched the book from the shelf and began frantically shuffling through its pages. Presently, I realized that Loewen had elucidated the exasperation of countless teachers of American history, and I could barely wait to get the book home where I could pore over his words without interruption. A sociologist by trade, Loewen articulates brilliantly the effects upon a society when its citizens are ignorant of their history and shines an almost blinding light on some of the most sacrosanct American historical legends.

By and large, Americans do not consider themselves ignorant of their history. Yet, most are still under the influence of grammar-school indoctrination in the "discovery" of America by Columbus and the myth of George Washington's confession to his father that he, indeed, could not tell a lie and did, in fact, cut down the cherry tree. Sadly, in the technologically-obsessed twenty-first century, any knowledge of history beyond these mythical snippets is considered "onerous" or simply "extraneous" to the "real" world.

Overwhelmingly, what I hear from my college history students is that high school history was boring, irrelevant, and largely taught to them by teachers who had little or no passion for the subject. The classic situation is the high school coach who is hired to supervise athletic programs on the condition that he/she teaches a designated number of social studies courses of which history usually comprises the majority.

In my own experience, high school history was taught by male coaches who authoritatively lectured about U.S. history as a parent would a child, then barked commands, like: "All right, everybody be quiet and write the answers to the questions on Page 29." While we submissively complied, the coach sat at his desk, clipboard and pencil in hand, diagramming football plays, resentfully offering obligatory answers to any questions we might ask.

Nevertheless, some of us, thanks to stimulating college instructors, learned to love history. We studied the subject in the context of the social upheaval and cultural transformation of the 1960s and 70s. Moreover, in awe-stricken wonder at the relevance of history to our lives and our world, we vowed that our teaching of it would be passionate, vital, and illuminating. We could not wait to incite a similar voracity for historical knowledge in our students.

So upon all of the above I reflect when I hear Henry Ford's proclamation that history is bunk. I believe that rather than simply defending against Ford's comment, the diligent historian must analyze it more deeply. First, we must ask ourselves what would cause someone to proclaim that history is bunk? What more should we know about Ford that might shed light on his dismissal of history? Is it not extraordinarily relevant to understand that Ford was passionately anti-semitic and an ardent admirer of Hitler? In fact, when Hitler penned his infamous *Mein Kampf*, a portrait of Ford rested on his writing desk.

What might happen if this detail *were* included in conventional history texts? Might it not lead to discussion of the reality that Ford was only one of hundreds of corporate tycoons during the 1930s who admired Hitler and helped finance his rise to power? And if Ford was only one, who were the others? Why did they support Hitler? How did they become admirers of the most treacherous butcher in modern history? And what happened to their support for Hitler during World War II and after? Does their identification with his cause have anything to do with the turn of events following World War II or even the unfolding of events in the early twenty-first century? Are there implications that connect with current events such as the fact that at this writing, the sitting American president's grandfather, Prescott Bush, a contemporary of Ford, was one of those numerous corporate financiers of Hitler?

These are questions that historians are obligated to ask, and I do, and in the following pages, I offer answers to those questions—or at least plausible explanations which may not be "right" in the conventional sense, but which provide an alternative not found in "official" versions of American history. This work is unequivocally controversial, and it is meant to be, but as one of my students remarked after a lively discussion of its contents: "We may not agree with you or this abstract, but we will never forget this course." For me, the impact of the questions raised is far more momentous than my students' or readers' agreement with my answers.

At the opposite end of the spectrum from Henry Ford is the philosopher, George Santayana, whose famous quote is ubiquitous in history books and holocaust museums: "Those who cannot remember the past are condemned to repeat it." Unfortunately, some students use this quote to attempt to validate the irrelevance of studying history. The logic goes something like: "Well, the only thing I learn from history is that people learn nothing from history." At that point, I am quick to challenge the student to tell me what he/she personally has learned from history. Almost always, the student discloses that she has learned a great deal from history but also confesses that it feels meaningless if the rest of society does not also learn similar lessons. At that point, I hasten to remind the student that one cannot compel society to learn from history, but one can learn one's own lessons from history, and since society is comprised of individuals, what each person learns from history has the potential to make an enormous difference in society.

I personally feel great empathy with the student who argues in this manner because he is articulating frustration with a society that does not value historical knowledge. College and university budgets incessantly decrease funds for humanities and social sciences while increasing them for engineering and technological programs. Academia appears to be screaming loudly that only the present and future matter. Whenever a tragic event occurs nationally, one of the most telling and frequently-repeated mantras is "we want to put this behind us" thereby revealing our collective belief in the irrelevance of the past—a place where dark, painful events are buried, never to be unearthed and examined for their meaning and relevance.

In my opinion, the relegating of history to an antiquated closet of insignificance is not only intellectually unsound but fundamentally dangerous. A people ignorant of their own history are easily deceived and exploited. For example, our Founding Fathers wrote and spoke profusely of the eighteenth-century Enlightenment concept of *inalienable rights*. It permeates our Declaration of Independence and Constitution. For them, the term was synonymous with human rights held by each individual by virtue of nothing more than his/her existence. That is, one possesses inalienable rights because one breathes air and walks on the earth. Currently, however, members of the Bush Administration, including former Homeland Security Chief, Tom Ridge, and Chief Justice of the Supreme Court, Antonin Scalia, argue that government *bestows* the rights guaranteed in the Constitution upon its citizens.

In almost every history class I teach, I ask students to explain the origin of their rights as American citizens. Typically, most assume that their rights are "given" to them by their government. It is a rare student who has ever considered that if the government can "give" these rights, the government can also take them away. Few traditional history textbooks clarify the concept of inalienable rights which has contributed, in my opinion, to several generations of Americans who assume that the rights they daily enjoy and take for granted are somehow bestowed by their nation's leaders.

It is important to understand that history textbooks are the products of corporate media, and corporate media, whether it be CNN, the *New York Times*, or Bedford St. Martins Publishers is much more concerned with selling a product than agonizing over accuracy. This is why hundreds of thousands, perhaps millions of Americans, no longer acquire their daily news from mainstream sources but rely on alternative sources on the internet to inform them of local, national, and world events.

Moreover, as Loewen explains in *Lies My Teacher Told Me*, public school systems are not interested in making waves in terms of questioning the accuracy of history textbooks. Particularly in an era of backlash against the teaching of the theory of evolution or sex education, educators are loath to scrutinize American history textbooks which teach, as virtually all traditional ones do, that the United States of America is the most tolerant, moral, non-aggressive, and benevolent nation on earth. Insufficient detail, if any, is offered regarding Native American genocide by European settlers or the rabid racism that motivated them from the moment they set foot on the continent. Few textbooks analyze the persecution of labor and social justice movements by the wealthy and powerful in America, or American imperialism which came to fruition in the Spanish-American War, steadily burgeoning throughout the twentieth century and which in the current moment, constitutes the fundamental lynchpin of international relations.

To analyze these issues in depth, which most certainly results in learning that the history of the United States contains a very dark, as well as lighter past, is now considered disloyal, unpatriotic, and earns the analyst the label of "terrorist" or "enemy combatant." In response to these accusations, the dedicated historian must always ask: How did this happen? How did we arrive at such a state of affairs in our history? How is it that we are increasingly kept ignorant of the dark side of American history and even discouraged from studying our history at all?

History Uncensored asks these questions and offers responses to them evoked by historical facts. Repeatedly, it presents historical events which are rarely discussed in traditional textbooks and asks the reader to think critically about them. I have taken great pains to document the information presented here so that the reader may investigate the information in order to validate its historical accuracy and also research it further if inclined to do so.

Unquestionably, what is presented here is unsettling, if not blatantly disturbing, and that is my direct intent. I have been and will continue to be accused of hating America and lacking gratitude for the benefits of being born in this nation. To this accusation I can only call on the wisdom of the great American writer Mark Twain who stated that "We should be loyal to our country at all times and to our government when it deserves it." As I adamantly declare to my students of U.S. history, I love my country dearly, but I fear that my government has been and is in the process of destroying it. Americans who genuinely revere their national heritage do not blindly deify it, but rather, in the words of another great American, the former slave, Frederick Douglass, realize that "We should be lovers of our country who rebuke and do not excuse its sins.

As this abstract will reveal, numerous former officials of the U.S. government have resoundingly criticized it within the past five years, not the least of whom was former Supreme Court Justice, Sandra Day O'Connor, who in March, 2006 stated that the United States is edging ever closer to becoming a dictatorship. She pointed to the incessant attacks on the U.S. judiciary by the right wing of the Republican Party which appointed her to the high court in the 1980s. "Statutes and constitutions do not protect judicial independence—people do," O'Connor emphasized in her scathing Georgetown University speech.[1]

Founding Father and second President of the United States, John Adams, wrote that "the historian must have no country". Adams meant that we must be so committed to discovering the truth that history reveals, painful as it may be, that we put aside nationalistic prejudice and apply the scalpel of historical research. By doing so, we help heal, not harm, the nation we revere. If we insist on "having a country" when studying history, such healing cannot occur.

---

[1] *The Guardian Unlimited*, (http://www.guardian.co.uk/usa/story/0,1729396,00.html)

Perhaps the most momentous historical event of the twenty-first century thus far was the fraudulent selection of George W. Bush, Jr. as President of the United States in 2000. This abstract addresses the event and offers overwhelming evidence of fraud and criminal behavior in the 2000 election. The reader may immediately wonder why I choose to label the 2000 election more momentous than the attacks of September 11, 2001. My answer is that I do not consider the two events to be unrelated. The connection is explained more fully near the end of this work, but the significance of both events is that, taken together, they launched a coup d'etat in the United States which dramatically accelerated America's trajectory toward empire, diverging with dizzying velocity away from its Founders' original intent, a democratic republic whose purpose was to provide for the general welfare of its citizens. What could be more despicable? For the analytical historian, the only appropriate response is to diligently explore the process of the nation's demise from the signing of the U.S. Constitution in 1787 to the termination of that experiment in November, 2000. Beginning with the year 1865, that is precisely what this abstract intends to do.

I emphasize that the devolution from republic to empire has been a process and not an event. Throughout recent American history, particularly the history of the twentieth century, certain markers or "tipping points" have signaled the collapse of the Founding Fathers' experiment. One date in particular looms larger than life for the attentive student of history. That is 1947 when the National Security Act was signed into law creating the Central Intelligence Agency and a black budget, which absolved the Agency from all accountability to Congress or the American people regarding its activities and expenditures. During the Reagan Administration of the 1980s, other government agencies were allowed to create black budgets which opened the door for unprecedented corruption in the federal government. Yet another marker—the assassinations of John F. and Robert Kennedy and Martin Luther King, Jr. And then the consummation of empire: the 2000 elections and September 11, 2001.

I contend that if one does not understand that the United States of America in 2006 is an empire, one can understand neither its history nor its future. To meticulously analyze its history, which traditional textbooks do not do, is to witness that empire taking shape. In fact, like the correct placing of scattered fragments of a puzzle, *History Uncensored* endeavors to put the puzzle together and construct a "map" which not only connects past and present events, but causes them to make perfect sense.

One imperative I offer the reader before beginning the journey through the abstract is: Please remove rose-colored glasses. Be willing to entertain new definitions of loyalty, patriotism, and national pride. What you will learn here is not pleasant, nor is it unparalleled. My intention is not to portray the United States as uniquely evil. Nor do I wish to portray other modern regimes as exclusively honorable. Unquestionably, Stalin of the Soviet Union and Chairman Mao of China behaved despicably and murdered tens of thousands of people in the name of the communist cause. Have other nations behaved as badly or worse than the United States? Absolutely. But I do not live in those nations; I live in the United States. My obligation, indeed my duty as an American citizen, according to the Constitution, is to dissent when I see its principles of liberty violated. For as Jefferson wrote, "Dissent is the highest form of patriotism." More recently a similar maxim has become prominent among activists in American society: "Dissent *protects* democracy."

Perhaps what Americans most need to understand is that their nation is not "special." We have been taught to mouth platitudes such as "America is the greatest country in the world" or "people all over the world sacrifice everything they have, including their lives to come here." From the days of the Puritans who viewed the New World as "a city set on a hill" or "a new Jerusalem" or "a light unto the world," Americans have been enculturated to believe that other countries have dictatorships, but we don't; that other countries are imperialistic, but we aren't; that other countries have corrupt elections, but we don't; that other countries torture and maim prisoners of war or their own citizens, but we don't; that other countries perform lethal scientific experiments on their own citizens, but we don't; that other countries would incite and conduct wars for natural resources or commercial markets abroad, but we don't.

In my own personal history, I have ancestors who fought in the American Revolution, some who were conductors for the Underground Railroad, and others who were members of the Ku Klux Klan. I wish that I could eliminate the reality of the latter, but I cannot. History, like the individuals who make it, is remarkably complicated. It contains the good, the bad, the ugly, the indifferent, and everything in between. I passionately contend that as Americans we must revere that in our history which is extraordinary, honorable, praiseworthy, and yes, unique, yet at the same time, we must be willing to comprehend the long and tragic journey away from those incipient virtues to the depraved ground on which we now stand.

Some readers will undoubtedly label this work "conspiracy theory"—an accusation which I no longer take seriously given the fact that conspiracies do happen every day of our lives and that the "conspiracy theory" allegation is so unremittingly utilized as an attempt to marginalize arguments which question or confront "official history." As my friend, investigative journalist, Mike Ruppert is fond of saying, "I don't deal in conspiracy *theory*; I deal in conspiracy *fact*." A former Los Angeles Police Department Narcotics Investigator, Ruppert has become known to many as an "information cop", a term which refers to law enforcement investigative procedures, where pieces of evidence are gathered and configured, so that when the configuration is sufficiently indicative of who might have committed the crime, the evidence is presented to a district attorney or a grand jury. An information cop relates similarly to information. I encourage the reader of this abstract to become his/her own information cop and carefully examine the pieces of evidence here, configure them, or as we say, "connect the dots", and draw one's own conclusions.

Indeed, I have selectively included certain historical events and omitted others. I have done so because like any other historian, I have an opinion, and unlike some historians, I see history "going somewhere", and where it appears to be going is more than a little disturbing to me. Present, past, and future are inextricably connected and, in my world view, constantly influence each other. I firmly believe that we cannot understand current issues of global climate change, the end of the age of hydrocarbon energy, the events of September 11, 2001, the current wars in Iraq and Afghanistan, the globalist economy which is in the process of obliterating national economies, including our own, the draconian evisceration of the Bill of Rights of the Constitution of the United States, the proliferation of poverty, prisons, and people without health care, to mention only a few national and planetary perils, unless we incisively examine the history of our nation, particular from the end of the Civil War to the present moment.

History Uncensored is meant to supplement, not replace, any textbooks or readings required by the institutions in which this course is being taught. The reader may be astonished at what is omitted in this work, but please bear in mind that my intention was not to write a history textbook covering every historical event from 1865 to the present, but to insert events that are typically excluded from traditional textbooks. For example, I have written little about the actual events of World War II, but I offer details regarding the Pearl Harbor attacks, the triggering event of America's involvement in the war, and the role of the United States in the world in the aftermath of the war and the war's effect on the U.S. domestically. For this reason, I have chosen to refer to the work as a *curriculum abstract*.

I have designed the abstract to be standard notebook size in order to facilitate note-taking and insertion in a notebook. I have found that students greatly appreciate having a printed abstract in front of them so that they do not have to hurriedly take notes but can simply relax and follow along, making additional notes in the margins if they like.

The abstract contains several handouts which I use as study guides for essay exams. I inform the students that the topic of that handout will appear as an essay question on the forthcoming exam and that knowing what is on the handout will be very helpful in writing a successful essay answer. I encourage instructors to add to the collection of handouts by making their own from the material in the abstract or from other sources. I wholeheartedly support instructors in adapting this work to their specific needs.

ACKNOWLEDGEMENTS

I wish to thank those who have been my teachers in the saga of the American experience. I am indebted to Norm Pollack, Professor Emeritus of History, Michigan State University; Richard Wunderli, Professor of History, University of Colorado; Howard Zinn, author of *A Peoples' History Of The United States;* Stanley Schultz, Professor of History, University of Wisconsin; Gabriel Kolko, Michael C. Ruppert, investigative journalist and editor of *From The Wilderness* (www.fromthewilderness.com); Catherine Austin Fitts, former Managing Director of Dillon Reed and former Assistant Secretary of Housing and Urban Development, creator of the Solari concept for transforming economies and communities (www.solari.com), my students, who teach me more than I could ever teach them, and all of my ancestors throughout time and infinity who have contributed to my personal and cultural history.

PREFACE

The historian must have no country.

—John Quincy Adams—

ELEVEN REASONS TO STUDY HISTORY

1) **TO ENHANCE CRITICAL THINKING**—Do you want to be a gullible human being or a thinking human being? Studying history teaches us to Analyze, Investigate and Make decisions (AIM) based on historical events, historical patterns and what people have learned or not learned from history. Above all, history teaches us to question all information.

2) **TO IMPROVE COMMUNICATION**—Studying history helps us think about, analyze, and express our ideas regarding history and its relevance to our lives in present time.

3) **TO VIEW KNOWLEDGE AS A WHOLE**—Frequently students ask: "Why do I have to study history when I'm going to be a computer engineer?" The very asking of that question indicates that our society has a big problem. That problem is an addiction to specialization—becoming an expert in one field of knowledge rather than having a full-spectrum education. Ask yourself: "Do I ONLY want to be a computer engineer, or do I want to be able to integrate knowledge so that I can be on the cutting edge of new information, new technology and new discoveries?" In other words, do you want to be just tolerated by your employer or *highly-valued* and more quickly considered for promotions and other perks?

4) **TO DEVELOP A GLOBAL PERSPECTIVE**—There really IS life beyond our local community. Studying history helps us see our place in time and in relation to the rest of the world. We begin to appreciate the interconnectedness of events on the other side of the world with our own personal world, wherever that may be.

5) **TO APPRECIATE DIVERSITY**—History exposes us to different cultures and ethnic groups. It helps us appreciate their place in creating OUR world. We can then understand our struggles in the context of theirs, which allows us to develop a healthy respect for cultural and individual differences.

6) **TO DEEPEN APPRECIATION OF ONE'S COMMUNITY**—Hopefully, the study of history will motivate us to learn more about the history of our own communities and cultures by reading local history, visiting museums, talking with our ancestors, creating genealogies, and supporting local artists and musicians.

7) **TO CLARIFY VALUES**—By studying issues such as Native American genocide, slavery, racism and sexism, corporate and government corruption, we will be able to examine our own beliefs on moral situations and make moral decisions in a meaningful and thoughtful way, based not merely on what we have previously been taught, but on our own analysis of issues.

8) **TO APPRECIATE AND DEVELOP ROLE MODELS**—By learning about how famous figures such as Thomas Paine, Frederick Douglass, Ida Tarbell, the Populists, Martin Luther King and many others have confronted the ignorance and injustice of their eras, we can develop an appreciation for their courage and perseverance. This can equip us to deal with difficult and trying times and hopefully, motivate us to challenge injustice in current time.

9) **TO KNOW WHAT IS ENDURING**—Through history, we discover what lasts and what humans have found meaningful throughout time. This helps us separate passing fads from enduring legacies and differentiate the meaningful from the meaningless.

10) **TO DEVELOP A "MAP" FOR TRAVELING THROUGH LIFE**—If you are going to New York, and you have never been there before, you'd better take a map, or you're going to get lost. Studying history can provide a map for how the world works and how to survive in it. My intention in writing this U.S. history curriculum abstract is not only to help open eyes and minds but to assist the reader in more skillfully journeying through life.

11) **TO BE INSPIRED**—The word "inspiration" is connected with "spirit" or "spiritual" which is not the same as religious. Hopefully, this abstract will awaken not only your mind, but your spirit and inspire you to create a better,more just, more humane, more meaningful world.

THOSE WHO CANNOT REMEMBER THE PAST ARE CONDEMNED TO REPEAT IT.

—George Santayana—

THE PAST IN THE PRESENT

The most important reason for studying history is that we absolutely cannot make sense of the present without understanding the past. Can you imagine not knowing where you came from? Can you imagine not knowing who your ancestors were or what culture you came from? In the same way, nations and societies must understand where they came from and how they became who they are.

William Faulkner, the great Southern novelist said, "Good history *is* not was," meaning that the past and the present are inextricably connected.

Following Faulkner's reasoning, an effective history teacher helps students connect the dots between what they learn in history class and what is going on today in the twenty-first century.

Another reason for studying history is most eloquently expressed in the words above by the philosopher, George Santayana: *"Those who do not understand the past are condemned to repeat it."* When you walk into any of the numerous holocaust museums around the world, somewhere in the museum, you are likely to see this quote.

It is frightening that many young people today know nothing about the holocaust or Adolph Hitler. We have Neo-Nazi groups declaring that the holocaust never happened, as well as the current president of Iran dismissing the holocaust as a myth. Racism is alive and well around the world and in the United States, but a thorough study of American history reveals conclusively that our nation was built upon the backs of minorities without whom America would never have become the prosperous nation that it is today.

From the moment that wealthy Europeans landed on these shores, they succeeded at the expense of peoples of color and lower classes. Columbus genocided thousands of Native Americans. European colonists who came later brought diseases that eventually eliminated 80-90% of the indigenous population. Europeans then began the slavery industry and subsequently expanded west and exterminated what was left of the native population there. Subsequently, a civil war was fought over the slavery issue, after which white Europeans created mega-corporations which discriminated against and exploited blacks and immigrants and everyone in lower classes. In the 1920s and '30s, thousands of blacks in the South were lynched and murdered in other ways as a new blight of racism swept across America. In the 1930s and 40s, America, turned a blind eye and deaf ear to the Nazi holocaust even when it knew what Hitler was doing to the Jews. Some Americans even sympathized with the extermination of Jews, and as you will learn in this course, some American corporation owners even financed Hitler's rise to power. During World War II, many Japanese American citizens were detained in concentration camps in the United States with the rationale that since Japan was one of America's enemies, Japanese Americans needed to be incarcerated in order to prevent espionage against the United States.

We all hope that never again in human history will we see anything like Hitler and his regime, but if we do not understand the holocaust and the fascist political system which unleashed it, we may repeat it ourselves. As a nation and as a planet, we now face enormous ethical problems such as the issue of cloning. If we do not understand what Hitler stood for, our ethics could easily descend to the same level as those touting "racial purity" in Nazi Germany. Cloning could feasibly begin as an "innocent" opportunity to choose a healthy child or to fight terminal illnesses, but in our search for perfection, it may be all-too tempting to begin creating a perfect race. If we do not remember the horrors of Nazism, we could easily be seduced into many misuses of all manner of technology.

Moreover, since the terrorist attacks against the United States, September 11, 2001, many Americans are questioning unprecedented curtailment of their civil liberties by such pieces of legislation as the *U.S.A. Patriot Act* and the currently-debated *Model Emergency Health Powers* Act[2], as well as fiat-like declarations from the Bush Administration regarding the government's "right" to invade the privacy of its citizens. While many Americans who are unfamiliar with the history of the totalitarian regimes of Hitler and subsequent right and left-wing dictators may not be alarmed by current threats to American civil liberties, many who are familiar with that history find legislation such as the *Patriot Act*, nothing less than appalling. Indeed, ignorance of the past condemns us to repeat it, and it is impossible to preserve our civil liberties if we do not study their origin in the two most important documents from our nation's inception, the Declaration of Independence and the Constitution.

WHY STUDENTS OFTEN DISLIKE HISTORY

One reason students dislike history has to do with the way history is taught in public schools. While I do not wish to blame teachers for an overwhelming distaste on the part of students for the subject, it is also true that in some cases, those who teach the subject are not sufficiently committed to it. For example, consider the high school athletic coach whose contract with the school district stipulates that he/she must teach social studies courses as well as coach. Frequently, the coach's passion lies with athletics and not history. Still other history teachers enjoy teaching the subject but have insufficient zeal or enthusiasm for the subject or do not know how to make history live and breathe for their students.

Yet another reason for students' dislike of history is that high school history textbooks not only present distortions of facts, they frequently present lies. In his groundbreaking work, *LIES MY TEACHER TOLD ME*,[3] by James Loewen, the author notes that many of our historical figures had a very dark side but are presented only as heroes in history textbooks. For example, in high school history textbooks, students learn that Thomas Jefferson and George Washington were champions of equality and democracy, but they are rarely told that virtually all of the signers of the Declaration of Independence, except John Adams, were slave holders. Textbooks almost never explain that the Founding Fathers were the ruling elite of their day and that they wrote the Constitution principally for people like themselves.

---

[2] Model State Emergency Health Powers Act (http://en.wikipedia.org/wiki/Model_State_Emergency_Health_Powers_Act and http://www.mercola.com/2001/dec/26/mehpa.htm)
[3] Loewen, James, *LIES MY TEACHER TOLD ME*, Touchstone, 1995.

In more recent American history, textbooks rarely associate the conquest of the American system of government by corporate interests with the plutocracy in which we live today. In fact, most students have never heard the word *plutocracy*, which means a society governed by the wealthy, not by the poor or middle-classes. In fact, most U.S. history textbooks teach that the so-called "abuses" of American society perpetrated by corporations in the late-nineteenth and early twentieth centuries have been "remedied", and that we should all be grateful that society has been "liberated" from the oppressive influences of industry.

SPECIFIC DISTORTIONS

Following are some of the distortions of American history that students have heard in high school:

- **There is equal opportunity in America**. This particular myth assumes that everyone starts from a level playing field in America and that she/he can pull him/herself up by the bootstraps because there are more opportunities, according to the myth, in America than in any other country. This fantasy is a delusion of the American middle and ruling classes. By the end of this abstract, the reader will understand the nature of opportunity in America and the historical roots of the indisputable limitations that women and minorities in America have faced since the nation's origin.

- Another myth is that of so-called **unbroken, uninterrupted progress**—that everything is getting better and better all the time. Few textbook authors grapple with the meaning of *progress* or address diverse definitions of it. For the single mother in an inner city housing project, "progress" may mean getting through another day without losing any of her children to crack-cocaine or drive-by shootings. For the textbook author, it may mean the enhancement of her investment portfolio and a more attractive 401K program. Moreover, the moral complexities of traditional capitalism, the North American Free Trade Agreement, and America's economic, political, and military hegemony in the world are rarely questioned. Nor do traditional history textbooks question the devastations of the ecosystems, attended by global warming, in the wake of unrestrained, unregulated, global capitalism. Nor are current textbook authors grappling with issues of the end of plentiful hydrocarbon energy on planet Earth or the likelihood of global economic collapse which is inextricably connected with energy depletion. Tragically, corporate media in America is producing textbooks which leave students with the impression that while gross inequalities and abuses of human, civil, and ecological rights may have existed in the past, such egregious behaviors are behind us.

- Traditional history textbooks and classes often subtley or blatantly teach students that **democracy is the same as free market capitalism**. According to this notion, "freedom" is synonymous with a capitalistic system. In the first decade of the twenty-first century, the Bush Administration praises the men and women in the military who are "fighting for our freedom", when in fact, what is meant by this tribute is that the U.S. military is defending and imposing the capitalistic system around the world, a reality explcitly detailed and documented in the following chapters.

- A particularly offensive illusion, in my opinion, is that **just because slavery ended, racism ended**. As this abstract will reveal, not only did American racism not end with the Civil War, it worsened after the Civil War and remained a brutal reality of our nation until the Civil Rights movement of the 1960s. James Loewen emphasizes that history textbooks are generally written from the Euro-centric perspective, with emphasis on European exploration and settlement of North America. However, in this abstract, I endeavor to present a fuller and more realistic picture of the adversities faced by minorities since the Civil War and into the current moment. More recently, since the September 11 attacks, allegedly committed by Middle Eastern hijackers, prejudice against Arabs and Arab-Americans has intensified. A thorough study of American history reveals the realities of institutionalized racism as a societal, not merely an individual or private affliction in America.

- Still another illusion, particularly disturbing post-September 11, is that if we criticize our historical characters and their actions, we are being unpatriotic, socialistic, Communistic or, even worse, sympathetic with terrorists. We must bear in mind that the majority of electronic media, print media and publishing houses in America are generally either multinational corporations themselves or are subsidiaries of them. Like other forms of corporate media, textbook publishers have an agenda: to sell textbooks and to promote the corporate perspective of the textbook's subject matter. Consequently, high school history books usually present a Disneyland view of history—a view of history that emphasizes only the positive in American history, and because it does not present the dark side, along with what is considered positive, this view is usually boring, bland, and emotion-less. Loewen says that EMOTION is the glue that causes history to stick[4]. One reason students hate high school history is that there is little emotion in it. It is frequently trite, insipid, simplistic, devoid of feeling and dedicated to a patriotic, chauvinistic America-can-do-no-wrong and America-is-getting-better-and-better perspective.

We should be lovers of our country who rebuke and do not excuse its sins.

~Frederick Douglass~

All men having power ought to be mistrusted.

~James Madison~

BEFORE USING THIS ABSTRACT IN CLASS…

Before beginning my courses in U.S. History (1865 to the present), I show the documentary DVD, **"The End Of Suburbia"** or the documentary **"Oil Crash"** which are detailed examinations of the issue of Peak Oil, that is, the end of cheap and abundant energy and the ultimate global energy crisis it will produce within the next ten to fifty years.

After viewing the documentary, I provide some time for discussion, followed by a clarification that we are actually beginning at the end of the course, with the twenty-first century issue of oil depletion, then going back to 1865 and moving forward to understand how we arrived at the current state of affairs.

The documentary **"The End of Suburbia"** is available at www.endofsuburbia.com, and **"Oil Crash"** is available at www.oilcrashmovie.com.

---

[4] Loewen, P.300.

Your Choice: THE RED PILL OR THE BLUE PILL?

"At last. Welcome Neo, as you no doubt have guessed, I am Morpheus."

"Its an honor to meet you."

"No, the honor is mine. Please come, sit. I imagine that right now you are feeling a bit like Alice tumbling down the rabbit hole."

"You could say that."

"I can see it in you eyes. You have the look of a man who acceptswhat he sees, because he is expecting to wake up. Ironically, this is not far from the truth…Do you believe in fate Neo?"

"No,"

"Why not?"

"Because I don't like the idea that I'm not in control of my life."

"I know exactly what you mean. Let me tell you why you're here. You're here because you know something. What you know, you can't explain. But you feel it. You've felt it your entire life. That there's something wrong with the world. You don't know what it is but it's there, like a splinter in your mind driving you mad. It is this feeling that has brought you to me. Do you know what I'm talking about?"

'The Matrix."

"Do you want to know what it is? The Matrix is everywhere, it is all around us, even now in this very room. You can see it when you look out your window or when you turn on your television. You can feel it when you go to work, when you go to church, when you pay your taxes. It is the world that has been pulled over your eyes to blind you from the truth."

"What truth?"

"That you are a slave Neo, like everyone else, you were born into bondage, born into a prison that you cannot smell or taste or touch. A prison for your mind. Unfortunately, no one can be told what the Matrix is. You have to see what it is for yourself. This is your last chance, After this, there is no turning back. You take the blue pill the story ends. You wake up in your bed and believe whatever you want to believe. You take the red pill you stay in Wonderland and I show you how deep the rabbit hole goes. Remember; all I'm offering is the truth. Nothing more."

Dialogue from the movie, ***The Matrix***

I

RECONSTRUCTION
(1865-1876)

After the Civil War, the new coalition of southern and northern elites developed, with southern whites and blacks of the lower classes occupied in racial conflicts, native workers and immigrant workers clashing in the North, and the farmers dispersed over a big country, while the system of capitalism consolidated itself in industry and government. But there came rebellion among industrial workers and a great opposition movement among farmers.

-Howard Zinn-
The Twentieth Century

This abstract begins with the Reconstruction period immediately following the Civil War. Students should be given a brief review of the events leading up to the Civil War and the major causes of it. Below is a summary of the principal causes of the Civil War. It offers a concise structure for review and may be easily adapted.

WHAT CAUSED THE CIVIL WAR?

For decades, conflict between North and South had been intensifying over slavery. On the one hand, there were several causes of the war besides slavery, but on the other hand, slavery was the truly defining issue; all other causes were related to it, and without it, the war would probably not have been fought.

- **The Constitutional question**: Abolitionists and many politicians of the North opposed slavery on moral grounds, but the South repeatedly argued that the Constitutional guarantee of "states rights" permitted it to maintain slavery and the Southern way of life surrounding slavery.

- **The Congressional question**: Each time a new territory became a state, the question of representation in Congress became an issue. Whether slave or free, the new state would have representation in Congress, and since the North and South were competing with each other for political power in Washington, each new state would tip the balance of power either in the direction of slavery or anti-slavery, depending on that state's position.

- **The Economic question:** The economy of the South was almost entirely based on cotton, and the South argued that slavery was necessary to maintain its economic base. The economy of the North was based on industry and banking. Southerners believed that if they were to lose their economic base, they would be at the economic mercy of the North.

- **The Moral question**: Militant abolitionists such as William Lloyd Garrison and John Brown fought against slavery as a moral outrage. Southerners defended slavery by insisting that slaves were "happy" with the conditions of slavery and that the plantation system was actually helping the slaves. Throughout his political career, Abraham Lincoln's opposition to slavery increased. By the end of his life, he was vehemently opposed to it and would not compromise in his opposition to it.

THE LAST STRAWS:

Three events provided the catalyst that ignited the Civil War:

- **The Fugitive Slave Law of 1850** which made the federal government responsible for apprehending fugitive slaves in the North. This meant that federal marshals could override the legal process in the North and drag fugitive slaves back to the South.
- **The Dred Scott Decision of 1857** by the Supreme Court, which said that blacks had no rights that whites had to recognize. The decision gave birth to the Republican Party and intensified the conflict between the Republicans of the North and the Democrats of the South.
- **John Brown's raid** on Harpers Ferry, Virginia in 1859 in an attempt to arm slaves. The rebellion failed and John Brown was martyred, but the event added fuel to the smoldering fires of Civil War.

The Abolition movement emerged triumphant from a Union victory in the Civil War. Many Republicans in Congress were of the abolitionist persuasion and used their political leverage to punish the South and subdue it economically. According to University of Wisconsin History Professor Stanley Schultz, Reconstruction raised three questions:

1) Can the U.S. be truly united?
2) Can blacks and whites live together?
3) Who runs the country?[5]

---

[5] Schultz, Stanley, U.S. History Lectures, University of Wisconsin: www.us.history.wisc.edu/

NOTE: Instructors should also be familiar with the three Reconstruction classics of American history:

- *RECONSTRUCTION AFTER THE CIVIL WAR*, by John Hope Franklin;
- *THE ERA OF RECONSTRUCTION*, by Kenneth Stampp; and
- *THE STRANGE CAREER OF JIM CROW*, by C. Vann Woodward.

The Thirteenth Amendment ended slavery, and was ratified in December, 1865. Subsequently, the **Fourteenth Amendment**, granting citizenship to former slaves and the **Fifteenth Amendment** which granted all American citizens the right to vote were passed. In a series on the life and accomplishments of black abolitionist, Frederick Douglass, the Thirteenth, Fourteenth and Fifteenth Amendments are discussed at: www.history.rochester.edu/class/douglass/part5.html

African Americans frequently refer to Reconstruction as the "First" and "Second" Reconstruction. In other words, the **First Reconstruction** was the period immediately following the Civil War which had as goals for blacks: voting, equality in politics and in the use of public facilities. The **Second Reconstruction** was the civil rights movement of the 1960s which more fully accomplished the goals of the First Reconstruction.

Additional notes on the Reconstruction Era may be found at:
http://www.odur.let.rug.nl/~usa/H/1994/ch6_p13.htm and at
http://odur.let.rug.nl/~usa/H/1994/ch6_p14.htm

The effects of the assassination of Abraham Lincoln:
The untimely death of Lincoln drastically altered what would most certainly have been a very different Reconstruction scenario for a number of reasons, not the least of which was the new President, Andrew Johnson, a Tennessee slaveholder with no college education. The assassination of Lincoln in relation to Reconstruction is discussed at:
http://www.socialstudieshelp.com/Lesson_36_Notes.htm
Additional essays and possible exam topics may be obtained at:

http://www.socialstudieshelp.com/Amer_History_Syallbus

Below is a concise handout which discusses the limited success of Reconstruction and which may be used as an essay question:

HOW SUCCESSFUL WAS RECONSTRUCTION?
(Handout)

During the Reconstruction period following the Civil War, some attempts were made to address the social concerns of freed slaves, but in reality, these attempts did not go far enough or last long enough to make blacks economically and politically equal with whites. In fact, there was never any intention of making blacks equal. Fundamental issues of equality would not be addressed for another one hundred years.

ECONOMIC PROBLEMS OF NEWLY-FREED SLAVES:

- They had no education and could not read or write as a result of Slave Codes.

- Job opportunities were extremely limited. They had no skills.

- Often the only skills blacks had were in manual labor.

- Freed slaves had no money, clothing or food.

- Jobs were usually limited to *sharecropping* or *tenant farming*.

    Sharecropping—In this arrangement, former plantation owners, who also had no money to hire workers, allowed freed slaves to work the land and give them a portion of the harvest. The portion was usually quite high, and the freed slaves had difficulty saving enough to sell on their own.

    Tenant farming—Some sharecroppers actually made enough to begin renting the land. This was known as tenant farming. Often, former plantation owners would charge very high rent, and freed slaves had a difficult time making ends meet.

    Both sharecropping and tenant farming were essentially new versions of slavery.

WHAT WAS DONE TO HELP FREED SLAVES?

- The Freedmen's Bureau was created as a part of the Reconstruction Act of 1865. It was a federal agency for providing food, clothing, and shelter to freed slaves.

- In the arena of education, black and white school teachers came to the South from the North and began to teach freed black slaves.

- Membership grew in black churches of the South which often tried, with very limited funds, to help their members.

POLITICAL DEVELOPMENTS

16 blacks were elected to Congress; however, many white supremacist organizations like the Ku Klux Clan emerged for the purpose of terrorizing blacks. Southerners were forced to live with blacks, but they refused to treat them as equals, and what came to exist was a *de facto* segregation—separation of the races, not by law, but by the fact that it exists.

Jim Crow Laws—These laws developed throughout the South and North to keep the races separate and to dominate blacks socially, politically, and economically. In the South, they were passed to protest and curtail the effects of the Thirteenth, Fourteenth and Fifteenth Amendments. Most notable were laws designed to prevent blacks from voting and from marrying whites. A list of Jim Crow laws may be viewed and printed at: http://www.nps.gov/malu/documents/jim_crow_laws.htm

The U.S. Supreme Court—The *Plessy v. Ferguson* decision of 1896 officially launched the doctrine of "separate but equal" which remained in place until the overturning of the decision in 1954 with *Brown v. the Board of Education*. Additionally, in 1898, the Court determined in *Williams v. Mississippi* that states could make their own decisions regarding standards of voting. Details of the Plessy decision are elaborated at; http://www.watson.org/~lisa/blackhistory/post-civilwar/plessy.html.

The Ku Klux Klan, a terrorist organization, was formed during the Reconstruction period using violence in an attempt to nullify and control black efforts toward equality. Although the Klan began in the South, its membership swelled in many Northern states, particularly in the 1920s. A fascinating video documentary, **THE KU KLUX KLAN: A SECRET HISTORY** is well worth viewing as a supplement to lecture material on the Reconstruction Era. It may be ordered at: www.libraryvideo.com or by phone at: 800-843-3620. Also available is a Black American History Video Series which includes five volumes: Pre-Slavery; Slavery; Reconstruction; Civil Rights and Modern History. The Black American History series may also be purchased at www.libraryvideo.com

THE PROS AND CONS OF RECONSTRUCTION FOR AFRICAN AMERICANS
(Handout)

OFFICIAL GAINS

- 13th Amendment officially ended slavery.
- The Freedman's Bureau was established in 1865 to provide some economic aid to freed slaves.
- The Civil Rights Bill of 1865 gave full citizenship to blacks.
- The 14th Amendment officially guaranteed that no state could deny any person his or her full rights as an American citizen.
- The 15th Amendment was passed which gave blacks, officially, the right to vote.
- Free public education began, but schools were segregated, and low taxes provided poor education, especially for black children.
- Officially, blacks were no longer slaves, but they had no skills or education and therefore had few options for income except to become tenant farmers or sharecroppers.

CRUEL REALITIES

Behind the scenes of these "official" advances were the:

- Black Codes which prevented blacks from buying land or earning a fair wage.
- Impossible literacy tests were administered to blacks who tried to register to vote, as well as the use of poll taxes and grandfather clauses, leaving them disenfranchised.
- The Ku Klux Klan in most states began a reign of terror to keep blacks from the polls and in their pre-Civil War social place.
- Meanwhile, many abolitionist and radical Republicans in the North lost their will to fight for black equality. Louisiana was one of the most repressive states where in 1896, there were 130,000 black voters, but where by 1904, there were only 1,342.
- The *Plessy vs. Ferguson* decision of 1896 which ruled in favor of "separate but equal", meaning that blacks had to have separate facilities, but those facilities were considered equal even though they were not.
- The *Williams vs. Mississippi* decision of 1898 which, in the name of states rights, allowed the states to make their own decisions regarding standards for voting.

In summary, we can say that while Reconstruction was a time of "official" gains for African Americans, it was also a time of repression and backlash against the official end of slavery.

2

WESTWARD EXPANSION

Between 1865 and 1890, some 430 million acres of land in the American West were settled. More land was settled during this time than in the first 250 years of American history. That is to say that the land area occupied by Americans doubled in twenty-five years. Three empires, mining, farming and cattle, rose and fell, and ten new states entered the Union. It was also during this time that Native Americans were defeated by whites in the Indian Wars which resulted in the confinement of Native Americans to reservations by the end of the century.

WESTWARD EXPANSION
(Handout)

Concepts which help us understand the settlement of the West after the Civil War are:

The concept of **MANIFEST DESTINY** which arose soon after the area called the Louisiana Territory was purchased from France in 1803. Although France "claimed" the territory, the territory was not actually owned by France but by Native American tribes throughout the region.[6]

Essentially, **MANIFEST DESTINY** was the belief that Anglo-European settlers were destined by God to settle all territory from the Atlantic Ocean to the Pacific. There were three powerful influences at work in this belief:

- The **Religious Influence:** This was the idea that America had Divine Providence on its side. It had a future that was destined by God to expand its borders with no limits. In other words, it was "God's will" that Americans settle the entire continent. And because it was God's will, Americans and their cause were unstoppable. Furthermore, it was the duty of white people to Christianize and "civilize" the savage Native Americans and take freedom "from sea to shining sea."

- The **Conquering Influence:** Americans had a sense of mission and also a sense of greed. They were tempted by boundless tracts of land which would eventually open new trade routes. The idea of conquest gave them a feeling of romance, adventure, and national pride. Furthermore, the easiest way to make sure that there

---

[6] Lowen, P. 123.

would be no foreign intervention along American borders was to conquer those borders and expand American territory.

- **The Racist Influence**—The white man and his culture are more advanced, and therefore, the "backward" and "superstitious" traditions of Native Americans must be subjugated to the "enlightened" will of the civilized, progressive and morally superior Europeans

THE DARK SIDE OF MANIFEST DESTINY

The dark side of Manifest Destiny was an insatiable greed, rationalized by religion, which caused the white man to feel that he had a right to destroy anything and anyone, especially Indians, who stood in the way of westward expansion. The theory of Manifest Destiny was used to justify the genociding of millions of Native Americans and possibly the largest land-grab in the history of the Western world.

Nineteenth-century historian, Frederick Jackson Turner, developed a thesis of the significance of the frontier in American history.

Major points:

- Turner conceived of the West not as a place but a process—a series of "Wests" in a receding frontier line—the point where savagery meets civilization.

- For Turner, American history is largely about people leaving settled areas for the frontier, and their struggle to find new ways to live in new lands. This struggle, according to Turner, explains American development.

- The frontier produces American democracy and individualism—the frontier requires Americans to develop new institutions; therefore, "Free land makes free men."

- Finally, Turner claimed that in 1890 the frontier was closed, ending the first stage of American development. This created uncertainty, for if the frontier no longer existed, how would American democratic development be maintained?

In sum, Turner argues that civilization is a process in which society becomes ever more complex. As complexity increases, opportunities become more limited, and civilization inevitably subordinates individuals to society.[7]

At this point, we might ask the question: What does a country do when it has expanded to the fullest extent of its borders and has nowhere else to go? We will discover the answer in the last two decades of the nineteenth century when America joins the trend of imperialism alongside other Western nations.

The Social And Ecological Impact Of Westward Expansion

The Slaughter of the Indian Population—The Native American population in the 1600s had been estimated at 10 million. By 1865, 300,000 remained. Deaths were due largely to disease and warfare—both with the U.S. Army and among themselves. Also, many eastern tribes had to migrate west in order to survive.

---

[7] Schultz Lectures, Lecture 3 (http://us.history.wisc.edu/hist102/lectures/lecture03.html)

The Slaughter of the Buffalo—Many were slaughtered for their hides, many only for sport. Carcasses were usually left on the plains to rot. In the 1600s, there had been some 15 million buffalo in America, and by 1900, only a few thousand were left.

The Disappearance of the Open Plains—Railroads came by the dozens and laid track, spewing their coal smoke throughout the plains. Thousands of farmers and their families settled in the plains and had to put up fences to enclose their stock.

Native American Land And Culture Are Decimated—Christian missionaries deluged the West, converting thousands of Indians and putting their children in religious schools. The Dawes Act of 1887 provided for the gradual elimination of tribal ownership of land. Indians were "given" full U.S. citizenship, but they could not gain full title to their property for twenty five years, supposedly to keep them from selling their land to speculators.

The Dawes Act was based on the philosophy of assimilation—taking Indians away from the tribe onto their own plots of land, taking Indian children away from their families and forcing them to attend boarding schools run by missionaries. The government agency set up to manage the assimilation process was the Bureau of Indian Affairs (BIA) which exists today and is generally hated by most Native Americans as it was the in the late 19th century. In addition, in many Indian communities, religious ceremonies were "officially" banned, although Indian people continued to practice them

The Declining Position Of The Farmer—The social consequences of Westward expansion were not exclusive to Native peoples. The economic difficulties of the farmers and the isolation of farm life had a social impact. In addition to unbearable loneliness and boredom, many farmers lacked access to adequate education for their children as well as adequate health care. There was virtually no sense of community, and many children could not wait to leave the farm as soon as they were able in order to move to the city and be part of a society. A growing sense of malaise and disappointment that permeated the rural psyche was one of the contributing factors to the development of the Populist movement. Within only two generations, the sturdy farmer who had considered himself as the backbone of American life was becoming painfully aware that his position was declining in relation to the rise of the urban industrial society of the east.

Native Americans from 1865-1890

**The 1867 Peace Commission

This commission was an attempt to bring peace to the West by creating reservations for the tribes. In order to succeed, however, the United States Army would need to make war on Native Americans which makes obvious the contradiction in the term "Peace Commission." The three major areas where reservations were created were South Dakota, Oklahoma and Arizona. In an attempt to survive—to protect their peoples and cultures, leaders of various tribes consented to settle on reservations. Dozens of treaties were made with whites, yet white settlers continued to encroach on Indian lands in violation of the treaties. Numerous "Indian Wars" erupted:

- The defeat of the Comanche in 1874
- The defeat of Chief Joseph and the Nez Perce in 1877
- The defeat of Geronimo and the Apache
- The defeat of Custer at Little Big Horn in 1876
- Conflicts with the Sioux from 1876 to 1890

Dawes Severalty Act (1887)

This act was a major government policy toward the Indians until the 1930s. The goal was to create independent farmers out of tribal Indians. Indian families would be given tools and 160 acres of reservation land. If Indians accepted this grant they would be "given" citizenship. To prevent exploitation by whites, the Indians were prohibited from selling their land for 25 years.

Wounded Knee
During the 1890s, the Sioux created a new religion called the **"Ghost Dance."** It was brought to them by Wovoka, a Paiute Indian who claimed to have had a vision of a dance that would prevent further encroachment by whites. The Sioux danced for hours, sometimes days, sometimes until some of their people died of exhaustion. In December, 1890, at a Ghost Dance ceremony at Wounded Knee on Sioux land in South Dakota, government troops surrounded the dancing Sioux, and opened fire with machine guns. 300 innocent people were killed while 170 women and children were left to die in the snow.

The **significance of Wounded Knee** is that it was the last military confrontation between Native Americans and the U.S. government. From the white perspective, it was the final solution to the "Indian problem." From the Indian perspective, it was an egregious slaughter of innocents out of revenge.

<u>VIDEO SUPPLEMENTS</u>:

- *500 Nations Series* with Kevin Costner (www.libraryvideo.com) Documentary
- *How The West Was Lost* (www.libraryvideo.com) Documentary
- *Ishi: The Last Yahi* (www.libraryvideo.com) Documentary
- *Sun Of The Morning Star* (the story of the Battle of Little Big Horn from the Sioux perspective) (www.reel.com) Movie
- *Into The West*, TNT-TV mini-series, 2005, Stephen Spielberg, Producer, (http://www.amazon.com/gp/product/B000AQ6A9E/002-5223860-8734438?v=glance&n=130)

**I strongly recommend showing video documentaries or movies relating to Native American issues. Visual presentations are far more impactful than reading or discussion regarding the history of Indian and white relations.

3

WORSENING CONDITIONS IN RURAL AMERICA

During the 1870s, hundreds of Americans abandoned their farms. At the same time, enormous changes were taking place in the mechanization of agriculture. Consequently, more capital was needed for successful farming, and machines demanded upkeep and repair—all of which meant that independent farmers now had more risks to take. Likewise, new agricultural lands were opened because farmers hoped to pay off their debts by raising more crops. They were feeling the pinch of higher mortgage rates charged by urban businessmen. Moreover, while urban businessmen were diversifying, farmers by and large, were continuing to raise crops traditional to their regions which increased the risk of complete loss. But in addition to all of the above, the agricultural markets were becoming increasingly complex. For one thing, the United States was beginning to export farm products, and by 1900, they became 75% of the total U.S. export trade. Middlemen took advantage of the ignorance of farmers regarding business matters and charged higher prices. Hence, farmers were forced to become businessmen, yet some remained ignorant of basic business practices.

Having no control over the marketplace, farmers were at the mercy of:

- Business cycles
- Credit
- Transportation
- Labor supply
- Price structure
- Government policies

Consequently, farmers began taking political action.[8]

During the Civil War, the railroads developed into the principal industry of the United States as they carried men and supplies for the Union and became a significant factor in the defeat of the South. When we study the rise of industry shortly, we will learn the extent to which railroads became the foundation of other flourishing industries in America.

---

[8] Ibid., Lecture 10.

One reason for their thriving success after the Civil War was agriculture. Much of this, as mentioned above, came at the expense of farmers.

During the 1870s, farmers began organizing on their own behalf and formed the **Grange Movement.** They worked hard to pass pro-farmer legislation and began the cooperative movement which allowed them to pool their capital in order to purchase machinery, supplies, and insurance less expensively. Although they faced formidable opposition from business, they succeeded in getting a major piece of litigation into the Supreme Court in 1877. In *Munn v. Illinois*, the court upheld the right of a state legislature to regulate railroad rates.

Unfortunately, after this legislative and legal victory, the Grange Movement decreased its political activity and was succeeded by three regional organizations:

- The Farmers and Laborers' Union of America which was a regional association in the Southwest
- The Northwest Farmers Alliance originating in Chicago
- The Colored Farmers National Alliance which addressed the needs of black farmers in the South.

In 1889, these three groups held a convention in St. Louis, but so many regional differences prevailed that they could not form one united organization. However, in 1890, Southern farmers joined with local Democrats, and Midwestern farmers formed their own local parties. Together these groups united to form the People's Party or the **Populist Party**.

In 1892, three major farmers' organizations held a convention in Omaha, Nebraska and stated six principal demands. This came to be known as the **Omaha Platform**:

- A permanent union of all working classes
- Wealth for the workers
- Government ownership of railroads
- Government ownership of all communication systems
- More equitable distribution of the national currency
- The end of ownership of land by those who do not actually use it

The entire **Omaha Platform** may be viewed at:
http://www.geocities.com/progpop/omaha.html

In 1890, farmers elected five U.S. Senators, six governors, and forty-six Congressmen. Increasingly, they were becoming a force to be reckoned with.

The Populists believed that the nation was beginning to place too much emphasis on property rights and that businesses were rapidly becoming monopolies. They adamantly embraced equality and rejected **Social Darwinism** and *laissez-faire* economics. (The latter concepts will be defined and discussed subsequently.) Populists argued that industrial society had turned the individual into a commodity and that wealth was unevenly distributed. In addition, Populists called for the elimination of the gold standard in favor of silver. This would have made money cheaper and more available. Other measures favored by the Populists were the passage of an income tax, the end of life tenure of federal judges and the end of the printing of paper currency by nationally chartered private banks.

By 1896, the Populists were a strong third party. At the Democratic convention that year, Populist, William Jennings Bryan, a devout fundamentalist Christian who passionately fought for social justice, was nominated as the Presidential candidate. He lost to William McKinley but ran again in 1900, losing again to McKinley. He ran once again in 1908, losing to William Howard Taft.

AN ASSESSMENT OF POPULISM: *A Summary based on the writings of* Norman Pollack, Ph.D.

While Populism originated as an agrarian movement, it became a powerful urban movement, championing the rights of workers and immigrants. In his research on Populism, Norman Pollack, Ph.D. emeritus, Michigan State University, has offered some far-reaching conclusions regarding the significance of Populism in American history.

First, according to Pollack, we must note that Populism was a very diverse and complex movement. It was comprised of people with almost no education to very articulate and cogent thinkers who spoke and wrote freely about it. It had elements of racism, reaction, regionalism and religious conservatism as well as more sophisticated elements of liberalism and literary genius.

Secondly, Populism was concerned with the question of sovereignty. Their fundamental issue was: Who will govern in America? They feared that sovereignty would come to rest in the private, corporate realm instead of in the independent, public realm. Government as regulator should function on behalf of the people, not on behalf of corporations. But beyond that, Populists sought to restructure economic and class relations in order to secure social and economic balance. The corporation, Populism believed, should be brought into proper alignment with and regulated by the government. They were not anti-business; in fact, they called for public ownership of monopolist enterprises on the ground that they were hindrances to free economic activity. They were not socialists, as some people have erroneously labeled them, but rather people who intended to construct an economy and a supportive culture of democratic capitalism which would reject both monopolism and socialism. The individual was deemed more sacred than the law, and the individual, more than property was the antecedent source of sovereignty.

Pollack believes that one of the mistakes historians make in assessing Populism is to see it as a single-issue movement which was focused primarily on becoming a third party. On the contrary, it had a manifold program and was as much a social movement as a political one. Populists did not just mobilize for elections but continually educated people politically and socially with an ideology of democratic rights and equitable economic, political and social arrangements. For this, three conditions would be necessary:

- The rule of law
- The absence of economic privilege
- The maintenance of opportunity for all social strata

Populists did not believe that the choice lay between an agrarian and an industrial order. They grasped the political as well as the technological character of modernization. Their primary intent was to democratize the internal make-up of the business system, remove its powers over public policy, and end its ideological hegemony in defining the society's values and systemic course.

Populists saw themselves as mediators between the intransigence of the community and those who cried out for social revolution. The Populist idea of a middle-class standard did not look like today's classless abundance. Instead, they believed that the whole society had to be reconstituted to retain property while serving the people, realizing more lasting values centered not on property but on a decent competence, humane working conditions and individual security.

By incorporating a moral-legal influence into the structure of the society, Populists believed it would be possible for capitalism to realize the potential for abundance within reach in America. Populism failed, however, because it was no match for its enemies. They were dependent on the political process—a political process that they knew was unresponsive and fraudulent. In addition, they were vulnerable because for the most part, they were not vindictive, and their opponents knew that their aggression against Populism would not be reciprocated. And finally, some Populist leaders, such as Tom Watson, were anti-semitic, anti-black and anti-immigrant, bringing about conflicts within their own ranks that served their enemies' purpose.

Nevertheless, Pollack concludes: "Populists, under trying conditions, commenced a rational discussion of democracy that issued in, for an all-too-brief season, the vision of a peoples' government...Protest marked a journey of rediscovery in which Populists summoned what was best in the American past, for having done so, they were treated as subversive to America in their own time, testifying to more than a devotion to a property-based society."[9]

The above summary of Norman Pollack's remarks on Populism is a composite taken from his work, *THE JUST POLITY: Populism, Law and Human Welfare*. Other works by Pollack are:
- *The Populist Response To Industrial America, 1976*
- *The Populist Mind, 1967*

The following handout offers a concise summary and essay questions material on Populism for students:

---

[9] Pollack, Norman. *The Just Polity: Populism, Law, and Human Welfare*. Chicago, Urbana: University of Illinois Press, 1987.

Excerpts from *The Just Polity*, by Norman Pollack:

FACTS ABOUT POPULISM
(Handout)

1) Populism was a very **diverse movement** comprised of people with almost no education to some very articulate and intelligent thinkers who spoke and wrote freely about it. The movement had elements of racism, reaction, regionalism, and religious conservatism as well as more sophisticated elements of liberalism and literary genius.

2) Populism was a movement **concerned with the question of sovereignty**. Populists feared that sovereignty would come to rest in the private, corporate realm instead of in the independent, public realm. Government as a regulator, populists believed, should function on behalf of the people, not on behalf of corporations. They sought also to restructure economic and class relations in order to secure social and economic balance. The corporation, populism believed, should be regulated by the government. Populists were NOT anti-business. In fact, they called for public ownership of monopoly-like enterprises on the ground that they were hindrances to free economic activity. They were not socialists, as some people have erroneously labeled them, but rather people who intended to construct an economy and a supportive culture of democratic capitalism which would reject both monopolism and socialism. The individual was deemed more sacred than the law, and the individual, more than property was the antecedent source of sovereignty.

MISCONCEPTIONS ABOUT POPULISM

- Some historians believe that one of the mistakes we make in assessing populism is to see it as a **single-issue movement** which was focused primarily on becoming a third party. On the contrary, populism had a **varied program** and was as much a social movement as a political one.

- They **didn't mobilize solely for elections** but continually **educated** people politically and socially about democratic rights and just economic, political, and social arrangements. For this, three conditions were necessary:
    —The rule of law
    —The absence of economic privilege
    —The maintenance of opportunity for all social strata

- Populists **didn't believe that people had to choose** between an agrarian and an industrial order. They grasped the political as well as the technological character of modernization. Their primary intent was to **democratize** the internal make-up of the business system, remove its powers over public policy, and end its domination in defining the society's values.

THE MORAL INFLUENCE OF POPULISM

Populism saw itself as a mediator between the inflexibility of the industrial community and those who cried out for social revolution. They believed that the whole society had to be reconstituted to retain property while serving the people.

By incorporating a moral-legal influence into the structure of society, populists believed it would be possible for capitalism to realize the potential for prosperity within reach in America.

WHY POPULISM FAILED

Populism failed, however, because it was no match for its enemies. They were **dependent on the political process**—a political process that they knew was unresponsive and fraudulent. In addition, they were **vulnerable** because for the most part, they were not vindictive, and their opponents knew that Populists would not return evil for evil. And finally, some populist leaders, such as Tom Watson, were anti-Semitic, anti-black, and anti-immigrant, bringing about **conflicts within their own ranks** that served their enemies' purposes superbly.

PRESIDENT LINCOLN'S WARNING REGARDING CORPORATIONS

I see in the near future a crisis approaching that unnerves me and causes me to tremble for the safety of my country....corporations have been enthroned and an era of corruption in high places will follow, and the money power of the country will endeavor to prolong its reign by working upon the prejudices of the people until all wealth is aggregated in a few hands and the Republic is destroyed.

—President Abraham Lincoln, Nov. 21, 1864
(letter to Col. William F. Elkins)
Ref: The Lincoln Encyclopedia, Archer H. Shaw
(Macmillan, 1950, NY)

4

URBAN AMERICA AND THE RISE OF THE ROBBER BARONS (1865-1914)

The late-nineteenth century has often been called the "Gilded Age", meaning that it was a time when American society seemed to be gold-encrusted by the wealth and power of its ruling elite.

Two themes of tension during the late-nineteenth century:

**Laissez-Faire Economics

In the same year that Jefferson wrote the Declaration of Independence, 1776, Adam Smith wrote *The Wealth of Nations*, introducing the concept of **laissez-faire** economics. According to Smith, a nation's economy is self-adjusting and should not be interfered with by government regulation or control.

According to historian Stanley Schultz, 19th-Century American economists generally agreed that:

- Political economy is ruled by unchanging, everlasting laws which can be equated with laws of Nature or God.
- Self-interest as the only motive for human action is not only natural but beneficial.
- Free competition is a permanent and necessary law of economics.
- Government is an inefficient agency and should not be involved in economic matters.

**Concentration of power in the hands of the government

During the last three decades of the nineteenth century, abuse and exploitation by corporations reached unprecedented heights. A growing labor movement and socially conscious citizens began demanding government regulation of industry. The progressive movement was born which ultimately resulted in the creation of a variety of federal regulatory agencies.

An age of corruption:

- **Credit Mobilier**—Between 1872 and 1873, major stockholders of the Union Pacific Railroad formed the Credit Mobilier Company of America and gave it contracts to build railroads. They also sold or gave shares of stock to influential Congressmen to bribe them to pass laws enabling them to make huge profits.

- **The Grant Administration**—From 1869 to 1877, bribery of government officials was rampant. In fact, the Grant Presidency has one of the worst records of corruption in American history.

The new businessmen:
- Daniel Drew
- Jay Gould
- Jim Fisk
- Cornelius Vanderbilt
- John D. Rockefeller
- J.P. Morgan
- Andrew Carnegie
- Andrew Mellon

New ways of doing business—Whereas the typical way of doing business in America had been the sole proprietorship or small-scale partnership, the late-nineteenth century gives birth to the corporation which allowed individuals to limit their liability and maximize their profits as never before.

Corporations had been around for a long time. In fact, one of the first corporations in America was the British East India Company which transported thousands of European settlers to the New World in the seventeenth century and continued to transport European products to the colonies until Americans became self-sufficient. What we see in the late-nineteenth century, however, is a new breed of corporation the *mega* corporation which began merging with other corporations to form trusts. **Trusts** became so large and powerful that they destroyed healthy competition and monopolized the market of some goods and services. In 1934, historian, Matthew Josephson, wrote *The Robber Barons*, a study of the industrial giants who rose to wealth and fame at the end of the nineteenth century. Subsequently, some historians have referred to these industrial giants as "robber barons."[10]

- **The corporation becomes "a person."** (*Santa Clara vs. Southern Pacific Railroad, 1886*) We know that newly-freed slaves were made citizens and granted legal protections by the U.S. Constitution through the 14th Amendment in 1868. Nearly twenty years later, corporate managers, lawyers and lobbyists who wanted to remove restrictions on corporations eyed this development as an opportunity to advance their cause. In 1886, their efforts were rewarded with a Supreme Court decision declaring that the corporation was legally equivalent to a person with regard to the protections afforded by the 14th Amendment. For further information see:

Corporism: The Systemic Disease that Destroys Civilization, by Ken Reiner at:
www.informationclearinghouse.info/article3310.htm

Below is a history of U.S. corporations by Richard Heinberg, entitled, *A History of Corporate Rule and Popular Protest*, which can be found at
www.nexusmagazine.com/corporations.html and which I regularly use in class:

---

[10] Schultz Lectures, Lecture 5 (http://us.history.wisc.edu/hist102/lectures/lecture05.html)

A History of Corporate Rule and Popular Protest

By Richard Heinberg

In the 21st Century, a new populist movement has emerged to challenge corporate power and call for a more equitable economic order that protects traditional cultures and ecosystems and promotes sustainability.

Extracted from Nexus Magazine, Volume 9, Number 6 (Oct-Nov 2002)
PO Box 30, Mapleton Qld 4560 Australia. editor@nexusmagazine.com
Telephone: +61 (0)7 5442 9280; Fax: +61 (0)7 5442 9381
From our web page at: http://www.nexusmagazine.com/
by Richard Heinberg © 2002
Editor/Publisher
MuseLetter
1604 Jennings Avenue
Santa Rosa, CA 95401, USA
Email: heinberg@museletter.com
Website: http://www.museletter.com/

The corporation was invented early in the colonial era as a grant of privilege extended by the Crown to a group of investors, usually to finance a trade expedition. The corporation limited the liability of investors to the amount of their investment—a right not held by ordinary citizens. Corporate charters set out the specific rights and obligations of the individual corporation, including the amount to be paid to the Crown in return for the privilege granted.

Thus were born the East India Company, which led the British colonisation of India, and Hudson's Bay Company, which accomplished the same purpose in Canada. Almost from the beginning, Britain deployed state military power to further corporate interests—a practice that has continued to the present. Also from the outset, corporations began pressuring government to expand corporate rights and to limit corporate responsibilities.

The corporation was a legal invention—a socio-economic mechanism for concentrating and deploying human and economic power. The purpose of the corporation was and is to generate profits for its investors. As an entity, it has no other purpose; it acknowledges no higher value.

Many people understood early on that since corporations do not serve society as a whole, but only their investors, there is therefore always a danger that the interests of corporations and those of the general populace will come into conflict. Indeed, the United States was born of a revolution not just against the British monarchy but against the power of corporations. Many of the American colonies had been chartered as corporations (the Virginia Company, the Carolina Company, the Maryland Company, etc.) and were granted monopoly power over lands and industries considered crucial to the interests of the Crown.

Much of the literature of the revolutionaries was filled with denunciations of the "long train of abuses" of the Crown and its instruments of dominance, the corporations. As the yoke of the Crown corporations was being thrown off, Thomas Jefferson railed against "the general prey of the rich on the poor". Later, he warned the new nation against the creation of "immortal persons" in the form of corporations. The American revolutionaries resolved that the authority to charter corporations should lie not with governors, judges or generals, but only with elected legislatures.

At first, such charters as were granted were for a fixed time, and legislatures spelled out the rules each business should follow. Profit-making corporations were chartered to build turnpikes, canals and bridges, to operate banks and to engage in industrial manufacture. Some citizens argued against even these few, limited charters, on the grounds that no business should be granted special privileges and that owners should not be allowed to hide behind legal shields. Thus the requests for many charters were denied, and existing charters were often revoked. Banks were kept on a short leash, and (in most states) investors were held liable for the debts and harms caused by their corporations.

All of this began to change in the mid-19th century. According to Richard Grossman and Frank Adams in *Taking Care of Business*: "Corporations were abusing their charters to become conglomerates and trusts. They were converting the nation's treasures into private fortunes, creating factory systems and company towns. Political power began flowing to absentee owners intent upon dominating people and nature."[1]

Grossman and Adams note that: "In factory towns, corporations set wages, hours, production processes and machine speeds. They kept blacklists of labor organizers and workers who spoke up for their rights. Corporate officials forced employees to accept humiliating conditions, while the corporations agreed to nothing."

The authors quote Julianna, a Lowell, Massachusetts, factory worker, who wrote: "Incarcerated within the walls of a factory, while as yet mere children, drilled there from five till seven o'clock, year after year.what, we would ask, are we to expect, the same system of labor prevailing, will be the mental and intellectual character of future generations.a race fit only for corporation tools and time-serving slaves?…Shall we not hear the response from every hill and vale: 'Equal rights, or death to the corporations'?"

Industrialists and bankers hired private armies to keep workers in line, bought newspapers and (quoting Grossman and Adams again): "painted politicians as villains and businessmen as heroes. Bribing state legislators, they then announced legislators were corrupt, that they used too much of the public's resources and time to scrutinise every charter application and corporate operation. Corporate advocates campaigned to replace existing chartering laws with general incorporation laws that set up simple administrative procedures, claiming this would be more efficient. What they really wanted was the end of legislative authority over charters."

During the Civil War, government spending brought corporations unprecedented wealth. "Corporate managers developed the techniques and the ability to organise production on an ever grander scale," according to Grossman and Adams. "Many corporations used their wealth to take advantage of war and Reconstruction years to get the tariff, banking, railroad, labor, and public lands legislation they wanted."

In 1886, the US Supreme Court declared that corporations were henceforth to be considered "persons" under the law, with all of the constitutional rights that designation implies.

The Fourteenth Amendment to the Constitution, passed to give former slaves equal rights, has been invoked approximately ten times more frequently on behalf of corporations than on behalf of African Americans. Likewise the First Amendment, guaranteeing free speech, has been invoked to guarantee corporations the "right" to influence the political process through campaign contributions, which the courts have equated with "speech".

If corporations are "persons", they are persons with qualities and powers that no flesh-and-blood human could ever possess—immortality, the ability to be in many places at once, and (increasingly) the ability to avoid liability. They are also "persons" with no sense of moral responsibility, since their only legal mandate is to produce profits for their investors.

Throughout the late 19th and early 20th centuries, corporations reshaped every aspect of life in America and much of the rest of the world. The factory system turned self-sufficient small farmers into wage-earners and transformed the family from an interdependent economic production unit to a consumption-oriented collection of individuals with separate jobs. Advertising turned productive citizens into "consumers". Business leaders campaigned to create public schools to train children in factory-system obedience to schedules and in the performance of isolated, meaningless tasks. Meanwhile, corporations came to own and dominate sources of information and entertainment, and to control politicians and judges.

During two periods, corporations faced a challenge: the 1890s (a depression period when Populists demanded regulation of railroad rates, heavy taxation of land held only for speculation, and an increase in the money supply), and the 1930s (when a profound crisis of capitalism led hundreds of thousands of workers and armies of the unemployed to demand government regulation of the economy and to win a 40-hour week, a minimum-wage law, the right to organise, and the outlawing of child labour). But in both cases, corporate capitalism emerged intact.

In the words of historian Howard Zinn: "The rich still controlled the nation's wealth, as well as its laws, courts, police, newspapers, churches, colleges. Enough help had been given to enough people to make Roosevelt a hero to millions, but the same system that had brought depression and crisis.remained."[2]

World War II, like previous wars, brought huge profits to corporations via government contracts. But following this war, military spending was institutionalised, ostensibly to fight the "Cold War". Despite occasional regulatory setbacks, corporations seized ever more power, and increasingly transcended national boundaries, loyalties and sovereignties altogether.

In the 1970s, capitalism faced yet another challenge as postwar growth subsided and profits fell. The US was losing its dominant position in world markets; the production of oil from its domestic wells was peaking and beginning to fall, thus making America increasingly dependent upon oil imports from Arab countries; the Vietnam War had weakened the American economy; and Third World countries were demanding a "North-South dialogue" leading towards greater self-reliance for poorer countries. President Nixon responded by doing away with fixed currency exchange rates and devaluing the dollar, largely erasing US war debts to other countries. Later, newly elected President Reagan, at the 1981 Cancún, Mexico, meeting of 22 heads of state, refused to discuss new financial arrangements with the Third World, thus effectively endorsing their further exploitation by corporations.

Meanwhile, the corporations themselves also responded with a new strategy. Increased capital mobility (made possible by floating exchange rates and new transportation, communication and production technologies) allowed US corporations to move production offshore to "export processing zones" in poorer countries. Corporations also undertook a restructuring process, moving toward "networked production"—in which big firms, while retaining and consolidating power, hired smaller firms to take over aspects of supply, manufacture, accounting and transport. (Economist Bennett Harrison defined networked production as "concentration of control combined with decentralization of production".) This restructuring process is also known as "downsizing", because it results in the shedding of higher-paid employees by large corporations and the hiring of low-wage contingent workers by smaller subcontractors.

Jeremy Brecher and Tim Costello write in *Global Village or Global Pillage* that: "As the economic crisis deepened, there gradually evolved.a 'supra-national policy arena' which included new organizations like the Group of Seven (G7) industrial nations and NAFTA and new roles for established international organisations like EU, IMF, World Bank, and GATT. The policies adopted by these international institutions allowed corporations to lower their costs in several ways. They reduced consumer, environmental, health, labor, and other standards. They reduced business taxes. They facilitated the move to lower wage areas and threat of such movement. And they encouraged the expansion of markets and the 'economies of scale' provided by larger-scale production."[3]

All of this has led to a globalised economy in which (again quoting Brecher and Costello): "All over the world, people are being pitted against each other to see who will offer global corporations the lowest labor, social, and environmental costs. Their jobs are being moved to places with inferior wages, lower business taxes, and more freedom to pollute. Their employers are using the threat of 'foreign competition' to hold down wages, salaries, taxes, and environmental protections and to replace high-quality jobs with temporary, part-time, insecure, and low-quality jobs. Their government officials are justifying cuts in education, health, and other services as necessary to reduce business taxes in order to keep or attract jobs."

Corporations, no longer bound by national laws, prowl the world looking for the best deals on labour and raw materials. Of the world's top 120 economies, nearly half are corporations, not countries. Thus the power of citizens in any nation to control corporations through whatever democratic processes are available to them is receding quickly.

In November 1999, tens of thousands of students, union members and indigenous peoples gathered in Seattle to protest a meeting of the World Trade Organization (WTO). This mass demonstration seemed to signal the birth of a new global populist uprising against corporate globalisation. In the three years since then, more mass demonstrations—some larger, many smaller—have occurred in Genoa, Melbourne, Milan, Montreal, Philadelphia, Washington and other cities.

In January 2001, George W. Bush and Dick Cheney took office, following a deeply flawed US election. With strong ties to the oil industry and to the huge energy-trading corporation Enron, the new administration quickly proposed a national energy policy that focused on opening federally protected lands for oil exploration and on further subsidising the oil industry.

Enron, George W. Bush's largest campaign contributor, was the seventh-largest corporation in the US and the 16th largest in the world. Despite its reported massive profits, it had paid no taxes in four out of the previous five years. The company had thousands of offshore partnerships, through which it had hidden over a billion dollars in debt. When this hidden debt was disclosed in October 2001, the company imploded. Its share price collapsed and its credit rating was slashed. Its executives resigned in disgrace, taking with them multimillion-dollar bonuses, while employees and stockholders shouldered the immense financial loss. Enron's bankruptcy was the largest in corporate history up to that time, but its creative accounting practices appear to be far from unique, with dozens of other corporations poised for a similar collapse.

Following the outrageous and tragic attacks of September 11, Bush launched a "War on Terror", raising the listed number of potential target countries from three to nearly 50, most having exportable energy resources. With Iraq (holder of the world's second-largest proven petroleum reserves) high on the list of enemy regimes to be violently overthrown, the Bush administration's Terror War appeared to be geared toward making the world safe for the expanded reach of US oil corporations. Meanwhile, new laws and executive orders curtailed constitutional rights and erected screens of secrecy around government actions and decision-making processes.

It remains to be seen how the American populace will react to these new developments. Here again, a little history may help us understand the options available.

The Populism of the 1890s failed for two main reasons: divisiveness within, and co-optation from without. While many Populist leaders saw the need for unity among people of different racial and ethnic backgrounds in attacking corporate power, racism was strong among many whites. Most of the Alliance leaders were white farm owners who failed in many instances to support the organising efforts of poor rural blacks, and poor whites as well, thus dividing the movement.

"On top of the serious failures to unite blacks and whites, city workers and country farmers," writes Howard Zinn, "there was the lure of electoral politics. Once allied with the Democratic party in supporting William Jennings Bryan for President in 1896.the pressure for electoral victory led Populism to make deals with the major parties in city after city. If the Democrats won, it would be absorbed. If the Democrats lost, it would disintegrate. Electoral politics brought into the top leadership the political brokers instead of the agrarian radicals…In the election of 1896, with the Populist movement enticed into the Democratic party, Bryan, the Democratic candidate, was defeated by William McKinley, for whom the corporations and the press mobilised, in the first massive use of money in an election campaign."[4]

Today, a new populist movement could easily fall prey to the same internal divisions and tactical errors that destroyed its counterpart a century ago. In the recent American presidential election, populists faced the choice of supporting their own candidate (Ralph Nader) and thereby contributing to the election of the far-right, pro-corporate Republican candidate (Bush), or supporting the centrist Gore and seeing their movement co-opted by pro-corporate Democrats.

Meanwhile, though African Americans, Asian Americans, Hispanic Americans, European Americans and Native Americans have all been victimised by corporations, class divisions and historical resentments often prevent them from organising to further their common interests. In recent elections, ultra-right candidate Pat Buchanan appealed simultaneously to "populist" anti-corporate and anti-government sentiments among the working class, as well as to xenophobic white racism. Buchanan's critique of corporate power was shallow, but it was often the only such critique permitted in the corporate-controlled media. One cannot help but wonder: were the corporations looking for a lightning rod to rechannel the anger building against them?

While Buchanan had no chance of winning the presidency, his candidacy did raise the spectre of another kind of solution to the emerging crisis of popular resentment against the system—a solution that again has roots in the history of the past century.

In the early 1900s, workers in Italy and Germany built strong unions and won substantial concessions in wages and work conditions; still, after World War I they suffered under a disastrous postwar economy, which fanned unrest. During the early 1920s, heavy industry and big finance were in a state of near-total collapse. Bankers and agribusiness associations offered financial support to Mussolini—who had been a socialist before the war—to seize state power, which he effectively did in 1922 following his march on Rome. Within two years, the Fascist Party (from the Latin fasces, meaning a bundle of rods and an axe, symbolising Roman state power) had shut down all opposition newspapers, crushed the socialist, liberal, Catholic, democratic and republican parties (which had together commanded about 80 per cent of the vote), abolished unions, outlawed strikes and privatised farm cooperatives.

In Germany, Hitler led the Nazi Party to power, then cut wages and subsidised industries.

In both countries, corporate profits ballooned. Understandably, given their friendliness to big business, Fascism and Nazism were popular among some prominent American industrialists (such as Henry Ford) and opinion shapers (like William Randolph Hearst).

Fascism and Nazism relied on centrally controlled propaganda campaigns that cleverly co-opted the language of the Left (the Nazis called themselves the National Socialist German Workers Party—while persecuting socialists and curtailing workers' rights). Both movements also made calculated use of emotionally charged symbolism: scapegoating minorities, appealing to mythic images of a glorious national past, building a leader cult, glorifying war and conquest, and preaching that the only proper role of women is as wives and mothers.

As political theorist Michael Parenti points out, historians often overlook Fascism's economic agenda—the partnership between Big Capital and Big Government—in their analysis of its authoritarian social program. Indeed, according to Bertram Gross in his startlingly prescient Friendly Fascism (1980), it is possible to achieve fascist goals within an ostensibly democratic society.[2] Corporations themselves, after all, are internally authoritarian (courts have ruled that citizens give up their constitutional rights to free speech, freedom of assembly, etc., when they are at work on corporate-owned property); and as corporations increasingly dominate politics, media and economy, they can mould an entire society to serve the interests of a powerful elite without ever resorting to stormtroopers and concentration camps. No deliberate conspiracy is necessary, either: each corporation merely acts to further its own economic interests. If the populace shows signs of restlessness, politicians can be hired to appeal to racial resentments and memories of national glory, dividing popular opposition and inspiring loyalty.

In the current situation, "friendly fascism" works somewhat as follows. Corporations drive down wages and pay a dwindling share of taxes (through mechanisms outlined above), gradually impoverishing the middle class and creating unrest. As corporate taxes are cut, politicians (whose election was funded by corporate donors) argue that it is necessary to reduce government services in order to balance the budget. Meanwhile, the same politicians argue for an increase in the repressive functions of government (more prisons, harsher laws, more executions, more military spending). Politicians channel the middle class's rising resentment away from corporations and toward the government (which, after all, is now less helpful and more repressive than it used to be) and against social groups easy to scapegoat (criminals, minorities, teenagers, women, gays, immigrants).

Meanwhile, debate in the media is kept superficial (elections are treated as sporting contests), and right-wing commentators are subsidised while left-of-centre ones are marginalised. People who feel cheated by the system turn to the Right for solace, and vote for politicians who further subsidise corporations, cut government services, expand the repressive power of the state and offer irrelevant scapegoats for social problems with economic roots. The process feeds on itself.

Within this scenario, George W. Bush (and similar ultra-right figures in other countries) are not anomalies but, rather, predictable products of a strategy adopted by economic elites—harbingers of a less-than-friendly future—as the more "moderate" tactics for the maintenance and consolidation of power founder under the weight of corporate greed and resource exhaustion.

These circumstances are, in their details, unprecedented; but in broad outline we are seeing the re-enactment of a story that goes back at least to the beginning of civilisation. Those with power are always looking for ways to protect and extend it, and to make their power seem legitimate, necessary or invisible so that popular protest seems unnecessary or futile. If protest comes, the powerful always try to deflect anger away from themselves. The leaders of the new populist movement appear to have a good grasp of both the current circumstances and the historical ground from which these circumstances emerge. They seem to have realised that, in order to succeed, the new populism will have to:

- avoid being co-opted by existing political parties;

- heal race, class and gender divisions and actively resist any campaign to scapegoat disempowered social groups;

- avoid being identified with an ideological category—"communist", "socialist" or "anarchist"—against which most of the public is already well inoculated by corporate propaganda;

- direct public discussion toward the most vulnerable link in the corporate chain of power: the legal basis of the corporation;

- internationalise the movement so that corporations cannot undermine it merely by shifting their base of operations from one country to another.

As Lawrence Goodwyn noted in his definitive work, *The Populist Moment*, the original Populists were "attempting to construct, within the framework of American capitalism, some variety of cooperative commonwealth". This was "the last substantial effort at structural alteration of hierarchical economic forms in modern America".[6]

In announcing the formation of the Alliance for Democracy, in an article in the August 14, 1996 issue of *The Nation*, activist Ronnie Dugger compiled a list of policy suggestions which comprise some of the core demands of the new populist movement. These include: a prohibition of contributions or any other political activity by corporations; single-payer national health insurance with automatic universal coverage; a doubling of the minimum wage, indexed to inflation; a generic low-interest-rate national policy, entailing the abolition of the Federal Reserve System; statutory reversal of the court-made law that corporations are "persons"; establishment of a national public oil company; limitations on ownership of newspapers, magazines, radio and TV stations to one of any kind per person or owning entity; and the halving of military spending. The new populists are, in Ronnie Dugger's words, "ready to resume the cool eyeing of the corporations with a collective will to take back the powers they have seized from us".[7]

The new populism draws some of its inspiration from the work of the Program on Corporations, Law and Democracy (POCLAD), a populist "think-tank" that explores the legal basis of corporate power. POCLAD believes that it is possible to control—and, if necessary, dismantle—corporations by amending or revoking their charters.[8]

Since the largest corporations are now transnational in scope, the new populism must confront their abuses globally. The International Forum on Globalization (IFG) was founded for this purpose in 1994, as an alliance of 60 activists, scholars, economists, and writers (including Jerry Mander, Vandana Shiva, Richard Grossman, Ralph Nader, Helena Norberg-Hodge, Jeremy Rifkin and Kirkpatrick Sale), to stimulate new thinking and joint action along these lines.

In a position statement drafted in 1995, the International Forum on Globalization said that it: "views international trade and investment agreements, including the GATT, the WTO, Maastricht and NAFTA, combined with the structural adjustment policies of the International Monetary Fund and the World Bank, to be direct stimulants to the processes that weaken democracy, create a world order in the control of transnational corporations and devastate the natural world. The IFG will study, publish and actively advocate in opposition to the current rush toward economic globalization, and will seek to reverse its direction. Simultaneously, we will advocate on behalf of a far more diversified, locally controlled, community-based economics. We believe that the creation of a more equitable economic order—based on principles of diversity, democracy, community and ecological sustainability—will require new international agreements that place the needs of people, local economies and the natural world ahead of the interests of corporations."[9]

Leaders of the new populism appear to realise that anti-corporatism is not a complete solution to the world's problems; that the necessary initial focus on corporate power must eventually be supplemented by a more general critique of centralising and unsustainable technologies, money-based economics and current nation-state governmental structures, by efforts to protect traditional cultures and ecosystems, and by a renewal of culture and spirituality.

It would be foolish to underestimate the immense challenges to the new populism from the current US administration and from the jingoistic, bellicose post-September 11 public sentiment fostered by the corporate media. Nevertheless, POCLAD, the Alliance for Democracy and the IFG (along with dozens of human rights, environmental and anti-war organisations around the world) provide important rallying points for citizens' self-defence against tyranny in its most modern, invisible, effective and even seductive forms.

Endnotes:

1. Grossman, Richard and Frank Adams, *Taking Care of Business: Citizenship and the Charter of Incorporation*, pamphlet, 1993, available at http://www.poclad.org/resources.html.
2. Zinn, Howard, *A People's History of the United States: 1492 to Present*, Harper Perennial, 2001.
3. Brecher, Jeremy and Tim Costello, *Global Village or Global Pillage: Economic Reconstruction from the Bottom Up*, South End Press, 1998.
4. Zinn, op. cit.
5. Gross, Bertram, *Friendly Fascism: The New Face of Power in America*, South End Press, 1998.
6. Goodwyn, Lawrence, *The Populist Moment: A Short History of the Agrarian Revolt in America*, Oxford University Press, 1978.
7. The Alliance for Democracy website, http://www.thealliancefordemocracy.org/.
8. POCLAD website, http://www.poclad.org/.
9. IFG pamphlet, 1995; revised position statement at IFG website, http://www.ifg.org/.

About the Author:

Richard Heinberg is a journalist, educator, editor, lecturer and musician. He has lectured widely and appeared on national radio and TV in five countries. He is a core faculty member of New College of California, where he teaches courses on Culture, Ecology and Sustainable Community.

He is the author of: "*Memories and Visions of Paradise*"; "*Celebrate the Solstice*"; "*A New Covenant with Nature*"; and "*Cloning the Buddha: the Moral Impact of Biotechnology*". His next book, "*The Party's Over: Oil, War and the Fate of Industrial Societies*", is to be published by New Society in March 2003. His essays have been featured in *The Futurist, Intuition, Brain/Mind Bulletin, Magical Blend, New Dawn* and elsewhere.

Richard is also author/editor/publisher of MuseLetter, a highly regarded monthly, subscription-only, alternative newsletter which is now in its tenth year of publication. MuseLetter's purpose is "to offer a continuing critique of corporate-capitalist industrial civilization and a re-visioning of humanity's prospects for the next millennium". His article, "A History of Corporate Rule and Popular Protest", was originally published in MuseLetter in 1996 as "The New Populism", and was revised in August 2002. Visit the MuseLetter website at http://www.museletter.com/.

Few Americans know that Thomas Jefferson and James Madison struggled to include an 11th Amendment in our Constitution that would have prohibited "monopolies in commerce." Michael Byron, Ph.D., Professor of Political Science at California State University, San Marcos, in an article entitled *Jefferson Was Right*, published May, 2003, explains the proposed 11th Amendment and the historical significance of its defeat:

Jefferson Was Right

By: *Dr. Michael P. Byron-05/24/03*

Published by http://www.liberalslant.com

Most Americans don't know it but Thomas Jefferson, along with James Madison worked assiduously to have an 11th Amendment included into our nation's original Bill of Rights. This proposed Amendment would have prohibited *"monopolies in commerce."* The amendment would have made it illegal for corporations to own other corporations, or to give money to politicians, or to otherwise try to influence elections. Corporations would be chartered by the states for the primary purpose of *"serving the public good."* Corporations would possess the legal status not of natural persons but rather of *"artificial persons."* This means that they would have only those legal attributes which the state saw fit to grant to them. They would NOT; and indeed could NOT possess the same bundle of rights which actual flesh and blood persons enjoy. Under this proposed amendment neither the 14th Amendment of the US Constitution, nor any provision of that document would protect the artificial entities known of as corporations.

Jefferson and Madison were so insistent upon this amendment because the American Revolution was in substantial degree a revolt against the domination of colonial economic and political life by the greatest multinational corporation of its age: the British East India Company. After all who do you think owned the tea which Sam Adams and friends dumped overboard in Boston Harbor? Who was responsible for the taxes on commodities and restrictions on trade by the American colonists? It was the British East India Company, of course. In the end the amendment was not adopted because a majority in the first Congress believed that already existing state laws governing corporations were adequate for constraining corporate power. Jefferson worried about the growing influence of corporate power until his dying day in 1826. Even the more conservative founder John Adams came to harbor deep misgivings about unchecked corporate power.

A few years after Jefferson's unsuccessful attempt to incorporate this amendment into the Bill of Rights, the fourth Chief Justice of the US Supreme Court, John Marshall, unilaterally asserted the Court's right to judicial review in the seminal case of Marbury v. Madison in 1803. In practice this meant that the Supreme Court would have sole and unchecked power to determine what the Constitution meant. Jefferson was aghast. His fear lay in the knowledge that an unelected branch of government, one which is not subject to the will of the citizens, and is effectively immune from check by the two elected branches of government (Only one Supreme Court Justice has ever been impeached—none have ever been convicted and removed) was now solely responsible for determining the meaning of the Constitution. The meaning of the Constitution, and hence the very nature of our political system, was now in the hands of an un-elected and effectively uncontrollable body. *"The Constitution has become a thing of wax to be molded as the Court sees fit"* Jefferson lamented.

In 1886 Jefferson's twin Constitutional nightmares collided in a train wreck which has effectively derailed true democracy in this nation and indeed across the globe as other nations have either copied our unfortunate example, or have fallen under the dominion of our multinational corporations—or both.. The precipitating event was the case of Santa Clara County v. Southern Pacific Railroad. This case is cited to the present day as having conferred the status of *"natural"* as opposed to *"artificial"* personhood upon American corporations. In fact the Supreme Court declined to rule on the issue. J.C. Bancroft Davis, the Clerk of the Court, an attorney, who curiously was also a former railroad company PRESIDENT, used his position to simply write this conclusion into the head notes which summarized the case. Ever since this fateful event; this sleight-of-hand rewriting of the Constitution, corporations have had the status of *"actual"* persons whose rights are fully protected by the Constitution. It was a coup against democracy which succeeded because there were no real external checks and balances on the Court, and because the Court itself chose not to act to repudiate Davis' rewriting of the Constitution. The thing stood. Precedent was established. Jefferson's *"thing of wax"* nightmare had come to pass.

Consider the implications: Actual flesh and blood persons are indeed all roughly equal in overall attributes. But a corporation can possess MILLIONS of times greater resources than does any *"natural"* person, or even a group of such persons. Neither labor unions, nor any other category of *"special interest"* group possesses this attribute of personhood and so they too are fundamentally and intrinsically unable to compete against corporate *"persons."*

To make a long and sad story short: The concentrated power of corporate persons has overwhelmed our democratic system. The unsound decisions of our unchecked and unbalanced Supreme Court have handed the *"keys to the Kingdom"* over to our corporate overlords. An analogy with an AIDS infection is instructive: After 1886, our democratic *"immune system"* resisted Davis' corporate personhood infection of our national body politic by deploying the Sherman Anti-Trust Act, the Progressive Movement, the Labor Movement, and the New Deal. All of these bought time. But now, in the era of global mega-corporations, after a long struggle, our *"democratic immune system"* is finally being overwhelmed. Democracy, rule of, by, and for the people, is dying in America.

Contemporary America is a nation almost wholly under the dominion of plutocratically wealthy, corporate quarterly-profit über alles overlords. A seamless web of corporate power connects our multinational corporations with our mass media—now almost wholly owned by a handful of mega-corporations. This military-industrial-media complex largely determines which politicians will and will not get elected. Thus they control the government. They control access to money as well as determine how a candidate will be presented to the viewers. The very policies that our *"elected"* officials are *"allowed"* to espouse are rigorously circumscribed: Remember Clinton's national healthcare proposals? Our media will never tell us that every other developed nation on Earth has universal health care for their citizens. Arguably, our corporate media has seen to it that the average American is as brainwashed as is say, the average citizen of North Korea. Our primary role in this atrocious system is simply to consume. We are consumers, corporate subjects, not citizens. Under this materialistic system our lives are devoid of deep meaning as we are conditioned to work ever harder and go ever deeper in debt to accumulate ever more useless junk as though if we just piled up enough of this crap we would somehow, magically, become happy.

What is to be done? Let's open our eyes and admit that the emperor has no clothes. Let's admit that our democratic, constitutional, system was derailed more than a century ago. Until we return power to the hands of flesh and blood citizens EXCLUSIVELY, until corporations are summarily striped of *"personhood"*, until this legal obscenity is abolished, we can have no real freedom, democracy cannot flourish. Furthermore, to ensure that the will of the people is respected and reigns supreme, all members of our federal judiciary must face periodic reelection by the citizens—just as is the case for our judiciary here in California. Until and unless these things come to pass we cannot be a free people. Because we are fundamentally NOT a free people, because our ability to act and to build freely upon our inspirations is constrained by corporate forces beyond our present control, we cannot live up to our full potentials as human beings. Once these goals are accomplished there shall be such an explosion of innovation in economic and political and scientific entrepreneurship as to make Periclean Athens seem timid. It's up to each of us to act NOW. Freedom itself hangs in the balance.

The social philosophy of American businessmen

When Thomas Jefferson originally wrote the Declaration of Independence, he substituted the term "pursuit of happiness" for the original term, "pursuit of property." In the late-nineteenth century, corporations insisted that pursing property and profit was their Constitutional right.

Yet, society was growing increasingly distrustful and resentful of corporations and their abuses. According to Professor Schultz, there are four principal reasons why corporations were progressively viewed as evil entities:

- They were unprecedented in terms of **size and power**. The early American ideal was Jefferson's yeoman farmer or the small shop keeper.

- Corporations were an **artificial creation**. They were nothing more than an agreement between legislators and businessmen. Many Americans distrusted a legislative process that allowed a group of investors to create a money-making device that could never actually exist physically.

- Corporations **threatened to destroy competition**. Smaller entrepreneurs feared that they would be eliminated from the marketplace by corporate giants, and consumers feared that they would have fewer choices for obtaining goods and services.

- Corporations were **oppressing people**. Workers, small businessmen, and concerned citizens realized that industry was exploiting labor in terms of wages and working conditions and creating massive social and environmental problems for which it was willing to own no responsibility.

Laissez-faire, Social Darwinism, and Eugenics theory

We have already noted the acceptance of laissez-faire economic theory which embraces the notion of a self-adjusting economy which the government should not regulate or control. Laissez-faire economic theory became widely accepted during a time in history when it was believed that human behavior, as well as the physical world was governed by natural laws. Thus the social, as well as the physical sciences, began interpreting human behavior according to so-called natural laws.

In 1859, Charles Darwin introduced his *Origin of Species*, which included the theory of natural selection. Later, Herbert Spencer coined the phrase, *survival of the fittest*, which implies that Nature selects only the fittest beings for survival in the next generation. Individuals who applied Darwinian principles to human behavior became known as Social Darwinists. William Graham Sumner, an American Social Darwinist, held that weaker strains of humans should be eliminated while stronger strains should be encouraged.

In the late-nineteenth and early twentieth centuries, the **eugenics** movement was born. It claimed that cultural and social patterns were the result of heredity and could be controlled through selective breeding. The ruling elite of the era, another name for the Robber Barons, wildly embraced this rabidly racist movement and frequently contributed vast sums of money to promote eugenics "research," which reinforced their desire to eliminate "undesirable" human beings such as blacks, Jews, criminals, and in fact, all individuals who did not share their values. Today, we would call this so-called research simply, "junk science."

EUGENICS
(Handout)

The eugenics movement became popular among the ruling elite in the late nineteenth century. The same people who promoted the eugenics movement were the same people who used Social Darwinism to justify their accumulation of wealth through exploiting the poor, immigrants, women and children. They believed that there should be social control of reproduction and selective breeding to insure that more people from the same genetic stock as themselves would be born and that very few "undesirables" would be born. They successfully lobbied for involuntary sterilization of prisoners, retarded people and the mentally ill which many state legislatures voted for.

Some of the more famous Robber Barons supporting eugenics were:

1) ANDREW CARNEGIE—who made his fortune in railroads and steel. He funded a great deal of eugenics "research."

2) E.H. HARRIMAN—who made his fortune in railroads and whose estate gave $500,000 to the eugenics movement.

3) JOHN D. ROCKEFELLER—who made his fortune in the oil industry and funded elements in Germany which prepared the way for Hitler's rise to power.

4) JOHN HARVEY KELLOGG—who made his fortune in the cereal industry and sponsored three conferences on eugenics

Sterilization of the mentally ill continued into the 1970s by which time some 60,000 individuals had been involuntarily sterilized.

It is difficult for twenty-first century American citizens to grasp the level of corruption and exploitation of human beings by the Robber Barons of the late-nineteenth and early twentieth centuries. Although most of our contemporary regulatory agencies are not effectively serving the American people by adequately enforcing laws against corporations who exploit them, current working conditions have improved, and workplace health and safety laws do exist. For how much longer, we do not know, given current socio-political trends.

Traditional historians, while often criticizing the Robber Barons for their greed and insensitivity to human suffering, generally continue to hold them up as heroes or at least "necessary" captains of industry in the evolution of the American economy. However, many journalist contemporaries of the Robber Barons were highly critical of them and demanded that the American public question their character and business practices.

Such journalists became **muckrakers**, which means that they devoted their writings to exposing corruption and exploitation in industry.

Journalist and muckraker, Ida Tarbell, wrote a scathing essay in *McClure's Magazine* on John D. Rockefeller called "John D. Rockefeller: A Character Study." (1906).

Excerpt from Tarbell:

> *Now a man who possesses this kind of influence cannot be allowed to live in the dark. The public not only has the right to know what sort of a man he is; it is the duty of the public to know. How else can the public discharge the most solemn obligation it owes to itself and to the future, to keep the springs of its higher life clean? Who then is this John D. Rockefeller? Whence did he come? By what qualities did he grow to such power? Has he proved his right to the power? Does he give to the public whence he has drawn his wealth a just return in ideas, in patriotism, in devotion to social betterment, in generous living, in inspiring personal character? Has John D. Rockefeller made good? From time immemorial men who have risen to power have had to face this question. Kings, tyrants, chieftains, since the world began have stood or have fallen as they have convinced the public that they were giving or not giving a just return for the power allowed them. The time is here when Mr. Rockefeller must face the verdict of the public by which he lives.*

Foreign immigrants in industrial America

- **Xenophobia**—The fear of things foreign or different, i.e. a different race, different culture, different lifestyle. Xenophobia reigned among the ruling elite and Anglo-Americans who feared the influx of the masses of foreign-born immigrants. Immigrants were generally not welcomed outside of their own communities. Generally speaking, immigrants from England, France and Germany were more accepted than those from Italy, Ireland or Asia.

- **Horrific living and working conditions in American cities**—Industry tolerated immigrants because they provided a source of cheap labor. Since they were not American-born, immigrants generally tolerated their horrible living and working conditions, feeling that a low-paying job with exploitative working conditions was better than no job at all. They lived in inordinately crowded conditions in urban tenements often dying at an early age as a result of disease, employment-related injuries or simply working themselves to death.

The Nature Of Immigration

A dramatic population increase and economic crisis in Europe, the spread of commercial agriculture, the rise of the factory system and less expensive means of transportation such as steamships and railroads motivated European immigrants to repatriate in the United States.

Essentially, there were **three great waves of immigration**

- From 1815 to 1860—Five million immigrants settled in the U.S. primarily from northwestern Europe

- 1865 to 1890—Ten million immigrants settled, again from northwestern Europe

- 1890 to 1914—Fifteen million immigrants who came from Austro-Hungary, Turkey, Lithuania, Russia, Greece, Italy and Romania. Many of these immigrants were also Jewish. Many Americans were eager to blame Jewish immigrants, those from southeastern Europe and Asia for the unprecedented social problems the country was facing, particularly in overcrowded, urban areas. Moreover, many Protestant Americans discriminated against immigrants, not only because of their racial or cultural origins, but also because many were Catholic or Jewish.

The Dillingham Commission

Appointed in 1907 by the U.S. Senate to study immigration patterns, the commission assumed that immigrants of the third wave were "inferior" to those who had come before 1880 from northern and western Europe. The commission also determined that a literacy test would be used to deny "inferior" immigrants from entering the country.

Terror of socialism in America

From the origins of the Industrial Revolution in Europe, labor movements began evolving. In the late-nineteenth century, a political and class struggle was exacerbating in Russia. Many European labor movements had embraced socialism as an alternative to the brutal exploits of capitalism. Socialism demanded stringent control of the means of production by and for the people. Understandably, American capitalist Robber Barons were terrified of the possibility that socialism could become a viable political alternative in America. Not only had socialist movements succeeded in curtailing the exploitative activities of industry in Europe, but they had, in fact, become powerful political movements which had effectively overthrown governments and elected their own candidates to office. America's industrial giants were willing to annihilate any inklings of socialism in the United States, however slight, by any means necessary. Their intractable position, nevertheless, did not deter workers from organizing for higher wages and better conditions.

Workers organize

- **Labor organizations before the Civil War**—A few "Workingmen's Parties" were formed before the Civil War by men who had migrated to the city from rural areas. They had little awareness of the realities of urban life and tended to follow middle and upper-class leaders, not workers themselves. They sought to organize labor, not for the benefit of working people, but for the purpose of reforming society.

- **Labor organizations after the Civil War**—Following the Civil War, America began to industrialize as never before. Mass production developed which de-skilled the labor force. Moreover, after the Civil War, the American economy became much more urbanized, and cities grew to unprecedented proportions.

Working conditions in industrial America

Before and after the Civil War, workers worked approximately twelve to sixteen hours per day. In the early 1880s, a movement for an eight-hour day became popular. Employers bristled at this movement and also believed that workers should not earn much more than subsistence income because:

- High wages hurt profits.

- If the working class makes too much money, it will spend the money on alcohol, gambling and prostitutes.

Early labor movements

- **Samuel Gompers**—In the mid-1800s, Gompers was brought to New York by his working class parents from Holland. He joined the Cigarmakers Union and later became president of it.

- **The Knights of Labor**—Originally a tailor's union, the Knights of Labor became an industrial union. It was the first significant national labor organization. Its membership was open to anyone except lawyers, bankers, gamblers and liquor dealers. However, management was allowed to join. It was not a racist organization and had a black membership of about ten percent. Unfortunately, it was too inclusive and tried to become all things to all people.

- **The American Federation of Labor**—Founded in 1886 by Gompers was a national labor union and remained the largest until 1955. It was a union of skilled craft workers stressing workplace labor issues: better wages, shorter work hours and worker safety. It was much less concerned with reforming society.

How management responded to labor

- **Haymarket Strike**

  On May 3, 1886, violence erupted at the McCormick Reaper Works in Chicago during an assembly of strikers. Management was enjoying a 71% profit rate which they enhanced by cutting workers' wages 15%. The workers were striking.

  That evening, a small group of strikers met to plan a rally the next day in response to the cutting of their wages. The meeting took place in the Haymarket area, and as it drew to a close at about 10PM, some 176 policemen moved in demanding dispersal of the approximately 200 workers. Suddenly a bomb exploded.

  Chaos followed as police, and possibly workers fired shots. One police officer was killed, six officers died later, and sixty others were injured. A number of civilians were also injured, but no exact count was made because friends and relatives carried them away immediately.

  The sheriff of Cook County instructed the police to "make the raids first and look up the law afterwards." No investigation of the tragedy took place, but merely an assumption that the workers threw the bomb.

  Although the bomb thrower was never identified, eight workers were indicted and later convicted. Four of the accused were hanged, one committed suicide in prison, two had their sentences reduced to life in prison and one remained in prison even though there was no case against him.

  The Haymarket Tragedy triggered a national wave of fear of anarchism and terror. In Chicago and other cities, labor leaders, socialists and anarchists were rounded up. It was assumed that immigrants and those sympathetic to socialism were responsible for the tragedy.

  One of the accused strikers, August Spies, before being hanged said: "There will come a time when our silence will be more powerful than the voices you strangle today." Indeed, Haymarket was the beginning of louder and more numerous labor strikes.

- **Pullman Strike**

  The Pullman Strike of 1894 was the first national strike in American history. It involved over 150,000 persons; the entire rail labor force of the nation walked away from their jobs. Pullman, Illinois appeared to be a model town. It was owned by George Pullman, owner of the Pullman Palace Car Company, and the town of Pullman was comprised primarily of company workers and their families.

  After the economic panic of 1893, Pullman cut company wages some twenty-five percent. However, rents in his town were also about twenty-five percent above the normal average. Most rentals were shabbily built, and some had no plumbing. In order to work for Pullman, workers were required to live in his houses. After some workers formed a committee to ask for lower rents, they were fired. Moreover, since Pullman essentially owned the town, it was virtually impossible to shop in stores not owned by Pullman.

  On May 11,1894, three thousand Pullman workers went on a "wildcat" strike, that is, without authorization of their union. Many of the strikers belonged to the American Railroad Union (ARU) founded by Eugene V. Debs. Debs, who was from Indiana, had moved to Chicago where he became a railroad fireman. He became aware of the working conditions of his fellow laborers, and saw men working for low wages, some of whom were injured or killed because of unsafe equipment. He was determined to make things better.

On July 2, a federal injunction was issued against the ARU, and on July 3, President Cleveland sent federal troops to end the strike. The strike was broken, and the Pullman plant opened again on August 2. 12 people were shot and killed, and 71 people were arrested and sentenced on a federal indictment. While the Pullman Strike showed the power of unified national unions, it also showed the willingness of the federal government to intervene and support industry against labor.

On July 10, 1894, Debs and three other union leaders were arrested on charges of interferring with U.S. mail. They were released within a few hours, but Debs realized that continuing the strike would be a lost cause because of the federal troops.

Most railroad workers resumed their old jobs and received the same wages as before. Some workers were put on a blacklist, which meant that no railroad in the United States was allowed to hire them. On July 17, 1894, Debs was sent back to jail and served a term of six months in jail. When he was released from jail, he discovered that the union he had created no longer existed.

The Pullman Strike was important because it was the first time a federal injunction had ever been used to break up a strike. George Pullman was no longer regarded as an enlightened employer who took care of his workers, but as a greedy and intolerant man. Pullman considered himself a generous employer, and he was offended by his workers' "ingratitude". Pullman also worried that people would try to steal what was his, from him. Shortly before he died in 1897, he requested that his grave be lined in concrete to keep looters from robbing him.[11]

INDUSTRY'S RESPONSE TO LABOR STRIKES
(Handout)

The incredibly inhumane treatment of workers during the late nineteenth and early twentieth centuries forced workers to unite to create labor unions. These efforts were strongly and violently opposed by management. Factory owners used a variety of methods such as:

1. **Firing** union organizers and workers

2. Placing union organizers and workers on **blacklists.** The blacklist was circulated among factory owners, and no one on it would be hired. Eventually, as a result of ongoing efforts by labor, blacklists were made illegal.

3. New hires were forced to sign a **yellow dog contract,** which was a promise that that person would never join a labor union. Eventually, these contracts were made illegal.

4. Factory owners also used court injunctions to stop union activities. The courts used the **Sherman Anti-Trust Act** to stop union activity by using one phrase in the act. The act had been passed to stop trusts from any *conspiracy in restraint of trade.* Courts said that unions were such a "conspiracy."

5. Striking workers were often fired and replaced with **scabs.**

Most companies had their own police forces or goon squads, such as the Pinkertons, who used violence to break up strikes or union rallies as in the cases of the Haymarket Strike and the Pullman Strike.

---

[11] The Pullman Strike: (http://www.lib.niu.edu/ipo/ihy941208.html)

5

BLACKS IN WHITE AMERICA IN THE "GILDED AGE"

Beginning in the 1890s and lasting well into the 1970s, a migration of Southern blacks to the western and northern United States changed the demographic structure of the nation. Blacks were searching for jobs and acceptance, and their migration raised a great controversy in the black community about the place of blacks in white America.

- **Booker T. Washington**—was an educated Southern black who founded the Tuskegee Institute in Alabama. He was a staunch believer in industrial training for Negroes. He did not believe in agitating for social equality but rather encouraged black people to prepare themselves fully for taking their place in white America.

- **W.E.B. Du Bois**—was a New England-born black, educated at Fisk and Harvard Universities. He strongly disagreed with Booker T. Washington's accomodationist response to white racism and adopted a Marxist and pro-Soviet point of view. He promoted peaceful but militant struggle for racial equality.

- **Marcus Garvey**—was a Jamaican-born black who urged blacks to accept a black Deity and who exalted African beauty. He encouraged blacks to revere their African heritage and promoted a "back to Africa" movement.

Many Robber Barons funded "scientific racism"—the eugenics movement. In the summary of the Eugenics Movement above, the specific contributions of Robber Barons such as Carnegie, Rockefeller, Harriman and Kellogg to the eugenics movement were noted. It is important to understand that the late-nineteenth and early-twentieth centuries were times of xenophobia and scapegoating of immigrants and racial minorities. Thus, a variety of academic disciplines were manipulated to reinforce all manner of prejudice.

As we enter the twentieth century, it will be important to keep in mind that a second generation of Robber Barons, most notably of **the Harriman, Rockefeller, Ford,** and **Bush** families, not only maintained a quiet adherence to the notion of selective breeding, but actually supported the rise of Hitler to power in Germany in the 1930s. (See below the financial connections of Prescott Bush and other American ruling elite with Hitler before and during World War II.)

6

POLICING THE WORLD: THE DAWN OF IMPERIALISM

An excellent primer on imperialism is "Imperialism 101," an excerpt from *Against Empire*, by Michael Parenti. That chapter has been included here:

Imperialism 101

Chapter 1 of *Against Empire* by Michael Parenti

Imperialism has been the most powerful force in world history over the last four or five centuries, carving up whole continents while oppressing indigenous peoples and obliterating entire civilizations. Yet, it is seldom accorded any serious attention by our academics, media commentators, and political leaders. When not ignored outright, the subject of imperialism has been sanitized, so that empires become "commonwealths," and colonies become "territories" or "dominions" (or, as in the case of Puerto Rico, "commonwealths" too). Imperialist military interventions become matters of "national defense," "national security," and maintaining "stability" in one or another region. In this book I want to look at imperialism for what it really is.

Across the Entire Globe
By "imperialism" I mean the process whereby the dominant politico-economic interests of one nation expropriate for their own enrichment the land, labor, raw materials, and markets of another people.

The earliest victims of Western European imperialism were other Europeans. Some 800 years ago, Ireland became the first colony of what later became known as the British empire. A part of Ireland still remains under British occupation. Other early Caucasian victims included the Eastern Europeans. The people Charlemagne worked to death in his mines in the early part of the ninth century were Slavs. So frequent and prolonged was the enslavement of Eastern Europeans that "Slav" became synonymous with servitude. Indeed, the word "slave" derives from "Slav." Eastern Europe was an early source of capital accumulation, having become wholly dependent upon Western manufactures by the seventeenth century.

A particularly pernicious example of intra-European imperialism was the Nazi aggression during World War II, which gave the German business cartels and the Nazi state an opportunity to plunder the resources and exploit the labor of occupied Europe, including the slave labor of concentration camps.

The preponderant thrust of the European, North American, and Japanese imperial powers has been directed against Africa, Asia, and Latin America. By the nineteenth century, they saw the Third World as not only a source of raw materials and slaves but a market for manufactured goods. By the twentieth century, the industrial nations were exporting not only goods but capital, in the form of machinery, technology, investments, and loans. To say that we have entered the stage of capital export and investment is not to imply that the plunder of natural resources has ceased. If anything, the despoliation has accelerated.

Of the various notions about imperialism circulating today in the United States, the dominant view is that it does not exist. Imperialism is not recognized as a legitimate concept, certainly not in regard to the United States. One may speak of "Soviet imperialism" or "nineteenth-century British imperialism" but not of U.S. imperialism. A graduate student in political science at most universities in this country would not be granted the opportunity to research U.S. imperialism, on the grounds that such an undertaking would not be scholarly. While many people throughout the world charge the United States with being an imperialist power, in this country persons who talk of U.S. imperialism are usually judged to be mouthing ideological blather.

The Dynamic of Capital Expansion

Imperialism is older than capitalism. The Persian, Macedonian, Roman, and Mongol empires all existed centuries before the Rothschilds and Rockefellers. Emperors and conquistadors were interested mostly in plunder and tribute, gold and glory. Capitalist imperialism differs from these earlier forms in the way it systematically accumulates capital through the organized exploitation of labor and the penetration of overseas markets. Capitalist imperialism invests in other countries, transforming and dominating their economies, cultures, and political life, integrating their financial and productive structures into an international system of capital accumulation.

A central imperative of capitalism is expansion. Investors will not put their money into business ventures unless they can extract more than they invest. Increased earnings come only with a growth in the enterprise. The capitalist ceaselessly searches for ways of making more money in order to make still more money. One must always invest to realize profits, gathering as much strength as possible in the face of competing forces and unpredictable markets.

Given its expansionist nature, capitalism has little inclination to stay home. Almost 150 years ago, Marx and Engels described a bourgeoisie that "chases over the whole surface of the globe. It must nestle everywhere, settle everywhere, establish connections everywhere….It creates a world after its own image." The expansionists destroy whole societies. Self-sufficient peoples are forcibly transformed into disfranchised wage workers. Indigenous communities and folk cultures are replaced by mass-market, mass-media, consumer societies. Cooperative lands are supplanted by agribusiness factory farms, villages by desolate shanty towns, autonomous regions by centralized autocracies.

Consider one of a thousand such instances. A few years ago the Los Angeles Times carried a special report on the rainforests of Borneo in the South Pacific. By their own testimony, the people there lived contented lives. They hunted, fished, and raised food in their jungle orchards and groves. But their entire way of life was ruthlessly wiped out by a few giant companies that destroyed the rainforest in order to harvest the hardwood for quick profits. Their lands were turned into ecological disaster areas and they themselves were transformed into disfranchised shantytown dwellers, forced to work for subsistence wages—when fortunate enough to find employment.

North American and European corporations have acquired control of more than three-fourths of the known mineral resources of Asia, Africa, and Latin America. But the pursuit of natural resources is not the only reason for capitalist overseas expansion. There is the additional need to cut production costs and maximize profits by investing in countries with cheaper labor markets. U.S. corporate foreign investment grew 84 percent from 1985 to 1990, the most dramatic increase being in cheap-labor countries like South Korea, Taiwan, Spain, and Singapore.

Because of low wages, low taxes, nonexistent work benefits, weak labor unions, and nonexistent occupational and environmental protections, U.S. corporate profit rates in the Third World are 50 percent greater than in developed countries. Citibank, one of the largest U.S. firms, earns about 75 percent of its profits from overseas operations. While profit margins at home sometimes have had a sluggish growth, earnings abroad have continued to rise dramatically, fostering the development of what has become known as the multinational or transnational corporation. Today some four hundred transnational companies control about 80 percent of the capital assets of the global free market and are extending their grasp into the ex-communist countries of Eastern Europe.

Transnationals have developed a global production line. General Motors has factories that produce cars, trucks and a wide range of auto components in Canada, Brazil, Venezuela, Spain, Belgium, Yugoslavia, Nigeria, Singapore, Philippines, South Africa, South Korea and a dozen other countries. Such "multiple sourcing" enables GM to ride out strikes in one country by stepping up production in another, playing workers of various nations against each other in order to discourage wage and benefit demands and undermine labor union strategies.

Not Necessary, Just Compelling
Some writers question whether imperialism is a necessary condition for capitalism, pointing out that most Western capital is invested in Western nations, not in the Third World. If corporations lost all their Third World investments, they argue, many of them could still survive on their European and North American markets. In response, one should note that capitalism might be able to survive without imperialism—but it shows no inclination to do so. It manifests no desire to discard its enormously profitable Third World enterprises. Imperialism may not be a necessary condition for investor survival but it seems to be an inherent tendency and a natural outgrowth of advanced capitalism. Imperial relations may not be the only way to pursue profits, but they are the most lucrative way.

Whether imperialism is necessary for capitalism is really not the question. Many things that are not absolutely necessary are still highly desirable, therefore strongly preferred and vigorously pursued. Overseas investors find the Third World's cheap labor, vital natural resources, and various other highly profitable conditions to be compellingly attractive. Superprofits may not be necessary for capitalism's survival but survival is not all that capitalists are interested in. Superprofits are strongly preferred to more modest earnings. That there may be no necessity between capitalism and imperialism does not mean there is no compelling linkage.

The same is true of other social dynamics. For instance, wealth does not necessarily have to lead to luxurious living. A higher portion of an owning class's riches could be used for investment rather personal consumption. The very wealthy could survive on more modest sums but that is not how most of them prefer to live. Throughout history, wealthy classes generally have shown a preference for getting the best of everything. After all, the whole purpose of getting rich off other people's labor is to live well, avoiding all forms of thankless toil and drudgery, enjoying superior opportunities for lavish life-styles, medical care, education, travel, recreation, security, leisure, and opportunities for power and prestige. While none of these things are really "necessary," they are fervently clung to by those who possess them—as witnessed by the violent measures endorsed by advantaged classes whenever they feel the threat of an equalizing or leveling democratic force.

Myths of Underdevelopment
The impoverished lands of Asia, Africa, and Latin America are known to us as the "Third World," to distinguish them from the "First World" of industrialized Europe and North America and the now largely defunct "Second World" of communist states. Third World poverty, called "underdevelopment," is treated by most Western observers as an original historic condition. We are asked to believe that it always existed, that poor countries are poor because their lands have always been infertile or their people unproductive.

In fact, the lands of Asia, Africa, and Latin America have long produced great treasures of foods, minerals and other natural resources. That is why the Europeans went through all the trouble to steal and plunder them. One does not go to poor places for self-enrichment. The Third World is rich. Only its people are poor—and it is because of the pillage they have endured.

The process of expropriating the natural resources of the Third World began centuries ago and continues to this day. First, the colonizers extracted gold, silver, furs, silks, and spices, then flax, hemp, timber, molasses, sugar, rum, rubber, tobacco, calico, cocoa, coffee, cotton, copper, coal, palm oil, tin, iron, ivory, ebony, and later on, oil, zinc, manganese, mercury, platinum, cobalt, bauxite, aluminum, and uranium. Not to be overlooked is that most hellish of all expropriations: the abduction of millions of human beings into slave labor.

Through the centuries of colonization, many self-serving imperialist theories have been spun. I was taught in school that people in tropical lands are slothful and do not work as hard as we denizens of the temperate zone. In fact, the inhabitants of warm climates have performed remarkably productive feats, building magnificent civilizations well before Europe emerged from the Dark Ages. And today they often work long, hard hours for meager sums. Yet the early stereotype of the "lazy native" is still with us. In every capitalist society, the poor—both domestic and overseas—regularly are blamed for their own condition.

We hear that Third World peoples are culturally retarded in their attitudes, customs, and technical abilities. It is a convenient notion embraced by those who want to depict Western investments as a rescue operation designed to help backward peoples help themselves. This myth of "cultural backwardness" goes back to ancient times, when conquerors used it to justify enslaving indigenous peoples. It was used by European colonizers over the last five centuries for the same purpose.

What cultural supremacy could by claimed by the Europeans of yore? From the fifteenth to nineteenth centuries Europe was "ahead" in a variety of things, such as the number of hangings, murders, and other violent crimes; instances of venereal disease, smallpox, typhoid, tuberculosis, plagues, and other bodily afflictions; social inequality and poverty (both urban and rural); mistreatment of women and children; and frequency of famines, slavery, prostitution, piracy, religious massacres, and inquisitional torture. Those who claim the West has been the most advanced civilization should keep such "achievements" in mind.

More seriously, we might note that Europe enjoyed a telling advantage in navigation and armaments. Muskets and cannon, Gatling guns and gunboats, and today missiles, helicopter gunships, and fighter bombers have been the deciding factors when West meets East and North meets South. Superior firepower, not superior culture, has brought the Europeans and Euro-North Americans to positions of supremacy that today are still maintained by force, though not by force alone.

It was said that colonized peoples were biologically backward and less evolved than their colonizers. Their "savagery" and "lower" level of cultural evolution were emblematic of their inferior genetic evolution. But were they culturally inferior? In many parts of what is now considered the Third World, people developed impressive skills in architecture, horticulture, crafts, hunting, fishing, midwifery, medicine, and other such things. Their social customs were often far more gracious and humane and less autocratic and repressive than anything found in Europe at that time. Of course we must not romanticize these indigenous societies, some of which had a number of cruel and unusual practices of their own. But generally, their peoples enjoyed healthier, happier lives, with more leisure time, than did most of Europe's inhabitants.

Other theories enjoy wide currency. We hear that Third World poverty is due to overpopulation, too many people having too many children to feed. Actually, over the last several centuries, many Third World lands have been less densely populated than certain parts of Europe. India has fewer people per acre—but more poverty—than Holland, Wales, England, Japan, Italy, and a few other industrial countries. Furthermore, it is the industrialized nations of the First World, not the poor ones of the Third, that devour some 80 percent of the world's resources and pose the greatest threat to the planet's ecology.

This is not to deny that overpopulation is a real problem for the planet's ecosphere. Limiting population growth in all nations would help the global environment but it would not solve the problems of the poor—because overpopulation in itself is not the cause of poverty but one of its effects. The poor tend to have large families because children are a source of family labor and income and a support during old age.

Frances Moore Lappe and Rachel Schurman found that of seventy Third World countries, there were six—China, Sri Lanka, Colombia, Chile, Burma, and Cuba—and the state of Kerala in India that had managed to lower their birth rates by one third. They enjoyed neither dramatic industrial expansion nor high per capita incomes nor extensive family planning programs. The factors they had in common were public education and health care, a reduction of economic inequality, improvements in women's rights, food subsidies, and in some cases land reform. In other words, fertility rates were lowered not by capitalist investments and economic growth as such but by socio-economic betterment, even of a modest scale, accompanied by the emergence of women's rights.

Artificially Converted to Poverty
What is called "underdevelopment" is a set of social relations that has been forcefully imposed on countries. With the advent of the Western colonizers, the peoples of the Third World were actually set back in their development sometimes for centuries. British imperialism in India provides an instructive example. In 1810, India was exporting more textiles to England than England was exporting to India. By 1830, the trade flow was reversed. The British had put up prohibitive tariff barriers to shut out Indian finished goods and were dumping their commodities in India, a practice backed by British gunboats and military force. Within a matter of years, the great textile centers of Dacca and Madras were turned into ghost towns. The Indians were sent back to the land to raise the cotton used in British textile factories. In effect, India was reduced to being a cow milked by British financiers.

By 1850, India's debt had grown to 53 million pounds. From 1850 to 1900, its per capita income dropped by almost two-thirds. The value of the raw materials and commodities the Indians were obliged to send to Britain during most of the nineteenth century amounted yearly to more than the total income of the sixty million Indian agricultural and industrial workers. The massive poverty we associate with India was not that country's original historical condition. British imperialism did two things: first, it ended India's development, then it forcibly underdeveloped that country.

Similar bleeding processes occurred throughout the Third World. The enormous wealth extracted should remind us that there originally were few really poor nations. Countries like Brazil, Indonesia, Chile, Bolivia, Zaire, Mexico, Malaysia, and the Philippines were and sometimes still are rich in resources. Some lands have been so thoroughly plundered as to be desolate in all respects. However, most of the Third World is not "underdeveloped" but overexploited. Western colonization and investments have created a lower rather than a higher living standard.

Referring to what the English colonizers did to the Irish, Frederick Engels wrote in 1856: "How often have the Irish started out to achieve something, and every time they have been crushed politically and industrially. By consistent oppression they have been artificially converted into an utterly impoverished nation." So with most of the Third World. The Mayan Indians in Guatemala had a more nutritious and varied diet and better conditions of health in the early 16th century before the Europeans arrived than they have today. They had more craftspeople, architects, artisans, and horticulturists than today. What is called underdevelopment is not an original historical condition but a product of imperialism's superexploitation. Underdevelopment is itself a development.

Imperialism has created what I have termed "maldevelopment": modern office buildings and luxury hotels in the capital city instead of housing for the poor, cosmetic surgery clinics for the affluent instead of hospitals for workers, cash export crops for agribusiness instead of food for local markets, highways that go from the mines and latifundios to the refineries and ports instead of roads in the back country for those who might hope to see a doctor or a teacher.

Wealth is transferred from Third World peoples to the economic elites of Europe and North America (and more recently Japan) by direct plunder, by the expropriation of natural resources, the imposition of ruinous taxes and land rents, the payment of poverty wages, and the forced importation of finished goods at highly inflated prices. The colonized country is denied the freedom of trade and the opportunity to develop its own natural resources, markets, and industrial capacity. Self-sustenance and self-employment gives way to wage labor. From 1970 to 1980, the number of wage workers in the Third World grew from 72 million to 120 million, and the rate is accelerating.

Hundreds of millions of Third World peoples now live in destitution in remote villages and congested urban slums, suffering hunger, disease, and illiteracy, often because the land they once tilled is now controlled by agribusiness firms who use it for mining or for commercial export crops such as coffee, sugar, and beef, instead of growing beans, rice, and corn for home consumption. A study of twenty of the poorest countries, compiled from official statistics, found that the number of people living in what is called "absolute poverty" or rockbottom destitution, the poorest of the poor, is rising 70,000 a day and should reach 1.5 billion by the year 2000 (San Francisco Examiner, June 8, 1994).

Imperialism forces millions of children around the world to live nightmarish lives, their mental and physical health severely damaged by endless exploitation. A documentary film on the Discovery Channel (April 24, 1994) reported that in countries like Russia, Thailand, and the Philippines, large numbers of minors are sold into prostitution to help their desperate families survive. In countries like Mexico, India, Colombia, and Egypt, children are dragooned into health-shattering, dawn-to-dusk labor on farms and in factories and mines for pennies an hour, with no opportunity for play, schooling, or medical care.

In India, 55 million children are pressed into the work force. Tens of thousands labor in glass factories in temperatures as high as 100 degrees. In one plant, four-year-olds toil from 5 o'clock in the morning until the dead of night, inhaling fumes and contracting emphysema, tuberculosis, and other respiratory diseases. In the Philippines and Malaysia corporations have lobbied to drop age restrictions for labor recruitment. The pursuit of profit becomes a pursuit of evil.

Development Theory
When we say a country is "underdeveloped," we are implying that it is backward and retarded in some way, that its people have shown little capacity to achieve and evolve. The negative connotations of "underdeveloped" has caused the United Nations, the Wall Street Journal, and parties of various political persuasion to refer to Third World countries as "developing" nations, a term somewhat less insulting than "underdeveloped" but equally misleading. I prefer to use "Third World" because "developing" seems to be just a euphemistic way of

saying "underdeveloped but belatedly starting to do something about it." It still implies that poverty was an original historic condition and not something imposed by the imperialists. It also falsely suggests that these countries are developing when actually their economic conditions are usually worsening.

The dominant theory of the last half century, enunciated repeatedly by writers like Barbara Ward and W. W. Rostow and afforded wide currency in the United States and other parts of the Western world, maintains that it is up to the rich nations of the North to help uplift the "backward" nations of the South, bringing them technology and teaching them proper work habits. This is an updated version of "the White man's burden," a favorite imperialist fantasy.

According to the development scenario, with the introduction of Western investments, the backward economic sectors of the poor nations will release their workers, who then will find more productive employment in the modern sector at higher wages. As capital accumulates, business will reinvest its profits, thus creating still more products, jobs, buying power, and markets. Eventually a more prosperous economy evolves.

This "development theory" or "modernization theory," as it is sometimes called, bears little relation to reality. What has emerged in the Third World is an intensely exploitive form of dependent capitalism. Economic conditions have worsened drastically with the growth of transnational corporate investment. The problem is not poor lands or unproductive populations but foreign exploitation and class inequality. Investors go into a country not to uplift it but to enrich themselves.

People in these countries do not need to be taught how to farm. They need the land and the implements to farm. They do not need to be taught how to fish. They need the boats and the nets and access to shore frontage, bays, and oceans. They need industrial plants to cease dumping toxic effusions into the waters. They do not need to be convinced that they should use hygienic standards. They do not need a Peace Corps Volunteer to tell them to boil their water, especially when they cannot afford fuel or have no access to firewood. They need the conditions that will allow them to have clean drinking water and clean clothes and homes. They do not need advice about balanced diets from North Americans. They usually know what foods best serve their nutritional requirements. They need to be given back their land and labor so that they might work for themselves and grow food for their own consumption.

The legacy of imperial domination is not only misery and strife, but an economic structure dominated by a network of international corporations which themselves are beholden to parent companies based in North America, Europe and Japan. If there is any harmonization or integration, it occurs among the global investor classes, not among the indigenous economies of these countries. Third World economies remain fragmented and unintegrated both between each other and within themselves, both in the flow of capital and goods and in technology and organization. In sum, what we have is a world economy that has little to do with the economic needs of the world's people.

Neoimperialism: Skimming the Cream
Sometimes imperial domination is explained as arising from an innate desire for domination and expansion, a "territorial imperative." In fact, territorial imperialism is no longer the prevailing mode. Compared to the nineteenth and early twentieth centuries, when the European powers carved up the world among themselves, today there is almost no colonial dominion left. Colonel Blimp is dead and buried, replaced by men in business suits. Rather than being directly colonized by the imperial power, the weaker countries have been granted the trappings of sovereignty—while Western finance capital retains control of the lion's share of their profitable resources. This relationship has gone under various names: "informal empire," "colonialism without colonies," "neocolonialism," and "neoimperialism."

U.S. political and business leaders were among the earliest practitioners of this new kind of empire, most notably in Cuba at the beginning of the twentieth century. Having forcibly wrested the island from Spain in the war of 1898, they eventually gave Cuba its formal independence. The Cubans now had their own government, constitution, flag, currency, and security force. But major foreign policy decisions remained in U.S. hands as did the island's wealth, including its sugar, tobacco, and tourist industries, and major imports and exports.

Historically U.S. capitalist interests have been less interested in acquiring more colonies than in acquiring more wealth, preferring to make off with the treasure of other nations without bothering to own and administer the nations themselves. Under neoimperialism, the flag stays home, while the dollar goes everywhere—frequently assisted by the sword.

After World War II, European powers like Britain and France adopted a strategy of neoimperialism. Left financially depleted by years of warfare, and facing intensified popular resistance from within the Third World itself, they reluctantly decided that indirect economic hegemony was less costly and politically more expedient than outright colonial rule. They discovered that the removal of a conspicuously intrusive colonial rule made it more difficult for nationalist elements within the previously colonized countries to mobilize anti-imperialist sentiments.

Though the newly established government might be far from completely independent, it usually enjoyed more legitimacy in the eyes of its populace than a colonial administration controlled by the imperial power. Furthermore, under neoimperialism the native government takes up the costs of administering the country while the imperialist interests are free to concentrate on accumulating capital—which is all they really want to do.

After years of colonialism, the Third World country finds it extremely difficult to extricate itself from the unequal relationship with its former colonizer and impossible to depart from the global capitalist sphere. Those countries that try to make a break are subjected to punishing economic and military treatment by one or another major power, nowadays usually the United States.

The leaders of the new nations may voice revolutionary slogans, yet they find themselves locked into the global capitalist orbit, cooperating perforce with the First World nations for investment, trade, and aid. So we witnessed the curious phenomenon of leaders of newly independent Third World nations denouncing imperialism as the source of their countries' ills, while dissidents in these countries denounced these same leaders as collaborators of imperialism.

In many instances a comprador class emerged or was installed as a first condition for independence. A comprador class is one that cooperates in turning its own country into a client state for foreign interests. A client state is one that is open to investments on terms that are decidedly favorable to the foreign investors. In a client state, corporate investors enjoy direct subsidies and land grants, access to raw materials and cheap labor, light or nonexistent taxes, few effective labor unions, no minimum wage or child labor or occupational safety laws, and no consumer or environmental protections to speak of. The protective laws that do exist go largely unenforced.

In all, the Third World is something of a capitalist paradise, offering life as it was in Europe and the United States during the nineteenth century, with a rate of profit vastly higher than what might be earned today in a country with strong economic regulations. The comprador class is well recompensed for its cooperation. Its leaders enjoy opportunities to line their pockets with the foreign aid sent by the U.S. government. Stability is assured with the establishment of security forces, armed and trained by the United States in the latest technologies of terror and repression. Still, neoimperialism carries risks. The achievement of de jure independence eventually fosters expectations of de facto independence. The forms of self rule incite a desire for the fruits of self rule. Sometimes a national leader emerges who is a patriot and reformer rather than a comprador collaborator. Therefore, the changeover from colonialism to neocolonialism is not without risks for the imperialists and represents a net gain for popular forces in the world.

ROOTS OF IMPERIALISM

Definitions: *Empire* is a political unit having an extensive territory or comprising a number of territories or nations and ruled by a single supreme authority. An empire extends its sovereignty externally through domination or control to subsume or conquer additional territories. Therefore, we say that it is *imperialistic* or that it engages in *imperialism*. Moreover, an empire, in addition to making war on other nations, makes war on its own citizens by limiting or eliminating their civil liberties, by maintaining severe economic restrictions and by utilizing media to propagandize its political, economic and military agenda by manufacturing and demonizing nations which it perceives as threats to its imperialistic designs.

- **Industrial expansion**
  In the late nineteenth century, U.S. corporations were producing more goods than Americans could consume. The economic Panic of 1893 was used by industry to justify industry's "need" for foreign markets in which to sell American products. Alternating business cycles of prosperity and recession, as well as foreign investment in the U.S. accelerated imperialist tendencies. Whereas European demand for American agricultural products had increased before 1880, the demand declined dramatically in the last two decades of the century.

- **The growth of the federal government**
  As we shall learn when we discuss Progressivism, increased federal government regulation prompted many corporations to secure markets in other countries where few regulations existed.

- **Rhetorical justifications for imperialism**

  ****Frederick Jackson Turner*
  Wrote, as mentioned above, "The Significance of the Frontier in American History," in which he argued that interaction with the frontier promoted democracy in America. Turner suggested that with the fulfillment of Manifest Destiny and the expansion of the empire to the Pacific Ocean, America would now face a crisis resulting from the loss of its frontier. Many interpreted his thesis to mean that overseas expansion was the next great frontier.

  ****The Anglo-Saxon myth*
  A belief in Anglo-Saxon superiority was the dominant intellectual justification for American imperialism. Generally speaking, the same individuals who supported Social Darwinism and eugenics theory, supported American expansionism. In fact, Senator Albert Beveridge moralized that America had a destiny and a duty to the world to carry democracy and American values and goods to the rest of the world.

  ****White Man's Burden/International Manifest Destiny*
  An Englishman, **Rudyard Kipling**, a staunch supporter of British imperialism coined the phrase, the "white man's burden," which encapsulated in three words, the Anglo-Saxon myth. In addition, after the Civil War, American Christian missionary work around the globe in Asia and Africa increased dramatically. The late nineteenth century was the beginning of a soul-saving/profit-making alliance between the American clergy and the American government on behalf of American corporations for securing new markets and territories around the world. Robert Spear, head of the Board of Foreign Missions of the Presbyterian Church, stated:

  The civilized nations are beginning to perceive that they have a a duty which is often contemptuously spoken of, to police the world. The recognition of this duty has been forced by trade."

  James Michner's historical novel, *Hawaii*, paints a grim picture of the white man's burden and its attendant abuses in the South Pacific. More recently, *Thy Will Be Done*, by Gerard Colby and Charlotte Dennett, an extremely well-researched study of the Christian missionary enterprise in South America in the 1950s, financed by the Rockefeller Family, documents the utilization of American missionary endeavors in the economic conquest of that continent by American corporations.

If all of this resembles the notion of Manifest Destiny which we discussed in our section on westward expansion, it is indeed just that. As we shall see, late-nineteenth and twentieth-century imperialism is essentially Manifest Destiny globalized.

The Anti-Imperialist movement

At the same time that the imperialist movement was growing, so too was an *anti*-imperialist movement made up of labor leaders, intellectuals, some Progressives and political organizers. One such individual was Scott Nearing (1883-1983), author of *The American Empire.* In Chapter 9, Nearing traces the development of American imperialism from 1898-1935 and concludes with this assessment:

> *The end of the nineteenth century saw the end of the Republic about which men like Jefferson and Lincoln wrote and dreamed. The New Century marked the opening of a new epoch—the beginning of world dominion for the United States.*

7

LIBERALISM, PROGRESSIVISM, NEO-LIBERALISM

Definition of the three "isms"

1) ***Liberalism***: *A political theory founded on the natural goodness of humans and the autonomy of the individual and favoring civil and political liberties, government by law with the consent of the governed, and protection from arbitrary authority.*

The Founding Fathers were profoundly influenced by the liberal socio-political ideas of the European Enlightenment such as those found in the writings of Locke, Hobbes, Rousseau and Montesquieu. Economic liberalism embraced the ideas of Adam Smith's "invisible hand," which discouraged government regulation of a nation's economy. Increasingly, in the United States, however, liberalism came to mean, according to Stanley Schultz that:

- That government should be more active in the well-being of its citizens
- That social problems are susceptible to government and legislative action
- That social problems could be eliminated by spending money on alleviating them.

2) ***Progressivism***: Although Progressives were never a unified group seeking a single objective, because many of them came from a long tradition of liberalism, they had many different, and sometimes contradictory, goals such as:

   a. An end to prostitution and sweat shops
   b. Prohibition
   c. The "Americanization" of immigrants
   d. Immigration restriction legislation
   e. Anti-trust legislation
   f. Rate regulation of private utilities

g. Full government ownership of private utilities

h. Women's suffrage

i. An end to child labor

j. Taylorism (See below, XIV, A)

k. Political reform

3) *Neo-liberalism*: During the last half of the twentieth century, neo-liberalism came to dominate the world economic scene. Following is a concise definition and history of neo-liberalism from Corp Watch at www.corpwatch.org (1997)

URL: http://www.corpwatch.org/issues/PID.jsp?articleid=376

What is Neoliberalism?

A Brief Definition for Activists

By Elizabeth Martinez and Arnoldo Garcia
National Network for Immigrant and Refugee Rights
January 1, 1997

"Neo-liberalism" is a set of economic policies that have become widespread during the last 25 years or so. Although the word is rarely heard in the United States, you can clearly see the effects of neo-liberalism here as the rich grow richer and the poor grow poorer.

"Liberalism" can refer to political, economic, or even religious ideas. In the U.S. political liberalism has been a strategy to prevent social conflict. It is presented to poor and working people as progressive compared to conservative or Rightwing. Economic liberalism is different. Conservative politicians who say they hate "liberals"—meaning the political type—have no real problem with economic liberalism, including neoliberalism.

"Neo" means we are talking about a new kind of liberalism. So what was the old kind? The liberal school of economics became famous in Europe when Adam Smith, an English economist, published a book in 1776 called *THE WEALTH OF NATIONS*. He and others advocated the abolition of government intervention in economic matters. No restrictions on manufacturing, no barriers to commerce, no tariffs, he said; free trade was the best way for a nation's economy to develop. Such ideas were "liberal" in the sense of no controls. This application of individualism encouraged "free" enterprise," "free" competition—which came to mean, free for the capitalists to make huge profits as they wished.

Economic liberalism prevailed in the United States through the 1800s and early 1900s. Then the Great Depression of the 1930s led an economist named John Maynard Keynes to a theory that challenged liberalism as the best policy for capitalists. He said, in essence, that full employment is necessary for capitalism to grow and it can be achieved only if governments and central banks intervene to increase employment. These ideas had much influence on President Roosevelt's New Deal—which did improve life for many people. The belief that government should advance the common good became widely accepted. But the capitalist crisis over the last 25 years, with its shrinking profit rates, inspired the corporate elite to revive economic liberalism. That's what makes it "neo" or new. Now, with the rapid globalization of the capitalist economy, we are seeing neo-liberalism on a global scale.

A memorable definition of this process came from Subcomandante Marcos at the Zapatista-sponsored <u>Encuentro Intercontinental por la Humanidad y contra el Neo-liberalismo</u> (Inter-continental Encounter for Humanity and Against Neo-liberalism) of August 1996 in Chiapas when he said: "what the Right offers is to turn the world into one big mall where they can buy Indians here, women there…." and he might have added, children, immigrants, workers or even a whole country like Mexico.

The main points of neo-liberalism include:

- **THE RULE OF THE MARKET.** Liberating "free" enterprise or private enterprise from any bonds imposed by the government (the state) no matter how much social damage this causes. Greater openness to international trade and investment, as in NAFTA. Reduce wages by de-unionizing workers and eliminating workers' rights that had been won over many years of struggle. No more price controls. All in all, total freedom of movement for capital, goods and services. To convince us this is good for us, they say "an unregulated market is the best way to increase economic growth, which will ultimately benefit everyone." It's like Reagan's "supply-side" and "trickle-down" economics—but somehow the wealth didn't trickle down very much.

- **CUTTING PUBLIC EXPENDITURE FOR SOCIAL SERVICES** like education and health care. REDUCING THE SAFETY-NET FOR THE POOR, and even maintenance of roads, bridges, water supply—again in the name of reducing government's role. Of course, they don't oppose government subsidies and tax benefits for business.

- **DEREGULATION.** Reduce government regulation of everything that could diminsh profits, including protecting the environment and safety on the job.
- **PRIVATIZATION.** Sell state-owned enterprises, goods and services to private investors. This includes banks, key industries, railroads, toll highways, electricity, schools, hospitals and even fresh water. Although usually done in the name of greater efficiency, which is often needed, privatization has mainly had the effect of concentrating wealth even more in a few hands and making the public pay even more for its needs.

- **ELIMINATING THE CONCEPT OF "THE PUBLIC GOOD" or "COMMUNITY"** and replacing it with "individual responsibility." Pressuring the poorest people in a society to find solutions to their lack of health care, education and social security all by themselves—then blaming them, if they fail, as "lazy."

Around the world, neo-liberalism has been imposed by powerful financial institutions like the **International Monetary Fund (IMF),** the **World Bank** and the **Inter-American Development Bank**. It is raging all over Latin America. The first clear example of neo-liberalism at work came in Chile (with thanks to University of Chicago economist Milton Friedman), after the CIA-supported coup against the popularly elected Allende regime in 1973. Other countries followed, with some of the worst effects in Mexico where wages declined 40 to 50% in the first year of NAFTA while the cost of living rose by 80%. Over 20,000 small and medium businesses have failed and more than 1,000 state-owned enterprises have been privatized in Mexico. As one scholar said, "Neoliberalism means the neo-colonization of Latin America."

In the United States neo-liberalism is destroying welfare programs; attacking the rights of labor (including all immigrant workers); and cutting back social programs. The Republican "Contract" on America is pure neo-liberalism. Its supporters are working hard to deny protection to children, youth, women, the planet itself—and trying to trick us into acceptance by saying this will "get government off my back." The beneficiaries of neo-liberalism are a minority of the world's people. For the vast majority it brings even more suffering than before: suffering without the small, hard-won gains of the last 60 years, suffering without end.

Elizabeth Martinez is a longtime civil rights activist and author of several books, including "500 Years of Chicano History in Photographs."

Arnoldo Garcia is a member of the Oakland-based Comite Emiliano Zapata, affiliated to the National Commission for Democracy in Mexico.

Both writers attended the Intercontinental Encounter for Humanity and against Neoliberalism, held July 27-August 3, 1996, in La Realidad, Chiapas.

CorpWatch
PO Box 29344
San Francisco, CA 94129 USA
Tel: 415-561-6568 Fax: 415-561-6493
URL: http://www.corpwatch.org/
Email: corpwatch@corpwatch.org

Essentially, there were four basic types of Progressive reform:

- Economic—to end monopolies
- Structural and political—to promote efficiency
- Social—to enhance democracy
- Moral—to bolster purity

According to Schultz, the **principle characteristics of Progressivism** were charity, reform, and regulation manifested in the following ways:

1) *Moralism*

2) *The belief that government, once purified, must act*

3) *The belief that the weakest element of society must be protected*

4) *No challenge to capitalism's basic tenets*

5) *Paternalism*

Many Progressives had roots in religious or transcendentalist belief systems. They believed that government must develop a moral conscience regarding the well being of its citizens, especially those that were disadvantaged, and use political power to protect them. However, Progressives never challenged the basic assumptions on which capitalism rested, and for all their rhetoric about human equality, they often treated the disadvantaged as "children" who needed to be "taught" Progressive (almost always white and middle-class) values.

Although poverty had always existed in American society, a number of urban reformers began calling for legislation to help the poor. Charity endeavors spread to major U.S. cities, along with a demand for the emancipation of women. The social settlement movement, founded by Jane Addams in Chicago, brought many university-educated women and men to urban areas to teach basic education and life skills. In addition, several clubs were organized in American cities to streamline government and end corruption.

Government regulation *in service of* corporations

Historians have made much of the political, economic and social changes brought about in American society by Progressivism. While it is true that government regulation of industry passed by legislators in response to their demands was unprecedented, it is also true that Progressives repeatedly failed to question the fundamental underpinnings of the capitalist system and, in fact, aspired to make government function as an "ideal corporation." Many revisionist historians, such as **Gabriel Kolko**, speculate that because the essential nature of capitalism was never questioned by the Progressives, regulation was put into place which brought about limited, specific reforms for the well being of workers, consumers and the poor, but which actually served to contain protest movements and maintain order and thereby, ultimately *served* business interests.

B. **Political Capitalism** and "The Triumph Of Conservatism," by Gabriel Kolko. The following handout on Progressivism summarizes the concept of **political capitalism**:

WHY "PROGRESSIVISM" WAS NOT PROGRESSIVE
(Handout)

The "progressive" movement has been so-named because during the first decade of the twentieth century, a number of reforms and regulations were enacted in American government affecting labor, commerce, and the health and safety of American workers and consumers. But what was the essence of those reforms? What was their purpose, and what social relationships were involved?

THE PURPOSE OF THE REFORMS

Gabriel Kolko, in his book ***THE TRIUMPH OF CONSERVATISM***, uses the words **"political capitalism"** to describe the end result of the Progressive Era. Kolko argues that regulation was put in place to *contain* protest movements and *maintain* order, and that they did not make fundamental changes in the American capitalist system. What emerged was regulated capitalism, which created minimal reforms for the working classes, but benefited business much more significantly and protected it from economic losses.

SOCIAL RELATIONSHIPS

"What was never explored or changed during the Progressive Era," Kolko concludes, "was the fabric of social relationships resulting from **political capitalism** and the dominance of a capitalist ruling elite. In other words, it was capitalist social relationships, not just economic factors that triumphed—the assumption that certain individuals, because of heritage, ethnicity, socio-economic status, etc. had the right to accumulate phenomenal wealth at the expense of other human beings and the environment. Although certain individuals who embraced socialism challenged the social relationships of political capitalism, by and large, progressives did not."

8

WOMEN IN PROGRESSIVE AMERICA

A. The "Cult Of True Womanhood" (See handout below compiled from the lecture notes of Stanley Schultz, Department of History, University of Wisconsin)

The main feminist movements

The first conference for women in the U.S. took place at Seneca Falls, New York in 1848. It was organized by **Lucretia Mott** and **Elizabeth Cady Stanton.** The conference produced "The Declaration of Sentiments," modeled on the Declaration of Independence and called for women's suffrage, the right of women to own property and equal access for women to education and employment. A number of feminist movements were born at Seneca Falls and came to fruition during the late nineteenth century. The three main feminist movements from 1870 to 1919 were:

- **The Suffragists**—who put all their energy into getting the vote for women. It was believed that the vote of women would purify politics.
- **The Social Feminists**—who agreed that women should have the vote but who also devoted themselves to social reforms other than suffrage. Prominent in this group were Jane Addams and Florence Kelley. Generally, social feminists saw the state as an agent for social welfare.
- **The Radical Feminists**—who offered a much stronger critique of American society, economics and politics. The most prominent was Charlotte Perkins Gilman, a sociologist, author and lecturer, who was also a socialist. Another facet of radical feminism was represented by Alice Paul, who organized the Woman's Party and introduced the first Equal Rights Amendment in 1916. The ERA campaign was so radical that most social feminists rejected it, fearing that the ERA would endanger protective legislation for women.

The Nineteenth Amendment

Passed by Congress in 1919, the 19th Amendment gave American women the right to vote. In addition to the ERA, another point of division among feminist groups was World War I. Jane Addams and others were vocal pacifists who opposed President Wilson's decision to enter the war. Other feminists, such as Carrie Chapman Catt, endorsed Wilson's decision, with the understanding that women would get suffrage after the war ended. Consequently, Wilson urged Congress to pass the 19th Amendment in return for women's loyalty to the war effort. It is worth noting that in order for American women to gain the right to vote, it was politically expedient for them to support a world war which opened the floodgates of American imperialism around the world.

Margaret Sanger

The founder of Planned Parenthood, Margaret Sanger, has often been accused of supporting eugenics. This assertion is unfounded. Sanger accomplished significant social reforms for women such as:

- Establishing the principle that a woman's right to control her own body is a basic human right.
- Bringing about the reversal the of Comstock laws which prohibited publication and distribution of information about sexuality and contraception.
- Helping to establish the protection of civil rights through non-violent civil disobedience
- Creating access to birth control for low-income, minority and immigrant women
- Organizing family planning centers across the U.S.

Sanger was not a racist nor an anti-Semite nor a eugenicist. In fact, her books were some of the first burned by the Nazis in their campaigns against family planning. Sanger actually helped several Jewish women and men escape the Nazi regime in Germany. In addition, Sanger opened a family planning clinic in Harlem staffed by a black physician and black social workers. In 1966, the year Sanger died, Martin Luther King acknowledged a kinship between the efforts of Margaret Sanger and the civil rights movement.

Feminism after 1919

In the 1920s, the women's rights movement died down, not only because of the achievement of the goal of suffrage but because of a general retreat from activism in post-WWI America. The twenties, as we will soon learn, became the "party decade" in which women were generally more interested in smoking, drinking, going without corsets, bobbing their hair and dancing the Charleston.

THE VICTORIAN CULT OF "TRUE WOMANHOOD"[12]
(Handout)

In the last half of the 19th Century, Victorian ideals were predominant in American society. The name Victorian comes from Victoria, who was Queen of England at that time. Among the middle and upper class of America, women were supposed to practice four cardinal virtues:

1) Piety—It was believed that women were far more spiritual in nature than men.
2) Purity—American women were supposed to be pure of heart, mind, and of course, pure in body, not engaging in sexual relations until marriage, and even then, not enjoying them.
3) Submission—Women were supposed to live in a kind of perpetual childhood, passively responding to the actions and decisions of men.
4) Domesticity—"Decent" women were supposed to stay at home, not work outside the home and take care of their husbands and children. Women who worked outside the home were considered somehow crass and vulgar. Thus, poor working class women were thought to be "indecent."

During the Victorian era, it was believed that women, being the "weaker" sex, had only a given amount of energy. They needed this energy for marriage, having and raising children. Therefore, it was believed, that getting an education or working outside the home would rob women of the energy they needed for the really "important" career of being a wife and mother. Thus, in upper and middle-class Victorian society, three things were feared in relation to women:

- —Dress reform
- —The education of women
- —Women working outside the home

---

[12] Schultz Lectures, Lecture 14, (http://us.history.wisc.edu/hist102/lectures/lecture14.html)

THE SOCIALIST IMPERATIVE

It is extremely difficult for twenty-first century Americans to comprehend the conditions of working people, immigrants, women and children in the urban areas of the United States during the late nineteenth century. Below are links to primary documents describing these conditions which contain links to additional historical websites:

> http://www.teacheroz.com/19thcent.htm#imperialism
> http://www.askeric.org/Virtual/Lessons/crossroads/sec2/essay07.html
> http://www.nv.cc.va.us/home/nvsageh/Hist122/Part1/WorkingMen.htm
> http://lcweb2.loc.gov/ammem/ndlpedu/features/timeline/riseind/work/work.html
> http://rs6.loc.gov/ammem/papr/west/westpres.html
> http://tenant.net/Community/LES/kleeck9.ht

The Appeal of Socialism

Readings by Socialist writers of the Victorian Era:

- http://www.fordham.edu/halsall/mod/1884hdlloyd.html, Excerpt from "Lords of Industry" by Henry Demarest Lloyd, *North American Review* 331 (June 1884)
- http://odur.let.rug.nl/~usa/D/1876-1900/reform/lloyd.htm,
  Excerpt From "Wealth Against Commonwealth", Henry Demarest Lloyd
- http://sunsite.berkeley.edu/Goldman/Writings/Anarchism/anarchism.html, "Anarchism: What It Really Stands For," by Emma Goldman
- http://www.marxists.org/archive/debs/works/1925/cppa.htm, Speech At 1925 Conference for Progressive Political Action, by Eugene V. Debs
- http://womenshistory.about.com/library/bio/blbio_mother_jones.htm, Resources on Mary Harris (Mother) Jones
- http://www.marxists.org/reference/archive/keller-helen/intro.htm, The Socialist Legacy of Hellen Keller

Additional Readings on Social Justice in The Progressive Era
- *The Robber Barons*, Matthew Josephson
- *The Jungle*, Upton Sinclair
- *The History of the Labor Movement In The United States*, Philip Foner
- *The Souls of Black Folks*, W.E.B. Du Bois
- *The Corporate Ideal In The Liberal States*, James Weinstein
- *The Search For Order,* Robert Wiebe
- *Aliens And Dissenters*, William Preston, Jr.
- *The Autobiography of Mother Jones*, Mary Jones
- *We Were There: The Story Of Working Women In America*, Barbara Wertheimer
- *How The Other Half Lives*, Jacob Riis

9

THE BEGINNINGS OF WORLD DOMINATION

A. Background

As explained above, the United States by 1850 had extended its influence to the Pacific Ocean. Turner's Frontier Thesis proclaimed that America would eventually face a dilemma, if not crisis, when it no longer had a "frontier." Even before the publication of Turner's Thesis, American capitalists were making dire predictions regarding the American economy if they could not acquire overseas markets and resources. Ironically, a severe economic downturn occurred in 1893, the same year that Turner published his thesis—a juxtaposition of events which reinforced the idea of global expansion in the minds of previously isolationist Americans. There were, however, a minority of Americans who opposed U.S. imperialism. They formed the **Anti-Imperialist League** in 1898. Their membership included Mark Twain, Samuel Gompers, William James, Carl Schurz and Scott Nearing.

Scott Nearing (1883-1983) was a leading leftist critic of imperialism throughout most of his long life. In his political autobiography he named four officers of the Philadelphia branch of the Anti-Imperialist League among the six people who most influenced his political beliefs in the period after his graduation from college. He was fired by the University of Pennsylvania in 1915 because of his outspoken opposition to World War I, and his case led to the movement to establish tenure for teachers and professors in the United States. A life-long anti-imperialist, Nearing would later oppose U.S. interventions in Cuba and the war in Vietnam in the 1960s and 1970s.

AMERICAN IMPERIALISM
(Handout)

Since its origin, America had been an **isolationist** country. Many Founding Fathers had warned the country of "entangling alliances." However, the **Monroe Doctrine of 1823** declared that European powers must not meddle in the affairs of any developing nation of the Western Hemisphere. Shortly, after the Civil War, with the purchase of Alaska in 1867, America gradually becomes an **expansionist** nation.

A number of factors contributed to American imperialism:

1) **"The White Man's Burden"**—the belief in Manifest Destiny applied to the rest of the world. It was the "destiny" of the United States to expand its interests into the rest of the world because of its racial superiority and in order to "save the world for democracy."

2) **Protestant missionary ideals**—Thousands of Protestant missionaries from the United States and Great Britain, moved into undeveloped country to convert the native peoples of those countries to Christianity. This was based on a sense of religious superiority, and these missionary efforts were often used by the governments of the United States and England to pave the way for economic exploitation and development of those countries.

3) **In 1893, America suffered a huge economic depression.**
   As a result, American industry realized that it needed an economic outlet for its goods and services. It desperately needed to increase its trade and shipping with other countries.

4) **The Turner Thesis**—Frederick Jackson Turner, the 19th Century historian had said that the frontier was the most significant element in the development of American democracy. However, with the frontier gone, America would have to find other "frontiers" in order to preserve its democratic tradition.

5) **The Roosevelt Corollary to the Monroe Doctrine**—President Theodore Roosevelt turned the Monroe Doctrine on its head by declaring that no country could interfere in the Western Hemisphere, but that the U.S. had the right to use police powers and military intervention in the Western Hemisphere to keep other nations out. In this way, he justified sending U.S. troops into the Dominican Republic, Cuba, the Philippines, Mexico and numerous other countries.

Most Americans were content to remain isolationist, but **yellow journalism** in the press fanned the flames of war hysteria. This was accomplished by such publishers as **William Randolph Hearst and Joseph Pulitzer.** As a result, the U.S. entered and won the **Spanish American War**, after which the **Anti-Imperialist League** was formed in the U.S. which opposed American acquisition of colonies as anti-democratic and destructive of American ideals.

Roosevelt and Wilson: America must take her place on the world stage: The Spanish-American War

In 1898, Spain was in decline, and the United States saw an easy opportunity to expand its economic, military and political influence by seizing Cuba and the Philippines. In 1898, the U.S. declared war on Spain after a suspicious explosion on the American **Battleship** *Maine*, docked in Havana Harbor. The war lasted only four months, at the end of which, Cuba was granted independence by the Treaty of Paris, and Spain surrendered Puerto Rico, Guam, and the Philippine Islands to the United States.

American business and religious missionaries exerted significant influence in Hawaii, which although never annexed by the United States, was dominated by it as America sought to keep others from extending influence over the islands. In addition, Theodore Roosevelt, determined to build a canal through the Isthmus of Panama, backed a revolution in that country, which declared independence in 1903. The canal was completed in 1914 at a cost of $400 million.

In the aftermath of the Spanish-American War, the United States became a world power. America could have returned its possessions acquired from Spain back to Spain; it could have sold Cuba, Guam, the Philippines, Wake Island and Puerto Rico to a European power; it could have left the islands to govern themselves. Predictably, however, the United States chose to keep them under its control.

At first, American corporations were not terribly interested in entering a war with Cuba. Nor did the American people support intervention because for them, the Cubans were fighting a revolutionary war similar to the one fought by Americans in 1776. Increasingly, however, U.S. businesses began to support intervention. Not only may they have begun to fear that, as Zinn says, "…the rebels would win on their own and keep the United States out", but the Cleveland Administration began talking about the potentially new republic of Cuba as a mixture of two races. Eventually, McKinley and the corporate community realized that their objective, to rid Cuba of Spain, could not be accomplished without war.[13]

Yellow Journalism

During the last two decades of the nineteenth century competition between newspapers grew fierce. As a result, a different type of journalism evolved which utilized sensational, scandalous news coverage, using drawings and comic strips. The two leading journalists using these tactics were **Joseph Pulitzer** of the *New York World* and **William Randolph Hearst** of the San Francisco *Examiner*.

Pulitzer and Hearst played an enormous role in influencing public opinion in the direction of American involvement in Cuba. They seized upon the opportunity to increase their circulations by fueling the flames of war. Together, they created a frenzy among the American people by reporting alleged brutality of the Spanish against Cuban rebels. War correspondent, Frederick Remington, upon visiting Cuba, reported to Hearst that there was no war taking place there. In reply, Hearst ordered Remington to remain in Cuba and added, "You furnish the pictures, I'll furnish the war." Subsequently, the *Examiner* dedicated at least eight pages per day to the war. By the time the *Maine* exploded in Havana Harbor, President McKinley feared what might happen to his political party if he did not engage in war with Spain.

---

[13] Howard Zinn: *The Twentieth Century, A Peoples' History*, Harper Collins, New York, 2003, pp. 8-9.

Significance of the Spanish-American War

According to Stanley Schultz[14], three lasting effects resulting from the Spanish-American War were:

- **The United States became more like European countries.**
  Clearly, after the Spanish-American War, the United States became a world power. The former "British colony" now had colonies of its own.

- **The nation was no longer a republic equal in all its parts**
  The question of equality for people living under the American flag in new territories was debated in the United States. Many anti-imperialists were also anti-immigrant, and they protested equality for citizens of the new territories. A number of cases on equality issues were heard by the Supreme Court which decided that ultimately, the U.S. Constitution need not apply equally to the populations of the territories. Consequently, the United States could legally withhold certain rights from the newly-conquered peoples

- **America's quick victory had lasting psychological effects on many people.**
  The Spanish-American War solidified the concept of Manifest Destiny in the American Psyche. British journalist, William Stead, wrote that: "The advent of the United States Of America as the greatest of the world's powers is the greatest political, social, and commercial phenomenon of our times."

Although Presidents Theodore Roosevelt and Woodrow Wilson disagreed on many issues, they both agreed that by the beginning of the twentieth century, it would be time for the United States to assume its place as a world power. Both believed that the United States should use whatever means necessary to see that its vision of democracy prevailed around the world.

Historians have made much of the differences between Roosevelt and Wilson, portraying Roosevelt as the brash "speak-softly-and-carry-a-big-stick" Rough Rider and Wilson as the quiet Christian professor from Princeton. For more in-depth analysis of the similarities between Roosevelt and Wilson in domestic policy, I refer the reader to *The Triumph Of Conservatism*, by Gabriel Kolko[15] who characterizes Wilson as "…antilabor, paternalistic conservative who nevertheless believed that child labor and factory laws were desirable if only to equalize competitive conditions."[16]

In fact, Wilson is a stellar example of political capitalism in action, functioning politically as Kolko notes as an "anti-Bryan [anti-Populist] Democrat who believed that reform was very largely a matter of good individuals replacing evil ones, and that only businessmen could ultimately understand business problems."[17] In a 1910 speech to the American Bar Association, he attacked the breaking up of trusts:

> If you dissolve the offending corporation, you throw great undertakings out of gear…to the infinite loss of thousands of entirely innocent persons and to the great inconvenience of society as a whole.…I regard the corporation as indispensable to modern business enterprise. I am not jealous of its size or might, if you will but abandon at the right points the fatuous, antiquated, and quite unnecessary fiction which treats it as a legal person.[18]

---

[14] Schultz Lectures, Lecture 13 (http://us.history.wisc.edu/hist102/lectures/lecture13.html)
[15] Gabriel Kolko, *The Triumph of Conservatism*, Macmillan, New York, 1963.
[16] *Ibid*, p. 204.
[17] *Ibid.*, p. 205.
[18] *Ibid.*, p. 206.

While Wilson did not subscribe to the notion of the corporation as a "person", he did believe that "giant business was axiomatic with efficiency."[19] Kolko concludes that it is too much to assume, given the intensity of Wilson's early conservatism and the narrow extent of his later liberalism, that he underwent a transformation in his political thinking to a perspective more aligned with social and economic justice.[20]

More recently, James Loewen devoted considerable space in *Lies My Teacher Told Me* to the personal characteristics of Wilson which have been sparsely presented in history books such as his racism and propensity for foreign intervention. Traditionally, he has been heralded as the great statesman who reluctantly led the nation into World War I and then after the war, led the struggle to establish the League of Nations.

A staunch Southern racist, Wilson racially segregated the federal government, and during his Presidency, the United States intervened in Latin America more often than at any other time in our history.[21] Whereas Roosevelt belligerently asserted that the United States must establish order, efficiency, and political, economic and military power in the world, Wilson approached international relations with a reserved, yet missionary zeal, proclaiming that the American system would save the world. By this Wilson meant that American economic goods, America's democratic political system and its blend of morality and Christianity could rescue the world from future wars and unstable conditions.

Arguably, Wilson's foreign policy harkens back to the Puritan origins of Manifest Destiny which perceived America as a "new Jerusalem," a "city set on a hill," a "light unto the world." Perhaps the most famous quote attributed to Wilson is: "The world must be made safe for democracy." A deeper examination of the man, however, forces us to conclude that for Wilson, "democracy" was synonymous with American capitalism reinforced by an aggressive American military establishment.

World War I

In the first decade of the twentieth century, extreme instability prevailed in Europe. The Turkish Empire was crumbling, and in Russia, revolution was brewing. Germany increasingly felt entitled to more imperial power, and Britain and France were feeling the rumblings of their neighbor to the east. War broke out in Europe in 1914, but America remained aloof. The main effect of the European war was to increase business for industries providing war supplies. When the United States finally did join forces with Britain and France against Germany, it established a pattern that would involve it in foreign intervention throughout the twentieth century. A significant reason for America's involvement in World War I was its economic relationships with Allied powers. American financial institutions had given over $2 billion in loans to Great Britain. Clearly, the United States capitalist establishment was interested in opening and maintaining new markets and obtaining resources around the world.

The United States had also lent massive amounts of money for the war effort to England and France, proclaiming neutrality. However, it entered the war when it became clear that without American involvement, European allies might lose the war, in which case, their debts to America could not be repaid.

The scepter of communism that had triumphed in Soviet Russia and that was hanging over a devastated Europe continued to intimidate European and American elites. As emphasized earlier, the American capitalist elite was willing to use whatever means necessary to quash any inroads of socialist or communist influence within the United States—hence the heavy-handedness with which it approached the labor movement in all contexts, the Haymarket debacle and the Pullman Strike being two notable examples.

---

[19] *Ibid.*, p. 206
[20] *Ibid.*, p. 205.
[21] Loewen, pp.22-31.

Comprehending its intractable paranoia of the left further illumines the fascination of America's ruling elite with German fascism and its willingness to finance German industry and Hitler's war effort against the Soviet Union well into World War II. For example, as will be discussed in our consideration of World War II, the Union Banking Corporation, under the directorship of Prescott Bush, father of George Herbert Walker Bush and grandfather of George W. Bush, Jr., was openly helping to finance the Nazi war effort. It was not until the United States government seized the assets of Union Banking in 1942 that Prescott Bush's financial support of the Nazi regime ceased. [22]

World War I was the result of the aggression of European leaders toward other countries on an unprecedented scale. Added to this volatile scenario was intensifying nationalism and economic and imperial competition attended by a perilous arms race. The United States claimed to remain neutral but suddenly entered the war in 1917 for reasons explained above. President Wilson articulated America's need to declare war on Germany as follows:

> It is a war against all nations. American ships have been sunk, American lives taken, in ways which it has stirred us very deeply to learn of, but the ships and people of other neutral and friendly nations have been sunk and overwhelmed in the waters in the same way. There has been no discrimination. The challenge is to all mankind. Each nation must decide for itself how it will meet it. The choice we make for ourselves must be made with a moderation of counsel and a temperateness of judgment befitting our character and our motives as a nation. We must put excited feeling away. Our motive will not be revenge or the victorious assertion of the physical might of the nation, but only the vindication of right, of human right, of which we are only a single champion.
>
> --President Woodrow Wilson's War Message, April 2, 1917--

In opposition to Wilson's statement, Nebraska Senator George Norris argued:

> We have loaned many hundreds of millions of dollars to the Allies in this controversy. While such action was legal and countenanced by international law, there is no doubt in my mind but the enormous amount of money loaned to the Allies in this country has been instrumental in bringing about a public sentiment in favor of our country taking a course that would make every bond worth a hundred cents on the dollar and making the payment of every debt certain and sure. Through this instrumentality and also through the instrumentality of others who have not only made millions out of the war in the manufacture of munitions, etc., and who would expect to make millions more if our country can be drawn into the catastrophe, a large number of the great newspapers and news agencies of the country have been controlled and enlisted in the greatest propaganda that the world has ever known to manufacture sentiment in favor of war.
>
> --Senator George W. Norris Opposition to Wilson's War Message, April 4, 1917--

We will consider the issue of propaganda raised by Senator Norris shortly, but first, let us consider the military developments that Schultz notes, resulting from World War I.

World War I produced a new kind of warfare:

- **War was fought more defensively** than previous wars had been. Whereas in the Civil War, troops frequently carried out engagement by marching toward one another, World War I began the practice of "taking cover" such as digging and firing from trenches.
- **World War I was more mechanized**, using tanks and airplanes which could drop bombs.

---

[22] http://www.tarpley.net, Chapter 6

- Unlike previous wars, **chemical weapons** were designed and used in World War I.
- In the United States, the **Selective Service Act of 1917** was passed which instated a military draft.

THE ROLE OF PROPAGANDA IN WORLD WAR I

What is propaganda?

1. The systematic propagation of a doctrine or cause or of information reflecting the views and interests of those advocating such a doctrine or cause.

2. Material disseminated by the advocates or opponents of a doctrine or cause, i.e., *wartime propaganda*. (www.dictionary.com)

World War I marked the beginning of the intentional use of propaganda by the American government. While yellow journalism assisted in the onset of the Spanish American War, no president prior to Wilson had actively created an office of propaganda to address public opinion. Below is an excerpt from twenty-first century social and political commentator, Gilles D'aymery, regarding propaganda during the Wilson presidency.

PROPAGANDA: THEN AND NOW

First published at SWANS.com at http://www.swans.com/library/art7/ga120.html

by GILLES D'AYMERY

"So far as individuals are concerned, the art of democracy is the art of thinking and discussing independently together."—Institute of Propaganda Analysis (1)

In January 1916, President Woodrow Wilson stated, "So far as I can remember, this is a government of the people, and this people is not going to choose war." (2) Later in the year, Wilson campaigned and won his re-election on a platform stressing a policy of neutrality, if not antiwar pacifism, toward the raging conflict on the old continent. The slogan used by his team, "He kept us out of the war," was factual though from 1914 to 1916 the US exports to Britain and France increased from $825 million to $3.2 billion. Months later, Wilson's request to declare war against the German government was approved in the Senate by 82 votes to 6 (April 4, 1917), and in the House of Representatives by 373 to 50 (April 6, 1917).

If "people [were] not going to choose war" then war would choose people, as Wilson's rhetoric drastically changed: "Lead this people into war, and they'll forget there was ever such a thing as tolerance. To fight, you must be brutal and ruthless, and the spirit of ruthless brutality will enter into the very fibre of national life, infecting the Congress, the courts, the policeman on the beat, the man in the street." (3)

One week later, as he was confronted with a deeply ambivalent public, Wilson created the **Committee on Public Information** (CPI) on April 13, 1917. According to a must-read study by Aaron Delwiche at the School of Communications, University of Washington, (4) "Under the leadership of a muckraking journalist named George Creel, the CPI recruited heavily from business, media, academia, and the art world. The CPI blended advertising techniques with a sophisticated understanding of human psychology, and its efforts represent the first time that a modern government disseminated propaganda on such a large scale. It is fascinating that this phenomenon, often linked with totalitarian regimes, emerged in a democratic state." "Invoking the threat of German propaganda," the study continues, "the CPI implemented 'voluntary guidelines' for the news media and helped to pass the Espionage Act of 1917 and the Sedition Act of 1918. The CPI did not have explicit enforcement power, but it nevertheless 'enjoyed censorship power which was tantamount to direct legal force.'"

"The CPI's domestic division was composed of 19 sub-divisions, and each focused on a particular type of propaganda." Scholars, novelists, moviemakers, artists, sociologists, psychologists, educators, advertisers, and all kind of professionals were recruited by the CPI to develop and disseminate its pro-war message, based on emotional appeals and demonization of the enemy. "On any given week, more than 20,000 newspaper columns were filled with material gleaned from CPI handouts." Pacifists and dissenters were silenced through threats and accusations of un-patriotism. Americans, once intensely divided, embraced the war with fervor and dedication.

On November 11, 1918, that mass insanity and slaughter, that "war to end all wars" came to a close with the Armistice signed at Compiegne, France. The next day, the CPI disbanded its domestic division and a few months later, following the Paris Peace conference that led to the Treaty of Versailles in June 1919, closed its foreign division.

The tools, techniques and processes developed by the CPI to manipulate the collective attitudes of the public did not disappear with the termination of the endeavor. The heads of the organization went on to apply the lessons learned in time of war to a country at peace. These former CPI agents moved on to Madison Avenue, joined the nascent Public Relations firms and became lobbyists.

"Two years later," the study states, (5) "the Director of the CPI's Foreign Division argued that 'the history of propaganda in the war would scarcely be worthy of consideration here, but for one fact-it did not stop with the armistice. No indeed! The methods invented and tried out in the war were too valuable for the uses of governments, factions, and special interests.' Sigmund Freud's nephew, Edward Bernays, took the techniques he learned in the CPI directly to Madison Avenue and became an outspoken proponent of propaganda as a tool for democratic government. 'It was, of course, the astounding success of propaganda during the war that opened the eyes of the intelligent few in all departments of life to the possibilities of regimenting the public mind,' wrote Bernays in his 1928 bombshell Propaganda. 'It was only natural, after the war ended, that intelligent persons should ask themselves whether it was not possible to apply a similar technique to the problems of peace.'"

The intelligent few....regimenting the public mind...Edward Bernays [1891-1995] is also known as the Father of Spin (6) and the godfather of modern public relations (the "father" of public relations is Ivy Lee whose firm, Ivy Lee & T.J. Ross, was hired for $25,000 a year by the German conglomerate, I.G. Farben, which invited him to meet Hitler and Goebbels. His son, James Lee went to work for Farben in Berlin.) (7)

The Institute for Propaganda Analysis, founded in 1937 to educate the public about the nature of propaganda, identified "seven basic propaganda devices: Name-Calling, Glittering Generality, Transfer, Testimonial, Plain Folks, Card Stacking, and Band Wagon." (8)

The techniques of Glittering Generality and Name-Calling are of particular interest as they are the two faces of the device that allows the forming of the public mind by manipulating, "guiding" people's emotions. The former relies on positive words such as freedom, democracy, liberty, patriotism, civilization, peace-loving country or people, etc.-all words that have been extensively repeated in the past few weeks by officials and main media alike-that have a potent commonality; that is, their meaning differs according to different people but they have a positive connotation. In reverse, Name-Calling emphasizes the negative, thus rousing fear, intolerance, profound dislike, even hate in people. Words like evil-doers, terrorists, fundamentalists, ethnic-cleansing, genocide-and depending on the circumstances, socialist, queer, gay, communist, liberal, radical, etc.-help create the "enemy." These "good names" and "bad names" are used deliberately and strategically to manipulate public opinion in order to achieve a specific goal (sell a product, create or cancel a policy or a law (cf. the Patriot Act of October 2001), go to war, discredit dissenters, etc.).

Goebbels, the mastermind of the Nazi propaganda machine was said to have read the publications of the Institute for Propaganda Analysis and carefully studied the techniques used by Madison Avenue.

We've come a long way since the 1930s and those studies. The techniques have been refined and perfected. Goebbels used to say that "Domination of the street [was] the first step to state power." Today, the first step to state power is domination of the media; a media, utterly controlled by mega-corporations, that takes advantage of the collective ignorance to disseminate the manipulated messages. In the past, dissenters like Mark Twain, Henry David Thoreau or Randolph Bourne were vilified and silenced. Today, they are mostly ignored or easily discredited in a few words. Here is an example in a recent article published in The New York Times, "Counterpoint to Unity: Dissent" (note the usage of the words Unity (Glittering Generality) and Dissent (Name-Calling):

"Another figure from the antiwar movement is Mr. Chomsky, who has never stopped criticizing American foreign policy as the major cause of hardship and harm in the world. He has long since stopped getting much notice among mainstream journals of opinion in the United States, but he retains an avid following among the numerous small leftist groups with magazines and Web sites and among the foes of so-called globalization." (9)

Or take Arundhati Roy. The famous Indian novelist, whose recent two powerful essays, (10) having reached a wide enough audience, was quickly discounted and discredited in another article published in The New York Times, "An Indian Novelist Turns Her Wrath on the U.S." Her essays were decried as "vain, shrill, unoriginal, oversimplified, hyperbolic and lacking any voices but her own." (11) Her words had to be considered serious or "subversive" enough-even though her pieces were not published in the United States-that she deserved an article not buried in the issue (as is usually the case) but featured in page A3!

In both cases, the arguments raised by Chomsky or Roy are not addressed. This is another tool of propaganda. The answers are *ad hominem*. Their arguments are judged "dangerous" enough that they need to be discredited. With Chomsky it suffices to bury him in the bowels of the paper on page 13 and to associate him with the minority. It is, like a friend puts it, "Well, his arguments can't be very compelling because they only persuade a small band of 'leftists'. Anyone of consequence doesn't listen to him…Therefore, neither should you." Roy, possibly regarded as a greater menace as she cannot be associated to a so-called fringe movement, is properly dispended of through vilification. In both cases, the result is the same: Mere discredit; but again their arguments are not touched with a ten-foot pole!

So, the evidence of Osama bin Laden "would not stand in court," says Secretary of State Collin Powell. Never mind such a detail. Simply keep repeating that bin Laden and the Taliban are "evildoers." Goebbels used to say, "Propaganda means repetition and more repetition!" "Repeat it until even the densest has got it."
So, civilians are being hit by our bombs. Deny it. Goebbels used to say, "Denials must always be categoric." The "collateral damage" is independently confirmed, therefore undeniable. No problem, have the networks show pictures of 9/11 after each and every report of civilian casualties. Goebbels used to say, "Denials alone won't work. You've got to counterattack."

Dissent is done with. Reason is done with. Intellect is done with. Common sense is done with. Everything the "Enlightenment" taught us is done with. We now live in an age, prescribed by Sigmund Freud's nephew, Edward Bernays, where "a leadership democracy administered by the intelligent minority who know how to regiment and guide the masses" has finally dawned upon humanity.

We, the "masses," should rejoice!

NOTES:

1. Institute for Propaganda Analysis. The Fine Art of Propaganda. New York: Harcourt, Brace and Company, 1939.
2. Harry Elmer Barnes, The Genesis of the World War. New York: Alfred A. Knopf, 1926.
3. Woodrow Wilson, quoted in Richard Hofstadter, The American Political Tradition And The Men Who Made It. New York: Vintage Books, 1948.

4. Aaron Delwiche, Propaganda, School of Communications, University of Washington. http://carmen.artsci.washington.edu/propaganda/home.htm
5. ibid.
6. Larry Tye, The Father of Spin: Edward L. Bernays and the Birth of Public Relations. New York: Crown Publishers, 1998.
7. The Latin America Solidarity Centre, Dublin, Ireland, Neoliberalism: The Balkans Scenario. http://www.eco.utexas.edu/faculty/Cleaver/wk2balkans.html and The Empire of I.G. Farben, Wall Street And the Rise of Hitler, by Antony C. Sutton. http://reformed-theology.org/html/books/wall_street/chapter_02.htm-Also, Charles Higham, Trading with the Enemy. The Nazi-American Money Plot 1933-1949. Delacorte Press, 1983. http://www.thirdworldtraveler.com/Fascism/Trading_Enemy_excerpts.html
8. Aaron Delwiche, Propaganda.
9. Richard Bernstein, Counterpoint to Unity: Dissent. The New York Times, October 6, 2001, A13 and A15.
10. Arundhati Roy, The Algebra of Infinite Justice, http://www.outlookindia.com/full.asp?sid=1&fodname=20011008&fname=Roy+%28F%29 and War Is Peace, October 23, 2001 in The Guardian of London, http://www.guardian.co.uk
11. Cecilia W. Dugger, An Indian Novelist Turns Her Wrath on the U.S. The New York Times, November 3, 2001, A3.

We should note that in subsequent U.S. wars, propaganda has been used successfully to accomplish a variety of political and military goals. More recently, it was used before the Gulf War but especially prior to the U.S. invasion of Iraq in March, 2003.

It is important to understand that out of World War I propaganda evolved the public relations firm and the use of PR firms by the Executive Branch of the U.S. government to influence public opinion. We will consider this phenomenon in more depth in our analysis of the Iraq War.

World War I ended in 1917 and was diplomatically concluded with the signing of the **Treaty of Versailles**, January, 1919. Of the 440 articles of the Treaty, the following four are particularly significant in terms of their shaping of subsequent events, particularly in relation to Germany:

- The German Army must not exceed 100,000 soldiers; its navy must not exceed six battleships, six light cruisers, twelve destroyers and twelve torpedo boats. Moreover, Germany is forbidden to have any submarines.
- Germany must pay for all wartime damages to the civilian population and property of Allied powers.
- The German territory west of the Rhine River will be occupied by allied troops for the next fifteen years.
- Germany must accept responsibility for causing all the loss and damage that the Allies and their citizens suffered.[23]

In summary, the consequences of the Treaty of Versailles in terms of its treatment of Germany were:

- Germany was for all practical purposes disarmed with regard to its military and naval power.
- Germany was severely crippled economically.
- A significant number of Allied troops would remain in Germany.
- Germany was scapegoated as the perpetrator and principal aggressor of World War I.

In events leading up to World War II, we will explore how Hitler used Versailles as the justification for the new German empire he vindictively sought to establish.

---

[23] http://www.historylearningsite.co.uk/treaty_of_versailles.htm

10

THE POLITICS OF PROSPERITY AND REACTION: THE 1920S

The Business Boom Of The 1920s

As is usually the case after a war, the United States after World War I experienced a time of transition from a war-time to a peace-time economy. In this challenging process, economic dislocation was caused for industrial workers, farmers, and renewed racism and nativism was stirred against Black Americans and foreigners. Nevertheless, the 1920s was a decade of unparalleled prosperity for the United States, particularly its ruling elite, as a result of an extraordinary financial boom in American industry.

Four factors of production *mass production, better machinery, higher production/higher wages,* and *more demand for consumer goods* constituted a spiral which led to a business boom.[24]

World War I had boosted improvements in technology and increased production. The industries of oil and steel were stimulated, as were new industries such as plastics and rayon. Moreover, a new form of "scientific management", known as *Taylorism*, provided a mathematical formula for labor, the streamlining of tasks and increased production. In the late nineteenth century, Frederick Winslow Taylor published a number of papers on scientific management in which he theorized methods for making human labor compatible with the machine age which would also give the employer increased control of the workplace to make employees less independent. Taylor suggested subdividing tasks in order to speed up production and make workers interchangeable, thereby diminishing an employer's dependence on any one worker. For example, if one worker knows how to do several different jobs, he/she is more valuable than a worker who only knows how to do one job. By hiring multi-trained workers, the employer can speed up production and cut overhead by not having to hire workers for each task.

Rapid increase in worker productivity meant that workers earned higher wages and became better consumers. Furthermore, consumption was enhanced with a new innovation, the installment plan. It is in the 1920s that we see

---

[24] Schultz Lecture 15 (http://us.history.wisc.edu/hist102/lectures/lecture15.html)

the beginning of encouraging consumers to build up debt to buy consumer goods. Consequently, a new psychology of consumption arose which Thorstein Veblen analyzed in his monumental work *The Theory of The Leisure Class*, published in 1898 but not widely read until the 1920s. It was Veblen who introduced the term *conspicuous consumption* which in the 1920s included the purchase of radios, the booming of the motion picture industry, a plethora of "must-have" new appliances, and of course, America's willingness to sacrifice almost anything for the purchase of an automobile. (*The Theory Of The Leisure Class* **is strongly recommended for an understanding of the 1920s psychology of consumption as well as the psychology of the ruling elite in the modern world.**)

Due to the steady decline in the price of the automobile until the mid-1920s, putting the automobile within virtually everyone's reach, and due to the accessibility of credit, nearly every American family had at least one car. Economically, the automobile promoted the growth of related industries such as petroleum, rubber and steel. Additionally, it necessitated a national system of highways and created a variety of service-related industries such as service stations, garages, restaurants and hotels. Socially, the automobile created a more mobile society and loosened the bonds of the family, allowing family members to go their own way.

The Symbiosis of Government and Corporations

When teaching U.S. History from 1865 to the present, I used to present a diagram on the overhead projector, depicting a 7-Headed Monster which illustrated the symbiosis between government and six other entities, revealing the tyrannical "beast" that America's institutions have become. The seven entities are: *corporations, the military, media, education, the intelligence community*, and *organized crime*—seven separate heads connected to one body.

I no longer use the illustration because the confluence of government and virtually all of our institutions is now so entrenched and so impenetrable that the "monster" analogy no longer serves to adequetly depcit the symbiotic relationships between them. One has only to research the dizzying rate at which thousands of individuals move through the revolving doors between the corporate sphere and government and back to the corporate sphere, to comprehend the comingling of the two worlds.

One of the legacies of the Civil War was the burgeoning convergence of government and industry which during the late-nineteenth and early-twentieth centuries foisted untold abuse upon American society. While the severity and frequency of the exploitation was in many instances curtailed during the Progressive Era, it was never eliminated because the symbiotic relationship between government and industry (political capitalism) was never thoroughly addressed, except by groups marginalized from the government-corporate mainstream.

As we consider the decade of the 1920s, we must explore more closely the relationship between government and corporations. As Kolko reminds us (see the above section on Progressivism), the so-called *regulation* of the Progressive Era "was put in place to contain protest movements and maintain order, and…they did not make fundamental changes in the American capitalist system. What emerged was regulated capitalism, which created minimal reforms for the working classes, but benefited business much more significantly and protected it from economic losses." The government-business symbiosis of *political capitalism*, born in the Progressive Era, matured and came to fruition in the 1920s.

Three Presidents, Harding, Coolidge and Hoover echoed, in one way or other, the sentiment that **"the chief business of the American people is business."** (Calvin Coolidge, 1925)

The Federal Reserve System

The Federal Reserve System was created in 1913 by the Federal Reserve Act to be the central bank of the United States. It includes a system of eight to twelve regional reserve banks. While most Americans believe that the Federal Reserve is a federal entity, it is indeed, a private bank which discloses the name and duties of its board chairman, but does not disclose the names of its board members. It oversees branch banks, sets monetary policy, interest rates, and oversees the printing of money. It is profoundly in charge of the economy of the United States.

While it is not in the scope of this abstract to examine the operations of the Federal Reserve in depth, it is important to understand that the money policy and supply of the United States is determined not by a government entity, but by a private corporation. For more in-depth research, see the DVD documentary, "The Money Masters"[25] or the "Articles" section of the website of Catherine Austin Fitts (http://www.solari.com) for further research on the Federal Reserve and its powers.

> *FASCISM SHOULD MORE PROPERLY BE CALLED CORPORATISM, SINCE IT IS THE MERGER OF STATE AND CORPORATE POWER.*
>
> Benito Mussolini~~~

---

[25] The Money Masters (http://www.themoneymasters.com/)

The above quote by Benito Mussolini reminds us of the danger of a government-corporate symbiosis. It has proven more often than not, to be the essence of a fascist state. The following handout outlines the corporate state of the 1920s and introduces the issue to which we now turn—the dark side of the Politics of Prosperity: *Reaction*.

THE CORPORATE STATE OF THE 1920s
(Handout)

During the 1920s, the relationship between corporations and the government was so close that the two were almost inseparable. Three Republican Presidents in a row, Harding, Coolidge and Hoover, virtually declared that "The business of America is business." Laissez-faire economics, little government regulation of business and less support of labor unions resulted in a virtual "corporate state" in which the government allowed business unrestrained greed and exploitation. In return, business financed politicians who would support its goals without reservation.

The federal government supported business in four major ways:

1) High tariffs—The federal government created the highest ever tariff policies on foreign-made goods in order to protect American business profits.
2) Reduction of income tax rates for corporations—Secretary of the Treasury, Andrew Mellon, son of a famous robber baron family, demanded that Congress repeal excess profits taxes and corporate income taxes. A list of tax loopholes were created for corporations.
3) The Federal Trade Commission which had been created to regulate big business and to investigate unfair trade practices did almost none of this during the 1920s.
4) Herbert Hoover strongly advocated that the government is RESPONSIBLE for helping corporations profit.

During the 1920s, the prevailing philosophy in government was that the government should stay out of the affairs of corporations UNLESS it was going to help the corporations increase their profits.

The 1920s was also a time of increased racism, nativism and a dramatic return of the Ku Klux Klan. In fact, many politicians and businessmen were Klan members. While the popularity of the Klan and the corporate state diminished with the onset of the Great Depression of 1929, the idea of the corporate state resurfaced after World War II and from there became virtually institutionalized in American domestic and foreign policy.

The Politics of Reaction

Elected President in 1920, Warren Harding attempted to lead the country in a "return to normalcy" after World War I. White America longed for a nation free of labor conflicts, fewer immigrants, less radicalism, small-town values, Christian fundamentalism and less government interference. The 1920s was a decade of intensified racism, nativism, cultural fundamentalism and anti-socialist hysteria. The widely read journalist and satirist of the era, H.L. Mencken's famous quote, "No one ever went broke underestimating the intelligence of the American people", was evoked by his disgust with the various forms of irrationality that ensued from America's desire for "normalcy." When people are frightened and threatened, they look for scapegoats—other ethnicities, immigrants, socialists, people whose religious beliefs differ from theirs.

According to Stanley Schultz, four events of the 1920s are particularly significant: The Red Scare, the trial of Sacco and Vanzetti, the rise of the Ku Klux Klan, and the Scopes Trial.[26]

- **The Red Scare**
  The Bolshevik Revolution occurred in Russia in 1917, bringing the Communist Party and its ideology to power. The lifeblood of the revolution was the workers' movement which pledged to take a workers' revolution all over the world. Although most Americans did not know who the Bolshevik leader, Lenin, was, politicians and the mainstream press portrayed "the Bolshevik menace" as a direct threat to the United States. America had already witnessed Haymarket and the Pullman Strike, and corporations and politicians played on fears of labor unrest and mob violence, asserting that America might fall to communism. These fears were only reinforced in 1919 by a huge wave of strikes, some attended by bomb threats.

  One of the targets of numerous bomb threats was none other than Attorney General, Mitchell Palmer. Such threats converted Palmer to the idea of a Red Scare. As a result, he organized a new group of crime fighters for investigating and deporting potential radicals and suspicious foreigners. In addition, he used the Sedition Act of 1918 to support his prosecutions[27] Incidentally, Palmer appointed the young J.Edgar Hoover, the future Director of the Federal Bureau of Investigation who would be a pivotal player in reaction to the Civil Rights Movement of the 1960s, as his head of the General Intelligence Division of the Justice Department.

  In his essay, The Case Against The Reds, Palmer stated:

  Behind, and underneath, my own determination to drive from our midst the agents of Bolshevism, I have discovered the hysterical methods of these revolutionary humans. I have been asked to what extent deportation will check radicalism in this country. Why not ask what will become of the United States Government if these alien radicals carry out the principles of the Communist Party?

  In place of the United States Government we would have the horror and terrorism of Bolshevik tyranny such as the destroying Russia now. The whole purpose of communism appears to be the mass formation of the criminals of the world to overthrow the decencies of private life, to usurp property, to disrupt the present order of life regardless of health, sex or religious rights.

  These are the revolutionary tenets of the Communist Internationale. These include the IWW's, the most radical socialists, the misguided anarchists, the agitators who oppose the limitations of unionism, the moral perverts and the hysterical neurasthenic women who abound in communism.

---

[26] http://us.history.wisc.edu/hist102/lectures/lecture16.html
[27] http://www.fordham.edu/halsall/mod/1916espionageact.html

On January 2, 1920 the Red Scare culminated in raids in thirty-three American cities in which the Justice Department arrested 3,000 people who they claimed were "Communists, anarchists, and aliens." In fact, most of these people were innocent of breaking any law. Nevertheless, they were held in violation of their Constitutional rights, held without bail and were not allowed to contact lawyers or family members. Still others were arrested on the grounds of "guilt by association." Thus, a total of 7,000 were arrested, but only 556 were deported or imprisoned. The **Palmer Raids** were so sweeping and so indiscriminate that even some scholars and famous humanitarians, such as Jane Addams, were arrested. Just a little over a month before the raids, Addams gave a compelling speech in Chicago regarding the violations of civil liberties with regard to dissenters:

Excerpt From Jane Addams Speech, Chicago, November, 1919

Hundreds of poor laboring men and women are being thrown into jails and police stations because of their political beliefs. In fact, an attempt is being made to deport an entire political party.

These men and women, who in some respects are more American in ideals than the agents of the government who are tracking them down, are thrust into cells so crowded they cannot lie down.

And what is it these radicals seek? It is the right of free speech and free thought; nothing more than is guaranteed to them under the Constitution of the United States, but repudiated because of the war.

It is a dangerous situation we face at the present time, with the rule of the few overcoming the voice of the many. It is doubly dangerous because we are trying to suppress something upon which our very country was founded—liberty.

The cure for the spirit of unrest in this country is conciliation and education—not hysteria. Free speech is the greatest safety valve of our United States. Let us give these people a chance to explain their beliefs and desires. Let us end this suppression and spirit of intolerance which is making of America another autocracy.

J. Edgar Hoover not only emerged from the Red Scare unscathed, but it became his claim to fame, and in 1924 during the Harding Administration, he was appointed Director of the FBI where he remained until his death in 1972. It is important to remember that Hoover rose to power in the FBI as a result of the Palmer Raids and that he would direct the FBI from a Red Scare paradigm for the rest of his life.

The classic work on the Red Scare of the early-twentieth century is *ALIENS AND DISSENTERS: Federal Suppression of Radicals, 1903-1933*, by William Preston, Jr.[28] I consider it a must-read for a complete understanding of the Red Scare of the 1920s. Moreover, Preston's work lends perspective to the renewed xenophobia (fear of other ethnicities and fear of the foreign-born).

As we consider America's current "war on terror" and its violation of the civil liberties of immigrants or even foreign-born American citizens, Preston's work gives us added historical perspective.

- **The Sacco and Vanzetti Trial**

Coinciding with a period of the most intense political repression in American history was the trial of two Italian workers, who also happened to be anarchist militants, deeply involved in labor strikes, political agitation and antiwar propaganda. In April, 1920, Sacco and Vanzetti fell into a trap laid for a suspect of a South Braintree, Massachusetts robbery who had robbed and murdered a local paymaster. As they were accustomed to do, both men were carrying

---

[28] William, Jr., *Aliens And Dissenters: The Federal Suppression of Radicals, 1903-1933*, Champaign-Urbana, University of Illinois Press, 1994.

guns which they claimed were for self-defense. While they were armed and while many witnesses could place them at the scene of the crime, many more incidents proved their innocence. Today, it is widely accepted that Vanzetti was innocent, but Sacco did not have a solid alibi. In 1921, both men were convicted, and in 1927, they were executed.

Experts have widely argued the innocence or guilt of the pair, but few dispute the reality that the trial was a travesty of justice and that they were railroaded to conviction because they were immigrant radicals. The trial revealed the dark side of cultural fundamentalism and caused many American intellectuals to question their government and its justice system.

- **The Rise Of The Ku Klux Klan**

As we recall from our study of the Reconstruction Era above, the Ku Klux Klan flourished after the Civil War, but it remained a small and regional organization until the 1920s. Given the prevailing attitudes of xenophobia and the Red Scare, Klan membership mushroomed from 100,000 to 1 million by 1922 and by 1925 to 2 million.

The Klan had three principal targets:

- **African-Americans.** As it had during Reconstruction, the Klan proclaimed "racial purity" and scapegoated African-Americans and immigrants as impure, disloyal, anarchist, and inherently inferior.
- **Roman Catholics.** The Klan was a solidly Protestant organization, declaring the Pope a "political autocrat." One could not be a loyal American, the Klan said, and also be a Catholic.
- **Jews.** Jews were scapegoated as "Christ killers" and financial wizards who were often involved with Bolshevism, labor unrest, or radical ideas.

No longer was Klan activity limited to the South. It became strongest in the State of Indiana where by the mid-1920s, many state legislators and even the governor himself were Klan members or sympathizers. The Klan captured six governorships including Oregon and Colorado. Although it never captured the Presidency, it split the 1924 Democratic National Convention. By 1925, membership was diminishing and Klan influence declining. It would regain strength in the 1930s and again after World War II.

(As mentioned above, the video documentary *THE KU KLUX KLAN: A Secret History*, is an excellent study of the organization from Reconstruction to the present time. The documentary is quite long, but it lends itself to being shown in two sections. I like to show the portion of the video dealing with Reconstruction when the class is studying that era. I then show the section covering the1920s revival of the Klan when we are studying the cultural fundamentalism of the 1920s.)

- **The Scopes Trial of 1925**

Known as "The Monkey Trial," the Scopes Trial was about academic freedom. It served to exacerbate the tension between a secular and a fundamentalist culture. The legislature of the State of Tennessee had passed the Butler Law which stated that no theory could be taught in public school which conflicted with the biblical story of Creation. However, by the 1920s, Darwin's theory of evolution was part of standard curriculum in colleges and universities. **John T. Scopes**, a 25 year-old teacher in Dayton, Tennessee challenged state law by teaching the theory of evolution in his high-school biology class. Scopes was arrested and was defended by a leading trial lawyer, **Clarence Darrow**. Financed by the American Civil Liberties Union (ACLU), Darrow was pitted against prosecuting attorney, **William Jennings Bryan**, Populist and three-time presidential candidate. Bryan was a fundamentalist Christian, while Darrow was an agnostic. The trial soon became not only an intense legal contest, but a media circus. Public sentiment was in Bryan's favor since rural Tennessee was a bastion of provincial, Christian fundamentalism.

The culture war we are witnessing in early twenty-first-century America is not unlike that of the 1920s as today's religious right and secularists polarize around issues of abortion, sexual orientation, contraception, gay and lesbian marriage, the teaching of intelligent design, and the right to die. Current culture war discourse almost eerily echoes the dialog below between attorneys Darrow and Bryan.

The American Studies Department of the University of Virginia describes the ideological contest between Darrow and Bryan:

> From the moment of Bryan's arrival in Dayton, the weight of public sentiment was in his favor. The records of the trial indicate that the townspeople came out for the trial in record numbers, packing the small country courthouse. Cries of "Amen" peppered the trial proceedings until the judge had to ask the observers to lower the noise level. Bryan planned to end the trial with a speech consummating his lifetime of preaching, one he had been preparing for seven weeks. Darrow, however, had other plans. Since the intention was to test the constitutionality of the Butler Law, Darrow wanted the jury to find Scopes guilty, so he could then appeal the decision in a higher court. He did not, however, plan to call Scopes to the stand, for if he were to do so, it might surface that Scopes had, in fact, not even been in school on the day mentioned in the indictment. He was meticulous in his effort to keep the trial free of technicalities. Just one could get the case thrown out with the law itself yet untested. Darrow also planned to call expert witnesses to give testimony about evolution. But when the judge ordered that Darrow could not call the scholars as witnesses, he shifted his plans.
>
> After the judge moved the trial outside because of the 100-plus degree heat inside and the instability of the courtroom floor under the weight of so many spectators, Darrow, in a fantastic gesture, called William Jennings Bryan to the stand. The interchange which follows targets the essence of Darrow's argument and signals the turning point in the trial, which brought public sentiment decisively over to Darrow's side:
>
> Q: "You have given considerable study to the Bible, haven't you, Mr. Bryan?"
> A: "Yes, sir; I have tried to…But, of course, I have studied it more as I have become older than when I was a boy."
> Q: "Do you claim then that everything in the Bible should be literally interpreted?"
> A: "I believe everything in the Bible should be accepted as it is given there…"
> Darrow continued to question Bryan on the actuality of Jonah and the whale, Joshua's making the sun stand still and the Tower of Babel, as Bryan began to have more difficulty answering.
> Q: "Do you think the earth was made in six days?"
> A: "Not six days of 24 hours…My impression is they were periods…"
> Q: "Now, if you call those periods, they may have been a very long time?"
> A: "They might have been."
> Q: "The creation might have been going on for a very long time?"
> A: "It might have continued for millions of years…"
>
> Darrow had set his trap and Bryan walked right in. Darrow asked for and was granted an immediate direct verdict, thereby blocking Bryan from giving his speech. Within eight minutes of deliberation, the jury returned with a verdict of guilty and the judge ordered Scopes to pay a fine of $100, the minimum the law allowed. In his last words to the court, Scopes, the man who was reluctant from the start, said, "Your Honor, I feel that I have been convicted of violating an unjust statute. I will continue in the future…to oppose this law in any way I can. Any other action would be in violation of my idea of academic freedom"[29]

---

[29] http://xroads.virginia.edu/~UG97/inherit/1925home.html

Just five days after the trial ended, Bryan lay down for a Sunday afternoon nap and never woke up. The diabetes with which he had contended for years had finally taken his life. Bryan, the former Populist-Democrat candidate for President, had retired from politics and began practicing law. In the above dialog with Darrow, we do not hear the impassioned activist who so articulately preached social justice and human rights in the Populist movement decades earlier, but the more puritanical Bryan who finds the teaching of human evolution reprehensible.

The trial itself also passed on when more than a year later, on January 14, 1927, the State Supreme Court in Nashville handed down a decision which reversed the earlier one. However, the court's decision stemmed from the very point Darrow sought to avoid-a technicality. By Tennessee state law, the jury, not the judge, must set the fine if it is above $50. The Butler Law, then, stood untested.[30]

The Significance of the Scopes Trial

It came at a crossroads in history. The trial itself mirrored the conflicts taking place in the society at large, the obvious one being evolution vs. religion. But as John Crowe Ransom notes, there were a series of tensions throughout the trial, including questions of collective vs. individual rights and academic vs. parental concerns, which have persisted in American culture since the birth of the nation.[31] At issue in both of these conflicts, not unlike the current milieu, was who had control of the society. Who controlled the schools, the masses, or the teachers? Who determined the law-the people or the leaders of the town? The outcome was even more unsettling because there was no final resolution. Scopes lost the case, but won the public's favor, and the Butler Law remained on the books in Tennessee.

The Scopes Trial was distinct not so much for its theme as it was for its presentation. Other school districts and other towns, struggling with this very issue, missed the media circus. Dayton, however, came to center-stage, with the lawyers and businessmen writing the script and the country enthralled with this true American drama.[32]

John Scopes lost the case and was fined $100, but later the case was overturned by the Tennessee Supreme Court on a technicality.

SUMMARY

The Red Scare, the trial of Sacco and Vanzetti, the resurgence of the Ku Klux Klan and the Scopes Trial are stellar examples of a decade of reaction and resistance to moving forward into the diverse and secular realities of the twentieth century. With their fears predominantly focused on immigrants and heretics, the American people were unable to discern the exploitation being foisted upon them by the corporate state. Presuming that the prolific Bull Market of the New York Stock Exchange was infinite and inexhaustible, middle and working-class Americans were ill prepared for the events of October, 1929

Racial Apartheid In America In The 1930s (The Tuskegee Study)

As we have seen, the 1920s and 1930s were times of egregious racism in the United States. In the twenties, the Ku Klux Klan had reclaimed power in the first few years of the decade and achieved higher numbers of membership than ever before in American history.

---

[30] *Ibid.*
[31] Scopes Evolution Trial (reprinted from Tennessee Historical Quarterly, Summer, 1981) 13.
[32] http://xroads.virginia.edu/~UG97/inherit/1925home.html

In the 1930s, an appalling experiment with African Amercian males in the state of Alabama exemplifed the level of racism sanctioned and carried out, not by the Klan, but by the United States government itself. In what came to be known as the Tuskegee Experiment, the United States Public Health Service, beginning in 1932 and lasting some forty years, conducted experiments on 400 black men with syphillis without their knowledge. Not told that they had syphillis and thus denied treatment of the disease, one hundred of the four hundred men died of the disease, and wives and grandchildren of the infected men contracted the disease or were born with it. A detailed summary of the Tuskegee Experiment may be read at: http://www.infoplease.com/ipa/A0762136.html Although President Clinton officially apologized to the African American community in the 1990s, the Tuskegee Experiment has left a permanent stain on America's past.

11

THE CRASH AND THE GREAT DEPRESSION

In 1928, Herbert Hoover was elected President. Since 1924, the U.S. stock market had been bullish. As we have seen, Americans wanted a "return to normalcy" and during the 1920s, ensconced themselves in the post-World War I economic boom, alleviating the shock and pain of the War with new appliances and the epitome of all purchases, the automobile. Optimism reigned, and the American people could see no reason why it should not. One of the most salient and also instructive realities of the 1920s is that the *appearance* of prosperity masked enormous economic inconsistencies. To say that the "good times" of the decade was largely accomplished with smoke and mirrors would not be an exaggeration.

The U.S. Stock Market

Stanley Schultz offers **six reasons why people invested** in the market from 1924 to 1929:

1) **New investors had been continually entering the market, perceiving the market as a way to get rich quickly.** But gradually the market became less fluid (that is, with new investors coming in and old investors going out) and became rather stagnant so that no new money was floating around.
2) **Americans experienced an increase in personal savings.** Good times meant that people had extra money to put into the stock market.
3) **Money was readily available at low interest rates.** Some evidence exists that people not only took out loans to buy cars but also to buy stocks.
4) **Overproduction profits were invested in new production which in turn led to more overproduction.** This cyclical pattern gave the illusion of more financial soundness for companies than was actually there, and this encouraged Americans to buy more stock.
5) **During the 1920s, there was not yet legal regulation** of buying and selling of stocks. Companies printed up more and more common stock, and many people began buying stock "on credit." Confident that stock value would rise, people made "down payments" on stock, expecting to be able to pay off the balance in a few months as a result of substantial profits. This exacerbated speculation in the market and made it increasingly like a pyramid scheme in which most of the money invested in the market was not actually there.
6) **The psychology of consumption** acted like a "drug" that gave people unquestioning faith in prosperity.[33]

---

[33] Schultz Lectures, Lecture 18, (http://us.history.wisc.edu/hist102/lectures/lecture18.html.)

The Crash

As a result of the above six factors, stock prices were out of proportion to actual profits. On October 24, 1929, (Black Thursday) investors began feverishly selling their stocks. A bull market rapidly became bearish, but by the end of the trading day, the market had stabilized somewhat. The House of Morgan (J.P. Morgan) began buying up stocks to ward off panic. On Friday, October 25, it appeared that the panic had ended; however, over the weekend, many investors pondered the situation and decided to sell their stocks. Tuesday, October 29 (Black Tuesday), the market hit bottom, and by November 13, over $30 billion disappeared from the American economy.

The Depression

America had seen many economic depressions, previously called "panics" but none like that of 1929. Nor was America alone in economic depression. All of the world's industrialized nations experienced it. Superb descriptions and images of the Great Depression worldwide and in the United States can be found at the website of the English Department of the University of Illinois at: http://www.english.uiuc.edu/maps/depression/depression.htm

A plethora of social problems tore at the American psyche during the Depression, including: personal suffering from losing employment, the breakdown of families, soaring high school dropout rates, homelessness, organized protests, farmers armed with guns marching on local banks to withdraw their money. The haunting images of the Depression have been captured in photos, songs, stories and literature of the era such as: bread lines, hoboes hopping freight trains, college graduates becoming gas station attendants, skyrocketing rates of mental illness and suicide, former businessmen selling pencils on the street corner, "Okies" or Oklahoma farmers seeking a new life as migrant workers on California farms, as depicted in John Steinbeck's novel, *The Grapes Of Wrath*.[34]

Causes

- **Unequal distribution of income and wealth**

    During the 1920s, 1% of the population possessed incomes 650% greater than the 11% at the bottom of the pyramid. Unprecedented concentration of wealth in the hands of a very few meant that the economy was increasingly dependent on high investment and the luxury spending of the wealthy. Both are given to fluctuations, far more so than the consistent expenditures of the common people on necessities of life such as food, clothing, and shelter. Thus, when the market crashed, both big spending and big investment crumbled.

- **Unequal distribution of corporate power**

    As implied above, the climate of regulation of corporations in the 1920s had reverted to pre-Progressive-era standards. During the administrations of Coolidge, Harding and Hoover, corporations virtually had a blank check to exploit anyone and anything in their paths. Consolidations and mergers were rampant. Two hundred of the largest corporations controlled 50% of the corporate wealth of America. This guaranteed that while a few companies might fail, the entire U.S. economy would be devastated.

- **Lack of banking regulation**

    Between 1923 and 1929, banks closed at the rate of two a day. No federal regulations existed to ensure start-up capital or to limit how much of their reserves banks could lend, resulting in many banks being highly insolvent. Such flaws in the banking system were disguised by the decade's ostensible prosperity.

---

[34] *Ibid.*

Moreover, there is compelling evidence that the policies of the Federal Reserve were instrumental in exacerbating the bursting of an enormous financial bubble in the U.S. stock market. In 1929, Federal Reserve board member, Paul Warburg, sent a secret directive to a number of financial elite, warning of a coming economic collapse. According to Clarence Barron in a 1930 *Harpers Magazine* article entitled, "They Told Barrons", Warburg had stated that: "If the orgies of unrestrained speculation are permitted to spread, the ultimate collapse is certain not only to affect the speculators themselves, but to bring about a general depression involving the entire country."

The revelation of the Federal Reserve Board's decision to trigger the Crash of 1929 appears, curiously, in the *New York Times* on April 20, 1929, in a story headlined, "Federal Advisory Council Mystery".

Moreover, after the stock market crash, the Federal Reserve did not loosen its currency policies to help relieve the suffering of the middle and working classes, but rather tightened them.

Congressman Louis T. McFadden (D-PA) stated:

> It was not accidental. It was a carefully contrived occurrence....The international bankers sought to bring about a condition of despair here so that they might emerge as rulers of us all.[35]

More recently, Nobel Prize-winning economist, Milton Friedman, stated that "The Federal Reserve definitely caused the Great Depression by contracting the amount of currency in circulation by one-third from 1929 to 1933."[36]

> ESSENTIALLY, THE GREAT DEPRESSION WAS A MASSIVE TRANSFER OF WEALTH BY THE CENTRALIZED BANKING SYSTEM FROM THE MIDDLE AND WORKING CLASSES TO THE FINANCIAL ELITE OF THE UNITED STATES AND A HANDFUL OF EUROPEAN NATIONS.

- **Foreign balance of payments**

    As a result of World War I, the U.S. was now a creditor, rather than a debtor, nation. It was lending more money than it owed to foreign nations. Protectionism and high tariffs kept foreign goods out of the United States but had a negative effect. If foreign countries could not pay their debts, they had no money to buy American goods.

- **The demise of laissez-faire**

    The doctrine of laissez-faire continued to dominate the American economy. Herbert Hoover's first remedy for the Depression was to ask business to decrease production and hire more people. However, if business could not sell its products to an economically depressed populace, how could it afford to hire more employees? The world had entered a new economic paradigm, but the United States was not on board. The Great Depression demonstrated unequivocally that laissez-faire was no longer a viable economic strategy.

---

[35] "The Money Masters" DVD Documentary, (www.themoneymasters.com)
[36] *Ibid.*

Howard Zinn in *Peoples' History Of the United States* writes that, "A socialist critic would…say that the capitalist system was by its nature unsound: a system driven by the one overriding motive of corporate profit and therefore unstable, unpredictable, and blind to human needs. The result of all that: permanent depression for many of its people, and periodic crises for almost everybody. Capitalism, despite its attempts at self-reform, its organization for better control, was still in 1929 a sick and undependable system."[37]

Unlike any contemporary historian, Zinn devotes an entire chapter "Self-Help In Hard Times," to the riots, rebellions, strikes, and unrest demonstrated by the working class, veterans, and the poor during the Great Depression. A decade of false prosperity culminating in economic disaster had pushed Americans to the breaking point.

(At this point, it may be useful to read aloud to one's class some anecdotes from Zinn's *The Twentieth Century*, especially Pages 114-115 where he documents the unrest and social upheaval taking place among citizens, particularly unemployed workers, farmers, and even children.)

The New Deal—The First New Deal (1933-1934)

In 1933, Franklin Delano Roosevelt was sworn in as President, bringing relief programs, measures to create jobs, and assistance for industrial and agricultural recovery. A pragmatist, like his distant cousin Theodore Roosevelt, FDR was committed to being liked and putting America back to work and constructing a strong economy.

In his first one hundred days, he launched the New Deal, an alphabet soup of programs designed to restore the economy. Historians frequently refer to the First New Deal, which was designed to resuscitate the economy from the top down with programs such as: The Agricultural Adjustment Act (AAA), The Civilian Conservation Corp (CCC), The Tennessee Valley Authority (TVA), and The National Industrial Recovery Act (NIRA) and the Second New Deal which was the attempt to restore America from the ground up through such programs as the Works Progress Administration (WPA), the Wagner Act, the Social Security Act, and the Wealth Tax.

Franklin Roosevelt has been touted as a champion of reform for the working and middle class during the Great Depression of the 1930s. Indisputably, all of his New Deal programs brought some relief to the American people in a time of unprecedented economic crisis. However, it must be emphasized that Roosevelt was a capitalist and as mentioned above, a pragmatist as well. Many of his reforms also enhanced the status of industry and the ruling elite. One notable case in point is the National Industrial Recovery Act (NIRA).

- **The National Industrial Recovery Act (NIRA)**

    The intention of the NIRA was ostensibly to stabilize prices and production by having American industries set up codes. Supposedly, these codes would be enforced by the federal government. In return for their cooperation, industry was promised that all anti-trust regulation would be suspended. While it did recognize the rights of labor to organize and to conduct collective bargaining with management, it did not ultimately champion the rights of labor. Schultz notes three reasons why the NIRA failed—all of which underscore the benefits of the act for industry:

    > **The NIRA assumed that business would comply with the codes which were ostensibly established for the benefit of workers and consumers but were drawn up by the largest corporations, thereby harming small business.

---

[37] Zinn, Howard, *Peoples History Of The United States*, New York, Harper Collins, 1980, pp. 377-378.

** The rights of labor to organize were never respected, and the right to collective bargaining was never enforced by the government.

**Rather than stabilizing prices by lowering production, what was needed was increased purchasing power for American consumers.[38]

(For an in-depth exploration of the NIRA and the ways it benefited industry, I recommend Sidney Fine's *The Automobile under the Blue Eagle: Labor, Management, and the Automobile Code*, Ann Arbor, University of Michigan Press, 1936.)

Two years after the NIRA was signed into law, it was declared unconstitutional.

- **The Securities and Exchange Commission (SEC)**

The Securities and Exchange Commission was established in 1934 to regulate the commerce in stocks, bonds, and other securities. After the October 29, 1929, stock market crash, reflections on its cause prompted calls for reform. Controls on the issuing and trading of securities were virtually nonexistent, allowing for any number of frauds and other schemes. Further, the unreported concentration of controlling stock interests in a very few hands led to the abuses of power that the unregulated exchange of stock supposedly eliminated.

The Second New Deal (1935-1941)

Beginning in 1935, Roosevelt sent Congress a new legislative package. This was the second phase of the New Deal or, as it later became known, the Second New Deal.

From 1935-1941, the Second New deal continued with relief and recovery measures and provided for social and economic legislation to benefit the mass of working people. A number of New Deal measures were invalidated by the Supreme Court; however; in 1935, as noted above, the NRA was struck down, and the following year the AAA was invalidated. Roosevelt unsuccessfully sought to reorganize the Supreme Court, but he did succeed in getting other laws passed which substituted for legislation that had been declared unconstitutional.

The entire New Deal agenda, which had received the endorsement of agrarian, liberal, and labor groups, met with increasing criticism. The rate of reform slackened after 1937, and there was a groundswell of Republican opposition to the huge public spending, high taxes, and centralization of power in the executive branch of government. Within the Democratic party itself there was strong disapproval from the "old guard" and from disgruntled members of the Brain Trust.

The "Brain Trust" were intellectuals from universities who had been Roosevelt's advisors. They were replaced with former corporate executives and members of the ruling elite. This pattern endures until this day, and as we shall see throughout the later twentieth century and into the twenty-first. As mentioned above, a revolving door increasingly rotates between corporate America and the federal government.

As Europe grew increasingly unstable, the emphasis of the U.S. government shifted to foreign affairs. There was little retreat from reform, and by the end of World War II, most of the New Deal legislation was still intact, and it remained the foundation of American social policy until the beginning of the twenty-first century when economic strategists of the George W. Bush, Jr. administration began working hard to permanently dismantle the New Deal. In summary:

---

[38] http://us.history.wisc.edu/hist102/lectures/lecture19.html.

> ROOSEVELT SET IN MOTION A PATTERN THAT CONTINUED THROUGHOUT THE TWENTIETH CENTURY AND ENDURES TODAY, NAMELY, THAT THE "BEST" WAY TO MAKE AMERICA PROSPER IS THROUGH MILITARIZATION AND THE USE OF WARFARE. THE FINAL "CURE" FOR THE GREAT DEPRESSION WAS WORLD WAR II.

Some of the specific programs comprising the Second New Deal were:

The WPA or The Works Progress Administration which established work projects for building streets, highways, bridges, airfields, and post offices. Forests were restored and electrical power extended to rural areas. During its seven-year duration, the WPA employed about 8.5 million Americans.

As well as developing infrastructure, the WPA assisted in promoting American culture. The Federal Theater, Arts, Dance and Writer's Projects brought music and drama to large and small communities. American writers such as John Steinbeck, Richard Wright, and Claude McKay were commissioned to write histories of the American people. This was highly significant because it was the first time in American history that the federal government took responsibility for supporting and promoting American art and culture.

The Wagner Act, also known as the National Labor Relations Act, guaranteed workers the right to form unions and the right to bargain collectively with management. For the first time, it mandated that the federal government would enforce these rights and that employers could no longer resist the formation of unions or retaliate against workers for unionizing.

The Social Security Act created a cooperative federal-state system of providing unemployment compensation and income for retired persons. Workers who paid Social Security taxes out of their wages would receive benefits upon retiring at age 65. Benefits would be paid from employee and employer contributions. The original Social Security Act did not make provisions for farm workers, domestic workers, employees of restaurant and service industries, or health-care providers. Although it was highly criticized as "socialistic," it never instituted payment by the government but rather, by employees and employers. The real significance of the Social Security Act was its acknowledgement that society at large was responsible to care for the less fortunate.

The Wealth Tax Act suddenly increased taxes on the wealthy and created larger taxes on excess business profits, inheritances, large gifts, and profits from the sale of property. It also increased regulation of trusts and holding companies.

Critics of The New Deal

As we have seen, the ruling elite of America had been for decades, terrified of any telltale signs of "creeping socialism" in the country. They wanted only to maintain and increase their corporate profits, and as we also noted, in earlier times, government regulation of business, the unionization of workers, or government programs which offered assistance to the disadvantaged and exploited citizenry were perceived as "socialistic" and detrimental to the agenda of industrial management.

Traditionally, historians have hailed the New Deal as a triumph for the workers and the poor in America, but as Howard Zinn observes:

The system responded to workers' rebellions by finding new forms of control—internal control by their own organizations as well as outside control by law and force. But along with these controls came new concessions. These concessions didn't solve basic problems; for many people they solved nothing. But they helped enough people to create an atmosphere of progress and improvement, to restore some faith in the system.[39]

> IT IS EXTREMELY IMPORTANT TO UNDERSTAND THAT THROUGHOUT AMERICAN HISTORY, REGULATION OF BUSINESS AND REFORMS ON BEHALF OF THE POOR OR WORKING CLASSES HAVE, ALMOST WITHOUT EXCEPTION, SERVED TO ENHANCE THE SOCIAL AND ECONOMIC POWER AND CONTROL OF THE BUSINESS COMMUNITY AND SERVED TO KEEP UNREST AND PROTEST IN THE LOWER CLASSES AT BAY. THE NEW DEAL IS YET ANOTHER EXAMPLE OF THIS HISTORICAL PATTERN.

Despite the popularity of the New Deal among the poor and within the Democratic Party, there were numerous critics of Roosevelt and the New Deal. Two of the most outspoken were:

- **Father Charles Coughlin**, a right-wing Catholic priest who was extremely sympathetic to Hitler's Nazi movement. Originally supporting FDR, Coughlin turned his back on him and created a political party called the National Union of Social Justice. He published a weekly paper called *Social Justice* and in his weekly radio programs, he praised Hitler and Mussolini. He ranted against Jews as "Christ Killers" and associated Jews and supporters of Roosevelt with Communists. Coughlin formed a nationwide fascist network, the Christian Front, which it was later discovered had planned to murder Jews, Communists, and at least a dozen Congressmen.[40]

- **Governor Huey Long** of Louisiana was a critic of Roosevelt's New Deal, not from the political right, but from the left. Long believed that the New Deal did not go far enough. While Long used his political power to expand the infrastructure of Louisiana, to build roads, hospitals, bridges, and a state university, he was steeped in corruption and was assassinated in 1935.
***A complete list of New Deal programs and agencies created by them can be found at:
http://www.nv.cc.va.us/home/nvsageh/Hist122/Part3/NewDeal.htm#highlights

Stanley Schultz summarizes Roosevelt's New Deal:

- FDR had no coherent blueprint for what he wanted to do. He was willing to experiment, to bend his own Constitutional authority, to wheedle and cajole Congress, to send apparently conflicting messages. Assaulted from both left and right, he was probably more conservative and more radically liberal than his opponents on either side would have admitted.

---

[39] Zinn, Howard, *Peoples History Of The United States*, New York, Harper Collins, 1980, p.393.
[40] Charles Edward Coughlin, (http://www.spartacus.schoolnet.co.uk/USAcoughlinE.htm)

- The New Deal did not end the Depression. FDR's programs improved life for millions and gave hope to many others, but it did not end or repair the underlying causes of economic problems. The massive government spending during World War II was what finally revived the economy.

- During FDR's Administration American voting patterns shifted dramatically. African Americans began to feel the hand of government lifting them up rather than pushing them down, and they shifted from voting about 80% Republican to 80% Democratic.

- The Democratic Party became the majority Party And dominated the White House, Congress, or both until the late twentieth century. For only a handful of years since 1933 have Republicans controlled the White House and Congress at the same time.[41]

** I STRONGLY SUGGEST THE VIEWING OF THE DVD DOCUMENTARY, "The Money Masters" FOR A MORE COMPLETE UNDERSTANDING OF THE HISTORY OF MONEY AND ECONOMIC POLICY IN THE UNITED STATES, BEFORE, DURING, AND AFTER THE GREAT DEPRESSION.

---

[41] Website of the History Department of the Community College of Northern Virginia
http://www.nv.cc.va.us/home/nvsageh/Hist122/Part3/NewDeal.htm#highlights

Assessing the New Deal

Was the New Deal the triumph of social justice and the curtailment of capitalism's abuses that historians have traditionally proclaimed it to be? Howard Zinn concludes[42]:

> WHEN THE NEW DEAL WAS OVER, CAPITALISM REMAINED INTACT. THE RICH STILL CONTROLLED THE NATION'S WEALTH, AS WELL AS ITS LAWS, COURTS, POLICE, NEWSPAPERS, CHURCHES, COLLEGES. ENOUGH HELP HAD BEEN GIVEN TO ENOUGH PEOPLE TO MAKE ROOSEVELT A HERO TO MILLIONS, BUT THE SAME SYSTEM THAT HAD BROUGHT DEPRESSION AND CRISIS—THE SYSTEM OF WASTE, OF INEQUALITY, OF CONCERN FOR PROFIT OVER HUMAN NEED—REMAINED.

Author and activist, Stan Goff, states more poignantly, that:

> …Franklin Roosevelt was elected the 33rd President of the United States in 1933 with a mandate to take extraordinary measures ostensibly to relieve the suffering of the American working class masses, but more importantly—from the point of view of U.S. elites—to take the increasingly revolutionary edge off of their agitations.[43]

While Roosevelt's New Deal remains predominant in traditional historians' consideration of American economic patterns in the 1930s and 40s, less attention is focused on what may be an even more stunning economic feat, namely Roosevelt's financial designs of fashioning the United States as a creditor nation.

According to Goff:

> The United States stayed out of the war [World War I] until it became likely that without US intervention, the Allies would lose and their debts to America would remain unpaid. Once the war was over, Great Britain and France were heavily indebted, and the US—far from being the benevolent post-war ally-behaved much like any Brooklyn loan shark, bleeding its former allies so severely that they in turn wrecked the post-war German economy with reparations to assist the allies in their debts. This led directly to the rise of Nazism and the Second World War.
>
> Whereupon, the US began its participation, *again*, not as a fellow combatant, but as a creditor to the other allies. It is now very clear that Franklin Roosevelt developed financial designs on the colonies of the British Empire, and that he maneuvered throughout the war to let others-particularly the Soviet Union, but also England and France-take the brunt of Hitler's aggression to weaken them, while he built up the geographically war-immune US industrial base, and positioned the US to be a post-war creditor and *the* new super-power.[44]

---

[42] Zinn, Peoples' History Of The United States, p. 394.
[43] Stan Goff article, "Today's Imperialism", (http://www.fromthewilderness.com/free/ww3/102804_todays_imperialism.shtml)
[44] *Ibid.*

Thus, Roosevelt positioned the United States to become the most powerful nation economically in the world. Moreover, Roosevelt abandoned the *gold standard* which strategically de-valued U.S. currency, using it as an economic weapon against its so-called allies in Europe—one of the first of many uses by the United States of economic warfare. The intent was never to destroy European allies, but as Goff says, "to bring Europe and ascendant Asia under the sway of the United States as sub-imperial powers in a new global hierarchy that would extend the influence of the U.S. beyond anything ever yet imagined by former empires—in a qualitatively new way."[45]

As we shall see shortly, the United States emerged from World War II with two daunting weapons, finance capital and the military, working together to begin creating the most powerful empire on earth.

The laissez-faire notions of Adam Smith were dead. Roosevelt's economic advisors were devotees of the British economist, John Maynard Keynes, who rejected the classical economics of Smith and the "self-regulating" theories of the free market. Rather then the "leave it alone" approach of Smith, Keynes advocated vast government spending, especially in times of recession, and when the economy had recovered, federal spending would be cut back.

> PERHAPS THE MOST ENDURING LEGACY OF THE NEW DEAL WAS THE **CORPORATE STATE**. THROUGH THE SO-CALLED "REGULATION" OF BUSINESS ACTIVITIES, BUSINESS AND GOVERNMENT WERE DRAWN MORE CLOSELY TOGETHER BY NEW DEAL LEGISLATION AND BY WORLD WAR II. FOLLOWING AND FLOWING FROM WORLD WAR II, A THIRD PLAYER EMERGES—THE MILITARY, WHICH ALONG WITH BUSINESS AND GOVERNMENT IS TRANSFORMED INTO THE **MILITARY INDUSTRIAL COMPLEX** AND IS SUBSIDIZED MORE EXTRAVAGANTLY THAN ANY OTHER INSTITUTION THROUGHOUT THE REST OF THE TWENTIETH CENTURY.

---

[45] *Ibid.*

12

THE RISE OF FASCISM

Hitler's Rise To Power

As noted above, Hitler used the Treaty of Versailles and its disastrous consequences for Germany to justify his rise to power and his creation of a racist, totalitarian state. It is important and necessary in order to fully understand U.S. history to grasp:

- How Hitler came to power
- How the ruling elite in the United States financed and assisted Hitler's rise to power

In 1932, three elections were held in Germany within five months. In the first two elections, Hitler did not receive the majority of the popular vote. The story of the elections and Hitler's failure to receive a majority is a complicated one, but essentially, Hitler was ultimately "installed" by demanding that the President of Germany appoint him Chancellor of Germany. This allowed him and his Nazi party to consolidate power and drive their opponents out of the government.

In addition, the **Reichstag,** or the home of the German Parliament was burned down shortly after Hitler came to power in 1933. Hitler and his Nazi associates dramatically accused German communists of setting the fire. Today, there is a strong suspicion that Hitler had the Reichstag burned in order to scapegoat the communists and increase his own popularity. Not unlike the situation in the U.S. following September 11, 2001, the German people were eager to support any leader who helped them feel secure. In 1934 the President of Germany died, and Hitler, promising security for Germany, destroyed the position of President, assuring that he would have absolute control of the country.

Keep in mind that Germany, like the United States, was economically reeling from a worldwide depression. The average non-Jewish German supported Hitler because he promised prosperity and a restoration of the country to a place of respect and honor among nations. Most German citizens merely wanted to work hard, take care of their families, and not involve themselves in political issues.

Although discrimination against Jews existed in Germany, it was not until the 1940s that Nazi death camps were established to systematically exterminate Jews. Meanwhile, Hitler promised to re-arm Germany and retake what had been lost at Versailles. Moreover, he promised a "German race" and racial superiority for Aryans which he said could not be accomplished until non-Aryans were removed from Germany. Moreover, the master race, according to Hitler, needed *Lebensraum* or living space and must, therefore, expand its territory and conquer other nations. But deportation and extermination of certain populations was a daunting and costly endeavor. Could Germany accomplish the task without external help?

In his award-winning book, *IBM And The Holocaust*, investigative journalist, **Edwin Black** has analyzed the intricate and complicated business connections between one of America's industrial giants and the German Nazi regime of the 1930s and 40s. Black superbly documents that the Nazis were able to keep precise records on European Jews and their genealogies, as well as keep track of their whereabouts as a result of the punch card system developed in the United States and shared with the Nazis by IBM. In fact, Black argues, the trains bound for concentration camps ran impeccably on time thanks to the efforts of IBM.

American Corporate Support of Hitler

IBM was one of the most blatantly complicit U.S. industries in the Nazi holocaust, but it was by no means the only American corporation doing business with or financing the Hitler regime.

Keep in mind our previous consideration of the world view and mindset of the American Robber Barons and their obsession with keeping America and the world insulated from socialism and socialist tendencies. Remember the Red Scare of the 1920s and the lengths to which industry had gone to protect its profits and prevent an equal distribution of income and resources among the general population.

Moreover, as we have seen, most of the ruling elite were extremely racist and blatantly, anti-semitic. Hatred and suspicion toward Jews existed among them not only because Jews were involved in organizing and supporting labor and social justice movements, but also because European Jewish bankers controlled most of the wealth of Europe and Asia.

One of the most famous American industrial giants was **Henry Ford** who unashamedly supported Hitler and the Nazis and who wrote freely of his hatred of Jews. A powerful expose of Ford's anti-semitism is found in Jonathan Logsdon's article, *Power, Ignorance and Anti-Semitism, Henry Ford's War Against The Jews*. (http://history.hanover.edu/hhr/99/hhr99_2.html)

Less blatantly, a plethora of U.S. businessmen verbally supported and economically financed the German Nazi regime in the 1930s. Two extremely signifcant names in the financing of Hitler's rise to power, were **E.H. Harriman**, the railroad typcoon of the late ninetenth century and oil magnate, **John. D. Rockefeller**—both contributors to the eugenics movement. In fact, during Hitler's rise to power in the early 1930s, one would have been hard pressed to find a famous American industrial giant who was *not* supportive of Hitler and the fascist agenda.

Because of its relevance to the first decade of the twenty-first century, it is important to mention that some of the most deeply entrenched financiers of Hitler were the ancestors of President George W. Bush, Jr., specifically his grandfather, **Prescott Bush**. This reality is meticulously documented in Kevin Phillips' *American Dynasty*, and in *The Unauthorized Biography of George Bush*, by Webster Tarpley and Antonin Chaitkin which can be read in its entirety online at www.tarpley.net Two equally well-documented studies of this issue have been published by a Canadian organization, the Coalition To Oppose The Arms Trade. Their works, "Facing The Corporate Roots of American Fascism" and "All In The Family", may be read at http://coat.ncf.ca/. Additional documentation may be found in an article by John Buchanan and Stacey Michael, "Bush—Nazi Dealings Continued Until 1951," published in the *New Hampshire Gazette*, November 7, 2003.[46]

---

[46] "Bush, Nazi Dealings Continued Until 1951,"
(http://www.nhgazette.com/cgi-bin/NHGstore.cgi?user_action=detail&catalogno=NN_Bush_Nazi_2)

Plotting a fascist coup d'etat in the United States

As mentioned above, not everyone in America supported Roosevelt's New Deal agenda. In addition to Father Charles Coughlin and Huey Long, some famous names among the ruling elite openly opposed Roosevelt and constructed a plot to overthrow him.

Some of the individuals involved were:

- **Irenee Du Pont**-Right-wing chemical industrialist and founder of the American Liberty League, the organization assigned to execute the plot.
- **Grayson Murphy**-Director of Goodyear, Bethlehem Steel and a group of J.P. Morgan banks.
- **William Doyle**-Former state commander of the American Legion and a central plotter of the coup.
- **John Davis**-Former Democratic presidential candidate and a senior attorney for J.P. Morgan.
- **Al Smith**-Roosevelt's bitter political foe from New York. Smith was a former governor of New York and a Co-director of the American Liberty League.
- **John J. Raskob**-A high-ranking Du Pont officer and a former chairman of the Democratic Party. In later decades, Raskob would become a "Knight of Malta," a Roman Catholic Religious Order with a high percentage of CIA spies, including CIA Directors William Casey, William Colby, and John McCone.
- **Robert Clark**-One of Wall Street's richest bankers and stockbrokers.
- **Gerald MacGuire**-Bond salesman for Clark, and a former commander of the Connecticut American Legion. MacGuire was the key recruiter to General Butler.

The plotters attempted to recruit **General Smedley Butler** in 1933 to lead the coup. They selected him because he was a World War I hero who had been extremely popular with the troops. The plotters felt his good reputation was important to make the troops feel confident that they were doing the right thing by overthrowing a democratically elected president. However, their plan failed miserably. Butler was popular with the troops because he *identified* with them. That is, he was a man of the people, not the elite. When the plotters approached General Butler with their proposal to lead the coup, he pretended to go along with the plan at first, secretly deciding to betray it to Congress at the right moment.

Later, General Butler went public with the plot and took the details to Congress. The result was that the Congress, strongly influenced by the ruling elite, failed to call any of the alleged plotters to testify. Moreover, the media failed to pick up the story, and today, the incident is largely unknown. Butler was vindicated, however, in 1967 when journalist, John Spivak, uncovered the Congressional Committee's secret report which clearly confirmed Butler's story.[47] Details of the coup may be read at: http://members.tripod.com/~american_almanac/smedley.htm

Butler is also famous for his groundbreaking publication, "War Is A Racket" in 1935, in which he explains that wars are "necessary" for the weapons industry in order to enhance their profits, advantageous for politicians in order to maintain power and prestige, and emotionally exhilarating for the masses whose nationalistic fervor is buoyed by military conflagration—that is, until the human and fiscal costs become overwhelming.[48]

---

[47] The Morgan British Fascist Coup Against FDR, (http://www.huppi.com/kangaroo/Coup.htm)
[48] "War Is A Racket", (http://www.ratical.org/ratville/CAH/warisaracket.html)

13

WORLD WAR II

Although Franklin Roosevelt and the U.S. government were well aware of Hitler's rise to power and his devastation of Europe, the U.S. refused to become involved in World War II. Traditionally, historians have argued that the American public was determined after World War I never again to enter another world war and that Americans were committed to isolationism and unwilling to be involved in world affairs.

While it is true that the American public had a strong aversion to U.S. involvement in world affairs, and particularly a world war, it is also true that Roosevelt's reluctance to enter World War II was thoroughly calculated. The U.S. continued to lend money and material for the war, as it had in World War I, knowing that the longer the war continued, the more debt would be accrued to the U.S. Moreover, as Goff has noted above, "The United States stayed out of the war until it became likely that without US intervention, the Allies would lose and their debts to America would remain unpaid."

Furthermore, Gabriel Kolko argues in his *Politics of War*, that "the American economic war aim was to save capitalism at home and abroad." In April, 1944, a State Department official said:

> As you know, we've got to plan on the enormously increased production in this country after the war, and the American domestic market can't absorb all that production indefinitely. There won't be any question about our needing greatly increased foreign markets.[49]

Roosevelt's intention was to make the United States the most powerful nation on earth economically and militarily. To have entered the war early on would have compromised this objective. Yet even in 1941, two years after Hitler invaded Poland, the American people were opposed to U.S. involvement in the war. What would or could change their opinion?

Not only was Roosevelt committed to American economic and military superiority, he also realized the threat to U.S. expansionism in the Pacific by Japan which had set its sights on Southeast Asia with the intention of dominating the Pacific economically.

---

[49] Zinn, Peoples' History of the United States, P. 404.

Robert Smith Thompson in *A Time For War: Franklin D. Roosevelt and the Path to Pearl Harbor* emphasizes that Roosevelt used economic warfare against Japan by prohibiting oil exports to that nation:

> During this period, Japan was economically very vulnerable. More than any other industrial power, it was unusually dependent on imports of oil and other essential raw materials, as well as on foreign markets for export. In the circumstances of the time, it was economically beholden to the United States. It was thus a jolt when, in 1939, the United States cancelled its 1911 trade agreement with Japan. Much more serious were the trade embargoes imposed in 1940, when the US halted exports to Japan of petroleum, petroleum products (including gasoline and lubricants) and all grades of iron and steel scrap.
>
> America's economic warfare against Japan came to climax on July 26, 1941, when President Roosevelt ordered the freezing of all Japanese assets and credits in the United States. This ended all trade between the two countries. (In coordination with this, Britain and the Netherlands followed quickly with similar measures of their own.) Because Japan was largely dependent on the US for petroleum and petroleum products, Roosevelt's order threatened her survival as an industrial nation. As British historian J.F.C. Fuller pointed out, "this was a declaration of economic war, and, in consequence, it was the actual opening of the struggle."
>
> Here was no mere deterrence; here was deterrence that amounted to provocation. Was the provocation deliberate? Three times, twice to Lord Halifax and once to British premier Winston Churchill, Franklin Roosevelt intimated that he was trying to force "an incident" that would bring America more deeply into the fray. He may have hated war, but he presided over policies that came to be indistinguishable from incitements to war.[50]

It is one thing to use economic warfare against a nation, and quite another to provoke that nation to attack one's own nation. The latter is precisely what World War II veteran and researcher, Robert Stinnett in his meticulously-researched work, *Day of Deceit*, argues, namely, that the Roosevelt administration provoked Japan to attack the United States and had explicit foreknowledge of the attacks. Stinnett writes that:

> Immediately after December 7, 1941, military communications disclosed American foreknowledge of the Pearl Harbor disaster were locked in U.S. Navy vaults away from the prying eyes of congressional investigators, historians, and authors. Though the Freedom of Information Act freed the foreknowledge documents from the secretive vaults to the sunlight of the national Archives in 1995, a cottage industry continues to cover up America's foreknowledge of Pearl Harbor.[51]

The United States declared war on Japan immediately after the Pearl Harbor attacks in December, 1941. The war lasted until the Japanese surrendered in August, 1945. For a detailed examination of World War II, please visit the links below:

http://www.bbc.co.uk/history/war/wwtwo/ww2_summary_01.shtml

http://gi.grolier.com/wwii/wwii_mainpage.html

http://www.grolier.com/wwii/wwii_i.html

---

[50] *A Time For War: Franklin D. Roosevelt and the Path to Pearl Harbor*, by Robert Smith Thompson. New York: Prentice Hall, 1991
[51] Stinnett, Robert, *Day of Deceit*, New York, Free Press, 2000

In May, 1945, Germany surrendered to the United States, but the war in the Pacific continued. That war ended when the United States dropped the atomic bomb on the Japanese cities of Hiroshima and Nagasaki in August, 1945. Historians continue to debate whether the dropping of the bomb could have been prevented.

Traditionally, historians and the American government have argued that dropping the bomb would help the war end more quickly and make an invasion of Japan by the United States unnecessary, thereby saving more lives. We now know, however, that Japan was already in the process of negotiating surrender with the United States. Some historians argue that the U.S. really didn't know that Japan wanted to surrender, yet it is inconceivable that American leaders did not know this given the fact that Japanese codes had been broken and Japan's messages intercepted.

The United States demanded *unconditional* surrender, whereas Japan asked only one condition for surrender: that its emperor, a holy figure to the Japanese, remain in office. The U.S. would not accept even one condition. Why?

Howard Zinn proposes that the U.S. was anxious to drop the bomb before the Russians entered the war against Japan:

> The Russians had secretly agreed (they were officially not at war with Japan) they would come into the war ninety days after the end of the European war. That turned out to be May 8, and so on August 8, the Russians were due to declare war on Japan. But by then the big bomb had dropped, and the next day, a second one would be dropped on Nagasaki; the Japanese would surrender to the United States, not the Russians, and the United States would be the occupier of postwar Japan.[52]

The dropping of the atomic bomb on Japan which ended World War II put the United States in position to dominate the world. Moreover, America's triumph, according to Zinn, created conditions for effective control at home. "The unemployment, the economic distress, and the consequent turmoil that had marked the thirties," writes Zinn, "only partly relieved by New Deal measures, had been pacified, overcome by the greater turmoil of the war. The war brought higher prices for farmers, higher wages, enough prosperity for enough of the population to assure against the rebellions that so threatened the thirties."[53]

For further articles on the issue of "necessity" in the dropping of the atomic bomb on Hiroshima and Nagasaki in 1945, see:

http://free.freespeech.org/americanstateterrorism/usgenocide/HiroshimaNagasaki.html

http://www.counterpunch.org/price08062004.html

**When studying the dropping the atomic bomb in 1945, I frequently show my classes the movie "Fat Man And Little Boy", the 1989 film which portrays the process of researching, testing, and dropping the bomb. Little Boy was the bomb dropped on Hiroshima, and Fat Man was the bomb dropped three days later on Nagasaki.

---

[52] Zinn, Peoples' History of the United States, pp. 414-415.
[53] *Ibid*, p. 416

14

THE DOMESTIC EFFECTS OF U.S. INVOLVEMENT IN WORLD WAR II

Stanley Schultz notes nine specific effects of World War II within the U.S.:

- Priority was increasingly given to **military spending** over spending for domestic reforms. Many pieces of reform legislation had been rolled back during wartime, and they would continue to be shelved during peace time.
- The war provided an **excuse to abolish segments of the New Deal**. The emphasis during wartime was on winning the war, not providing assistance to the disadvantaged. Obviously, the groups that suffered most were blacks, women, and the elderly.
- The **deficit rose** as social expenditures plummeted.
- The **poor were "put back in their place."** Poverty increased as New Deal programs were eliminated.
- The so-called **Brain Trust** of intellectuals who had been advisors to FDR became disillusioned with Washington's lack of interest in social reforms, and many of them left their posts. This vacuum was filled by **business executives** with good managerial skills but with little interest in reform. Generally, this trend continued throughout the twentieth century. As noted above, this is yet another example of the symbiosis between government and business.
- There was a marked **increase in the reach and power of the federal government and the Presidency**. Increasingly, important decisions were not made by Congress but by the Executive branch. Also, the Supreme Court refused to hear cases challenging increased Executive authority.
- The **Military-Industrial Complex** evolves. This is a systemic relationship between corporations, politicians, and the military. A synonym for this complex might be "war profiteering." It is has become a feeding frenzy for those in the private sector who seek government contracts for their participation in all aspects of war—before, during, and after a conflagration occurs.
  A further **solidification of the Corporate State**. Unions increased their power, but the power of corporations became unprecedented, as did the relationships between corporations and government. During the twentieth century, small business was permanently dwarfed by transnational corporations.
- America became an **urban and technological society**. During and after World War II, 15 million Americans moved from rural areas to the cities.[54]

---

[54] Schultz Lectures, Lecture 12, (http://us.history.wisc.edu/hist102/lectures/lecture21.html)

POLITICAL CONTINUUM OF 20TH CENTURY

<————————————————————>

| **Socialism** | Liberal | Centrist | Conservative | **Fascism** |
| **Communism** | Leftist | Moderate | Right Wing | **Nazi-ism** |

**Business controls government in order to benefit citizens

**Government and business form alliance in order to benefit each other

**Government exists for citizens

**Government exists for ruling elite

**Business profits surrendered to government for distribution to citizens

**Business makes profit and shares with government

**Abuses of human rights and civil liberties may occur in both systems.

15

THE BEGINNING OF THE COLD WAR

Retired Air Force Colonel, **L. Fletcher Prouty**, who served in World War II and for some years after in the Pentagon, has written two controversial books, *The Secret Team* and *JFK: The CIA, Vietnam, and The Plot to Assassinate John F. Kennedy*, the latter of which we will examine more closely below. Throughout his writings, Prouty emphasizes that following World War II in the wake of the invention and use of the atomic bomb, warfare was forever changed. No longer could nations recklessly engage in unlimited warfare because a new weapon now existed which could annihilate the entire planet. Therefore, although the United States had emerged from World War II as the most powerful nation on earth, particularly as a result of its use of the atomic bomb, it would be required, like every other nation, to temper its use of force by engaging not in all-out war, but in *low intensity conflict*. In other words, atomic weapons would only be used as a very last resort, and wars would necessarily be limited to strategic areas of the globe because world war had become unthinkable.

What Prouty also argues is that even before Japan surrendered in 1945, U.S. intelligence had its eye on Russia as the next adversary in world affairs. In order to understand this, we need only recall the many instances in this abstract where we have seen the fear and dread on the part of the American ruling elite, the U.S. military and the U.S. government of socialism wherever it might appear on earth. Remember how determined the United States was to prevent Russia from invading Japan and dropped the atomic bomb on Japan in order to prevent such an invasion?

Remember also the unprecedented prosperity that a wartime economy had brought to the United States. Americans, particularly those who had survived the Great Depression, would never be willing to settle for less in the future. The dilemma for the United States government and its ruling elite at the end of World War II seems to have been how to maintain a permanent wartime economy without being engaged in world wars which would only lead to the use of nuclear weapons.

Although Russia was an ally of the United States in World War II, the fear of "the red menace" had not left the American ruling elite or its friends in government. Therefore, even throughout the course of World War II, the United States was strategizing its next conflict with what was certain to become an increasingly powerful enemy, Russia.

Prouty writes that "One of the best-kept and least-discussed secrets of early Cold War planning took place sometime before the surrender of Japan. It had a great impact upon the selection of Korea and Indochina as the locations of early 'Cold War' hostilities between the 'Communists' and the 'anti-Communists.'"[55]

---

[55] Prouty, L. Fletcher, *JFK, The CIA, Vietnam And The Plot To Assassinate John F. Kennedy*, New York: Kensington Edition, 2003, p. 17.

Constructing a Cold War

In April, 1945, Harry Truman became President upon the death of Franklin Roosevelt. He immediately encountered, in Prouty's words, "a team of determined financiers, transnational industrialists, and their crack Wall Street lawyers." As Truman approached his gargantuan tasks, attempting to fill the shoes of the most popular President in American history to that point, he realized that his intelligence community was in dire need of reorganization.

At that time, the **Office of Strategic Services (OSS)** had been the primary intelligence gathering agency working with Army and Navy Intelligence during World War II. Truman was encouraged by the financiers, industrialists, and lawyers mentioned above to consolidate the intelligence gathering process and create one central agency for gathering all intelligence.

In 1947, Truman asked a friend, Clark Clifford, a Wall Street lawyer, to write the National Security Act, creating the Central Intelligence Agency. The primary purpose of the CIA was to gather intelligence from foreign sources, particularly in relation to the Soviet Union and its allies. **Very importantly, the CIA was forbidden by the National Security Act of 1947 to gather intelligence domestically on its own citizens.**

What Truman had not been told by his advisors was that an element of the CIA had been working, along with British intelligence, secretly with the Nazis and Nazi sympathizers in Europe as early as 1944 and that plans had been made to alienate the U.S. wartime ally, the Soviet Union, and create a hostile, bi-polar world. Unlike his British ally, Winston Churchill, Truman had little familiarity with the concept of a ruling elite, nor was he familiar with their influence in government.[56]

Clark Clifford Designs The CIA

Clark Clifford, author of the National Security Act, went on to become Secretary of Defense and a powerhouse in the Democratic Party. However, in the 1980s, Clifford was one of the key players in the corrupt CIA drug money laundering bank, the Bank Of Credit And Commerce (BCCI). Clifford and his banking partner, Robert Altman, were eventually indicted for their illegal acts involving BCCI.

The Dulles Brothers and The CIA's Questionable Allies

Two other Wall Street lawyers, Allen and John Foster Dulles, were close friends of Clifford. They essentially helped him "design" the CIA. After Dwight Eisenhower replaced Harry Truman as President in the early 1950s, John Foster Dulles became Eisenhower's Secretary of State.

Allen Dulles had been an OSS spy during World War II and frequently met with Nazi leaders. In addition, he took care of the investments of U.S. millionaires such as Prescott Bush and the Rockefeller family in Nazi Germany. He clearly helped build Hitler's war machine and helped Prescott Bush disguise his investments in Nazi Germany when Bush's investments were being investigated by the U.S. government in the early 1940s.

The hiring of Nazi war criminals

One of Dulles' Nazi associates was German General, **Reinhard Gehlen**. After Germany surrendered in 1945, Dulles arranged for Gehlen and several other former Nazi military and intelligence personnel to come to the United States to work for the OSS. The rationale for this was that since Germany had been spying on Russia for years, German intelligence officers would be ideal partners with the United States in spying on Russia. During the 1990s, an

---

[56] *Ibid.*, p. 20

investigation chaired by Congresswoman Elizabeth Holtzman of New York confirmed that in fact, the CIA had enlisted and employed former Nazi war criminals to assist in U.S. intelligence gathering against the Soviet Union.[57]

Nor was Gehlen the only former Nazi war criminal to be hired by the CIA. Over 700 such individuals were also hired, including **Klaus Barbie**, known as the "butcher of Lyons" who was part of the SS which was responsible for the death of thousands of French people under the Germany occupation.[58]

(I strongly recommend that classes view "Hitler And The Nazis", a History Channel Documentary explaining the role of Gehlen in the post-World War II CIA.)

Organized crime in France

During World War II, the OSS was heavily involved with organized crime leaders in the United States in order to prevent sabotage of East Coast ports. As we shall later discover, the CIA was and is deeply involved in the international drug trade and the laundering of drug profits. This involvement has been superbly documented in hundreds of places, one of which is the website:
http://ciadrugs.homestead.com/files/congress-cia-drug-history-doc.html

WORLD WAR II

The Office of Strategic Services (OSS) and the Office of Naval Intelligence (ONI), the CIA's parent and sister organizations, cultivate relations with the leaders of the Italian Mafia, recruiting heavily from the New York and Chicago underworlds, whose members, including Charles 'Lucky' Luciano, Meyer Lansky, Joe Adonis, and Frank Costello, help the agencies keep in touch with Sicilian Mafia leaders exiled by Italian dictator Benito Mussolini. Domestically, the aim is to prevent sabotage of East Coast ports, while in Italy the goal is to gain intelligence on Sicily prior to the allied invasions and to suppress the burgeoning Italian Communist Party. Imprisoned in New York, Luciano earns a pardon for his wartime service and is deported to Italy, where he proceeds to build his heroin empire, first by diverting supplies from the legal market, before developing connections in Lebanon and Turkey that supply morphine base to labs in Sicily. The OSS and ONI also work closely with Chinese gangsters who control vast supplies of opium, morphine and heroin, helping to establish the third pillar of the post-world War II heroin trade in the Golden Triangle, the border region of Thailand, Burma, Laos and China's Yunnan Province.[59]

Because the OSS, which then became the CIA, perceived communism as an international security threat, it went about intervening not only in national wars and elections throughout the world, but also in high-profile labor strikes. One of the earliest examples is the OSS involvement in the labor movement in Marseille in France.

1947

In its first year of existence, the CIA continues U.S. intelligence community's anti-communist drive. Agency operatives help the Mafia seize total power in Sicily, and it sends money to heroin-smuggling Corsican mobsters in Marseille to assist in their battle with Communist unions for control of the city's docks. By 1951, Luciano and the Corsicans have pooled their resources, giving rise to the notorious 'French Connection' which would dominate the world heroin trade until the early 1970s. The CIA also recruits members of organized crime gangs in Japan to help ensure that the country stays in the non-communist world. Several years later, the Japanese Yakuza emerges as a major source of methamphetamine in Hawaii.[60]

---

[57] CIA Admits Long Relationship With WWII German Gen. Reinhard Gehlen, Maria Alvarez, *The New York Post,* September 24, 2000. (http://www.rense.com/general4/gends.htm)
[58] Operation Paperclip, (http://www.thirdworldtraveler.com/Fascism/Operation_Paperclip_file.html)
[59] http://ciadrugs.homestead.com/files/congress-cia-drug-history-doc.html
[60] *Ibid*

1950

The CIA launches Project Bluebird to determine whether certain drugs might improve its interrogation methods. This eventually leads CIA head Allen Dulles, in April 1953, to institute a program for 'covert use of biological and chemical materials' as part of the agency's continuing efforts to control behavior. With benign names such as Project Artichoke and Project Chatter, these projects continue through the 1960s, with hundreds of unwitting test subjects given various drugs, including LSD. [61]

> THE SIGNIFICANCE OF THE NATIONAL SECURITY ACT OF 1947, CREATING THE CENTRAL INTELLIGENCE AGENCY, CANNOT BE OVEREMPHASIZED. IT WAS A TIPPING POINT IN THE HISTORY OF THE TWENTIETH CENTURY THAT PROFOUNDLY IMPACTED THE NATION AND THE WORLD FOR THE REMAINDER OF THE CENTURY AND HAS PRODUCED EXTREMELY NEGATIVE CONSEQUENCES FOR HUMANKIND IN THE TWENTY-FIRST CENTURY.

---

[61] *Ibid.*

16

THE COLD WAR: THE END JUSTIFIES THE MEANS

The Cold War, lasting from approximately 1945 to 1990, was yet another era of anti-socialist and anti-communist hysteria in the United States. Whereas in earlier years, the "war" against socialism had been conducted by the Robber Barons against the labor movement and radicals demanding more humane living and working conditions in America, or through the use of propaganda to depict socialism as the epitome of evil in the world, the Cold War saw the use or the threat of the use of military force against pro-socialist or pro-communist countries.

In a press conference of April, 1954, President Dwight Eisenhower used an expression that characterized the United States government's perception of the so-called communist threat:

> Finally, you have broader considerations that might follow what you would call the **'falling domino' principle**. You have a row of dominoes set up, you knock over the first one, and what will happen to the last one is the certainty that it will go over very quickly. So you could have a beginning of a disintegration that would have the most profound influences.[62]

In other words, communism, was an international malignancy that would reach its tentacles around the globe, and when one area of the world became "infected" with it, the disease would spread to the entire region. Therefore, for policy makers of the U.S. government, it became a matter of life and death to "nip in the bud" the slightest manifestation of pro-socialist or pro-communist tendencies. During the 1950s, on the domestic front, this was accomplished by way of the McCarthy Hearings. For the duration of the Cold War, combating communism was achieved through the CIA's use of mind control techniques, the creation of anti-communist propaganda, and covert activities in countries around the world using espionage, the overthrow of governments, and in some cases, assassinations.

---

[62] Domino Theory Principle, Dwight D. Eisenhower, 1954, Public Papers of the Presidents, Dwight D. Eisenhower, 1954, pp. 381-390 (http://coursesa.matrix.msu.edu/~hst306/documents/domino.html)

In the world view of the CIA and the Pentagon, whatever means were necessary to deter the spread of communism were ultimately justifiable given the incalculable "evil" of the communist system. Whatever it took to "fight communism" was utilized with virtually no questions asked.

THE Mc CARTHY HEARINGS

Wisconsin Senator, Joseph McCarthy, obsessed with fighting communism and convinced that hundreds of thousands of American citizens sympathetic to communism were working for the Soviet Union and the communist cause within the U.S., began an investigation in 1953 into the activities of the U.S. State Department. Convinced that the U.S. government was rampant with communists and communist sympathizers, McCarthy increasingly expanded his investigation of "communist activities" into the U.S. military and eventually into aspects of civilian society, including and especially, the activities of Hollywood actors and producers.

It is important to understand that McCarthy's obsession with the evils of communism drove him to absurd lengths in investigating people who were completely innocent of any connection with communism or the Communist Party. In some cases they may have casually associated with persons whom McCarthy suspected as sympathetic to communism or who may have been members of a profession which McCarthy believed was replete with communists. Such was the case with a number of individuals from the motion picture industry who had no connections with communists or the Communist Party, but whose lives and careers were ruined by the investigations.

Eventually, McCarthy was censured by the Senate for going too far, but not before he had damaged the credibility of numerous individuals. It is important to understand that the "McCarthy Era," as it has come to be known, was a period of renewed anti-communist hysteria of which the hearings were a product and which the hearings helped intensify.

I recommend viewing the movie, "Guilty By Suspicion," for a look at the damage done to the careers of innocent Hollywood personalities by the hearings and "Goodnight And Good Luck" for an understanding of McCarthy's attack on free speech in the media.

For further information on the McCarthy hearings, see these links:

"You Are the Un-Americans, and You Ought to be Ashamed of Yourselves": Paul Robeson Appears Before HUAC
"They Want to Muzzle Public Opinion": John Howard Lawson's Warning to the American Public
"The World Was at Stake": Three "Friendly" HUAC Hollywood Witnesses Assess Pro-Soviet Wartime Films
"A Damaging Impression of Hollywood Has Spread": Movie "Czar" Eric Johnston Testifies before HUAC
"Have You No Sense of Decency": The Army-McCarthy Hearings
"Communists are second to none in our devotion to our people and to our country": Prosecution and Defense Statements, 1949 Trial of American Communist Party Leaders
"Not Only Ridiculous, but Dangerous": *Collier's* Objects to Joseph McCarthy's Attacks on the Press
"I Cannot and Will Not Cut My Conscience to Fit This Year's Fashions": Lillian Hellman Refuses to Name Names
"Enemies from Within": Senator Joseph R. McCarthy and President Harry S. Truman Trade Accusations of Disloyalty
"I Have Sung in Hobo Jungles, and I Have Sung for the Rockefellers": Pete Seeger Refuses to "Sing" for HUAC
"We Must Keep the Labor Unions Clean": "Friendly" HUAC Witnesses Ronald Reagan and Walt Disney Blame Hollywood Labor Conflicts on Communist Infiltration
"National Suicide": Margaret Chase Smith and Six Republican Senators Speak Out Against Joseph McCarthy's Attack on "Individual Freedom"

MK ULTRA—THE CIA AND MIND CONTROL

As a result of contact with U.S. military prisoners of war during the Korean Conflict in the early1950s, the Pentagon and the Central Intelligence Agency became aware of a technique being used by the Soviet Union and Communist China called "brainwashing." As a result, the CIA began conducting in-depth experiments on brainwashing and mind control. The program was named MK Ultra and included experiments with LSD, electroshock therapy, truth serums, and mind and nervous system re-programming. From hindsight, it is now painfully obvious that the program soon became frighteningly out of control and conducted experiments on innocent human beings, for the most part, without their knowledge. In recent years, many MK Ultra documents have been de-classified and are accessible on the internet. One site, *Mind Control, LSD, the CIA and the American People* summarizes early CIA mind control programs and provides links to de-classified documents.[63]

Students are often appalled when in class we view the History Channel documentary, "Mind Control: America's Secret War" (1996) in which the abuses of MK Ultra are explained and victims of CIA mind control programs are interviewed. I highly recommend showing this documentary.

HUMAN EXPERIMENTATION AND PLUTONIUM

In 1994, *Albuquerque Tribune* reporter, Eileen Welsome, discovered boxes of old files stored at Kirtland Air Force Base in Albuquerque which contained detailed records of plutonium experiments conducted by the United States government on human beings. In her Pulizter Prize-winning book, *THE PLUTONIUM FILES: America's Secret Medical Experiments In The Cold War*, Welsome writes in detail about such procedures as:

* Exposing more than 100 Alaskan villagers to radioactive iodine during the 1960s.

* Feeding 49 retarded and institutionalised teenagers radioactive iron and calcium in their cereal during the years 1946-1954.

* Exposing about 800 pregnant women in the late 1940s to radioactive iron to determine the effect on the fetus.

* Injecting 7 newborns (six were Black) with radioactive iodine.

* Exposing the testicles of more than 100 prisoners to cancer-causing doses of radiation. This experimentation continued into the early 1970s.

* Administering radioactive material to psychiatric patients in San Francisco and to prisoners in San Quentin.

* Administering massive doses of full body radiation to cancer patients hospitalised at the General Hospital in Cincinnati, Baylor College in Houston, Memorial Sloan-Kettering in New York City, and the US Naval Hospital in Bethesda, during the 1950s and 1960s. The experiment provided data to the military concerning how a nuclear attack might affect its troops.

*Exposing 29 patients, some with rheumatoid arthritis, to total body irradiation (100-300 rad dose) to obtain data for the military. This was conducted at the University of California Hospital in San Francisco.

*Exposing almost 200 cancer patients to high levels of radiation from cesium and cobalt. The Atomic Energy Commission (AEC) finally stopped this experiment in 1974.

---

[63] Mind Control, (http://www.mindcontrolforums.com/lsd-mc-cia.htm)

Welsome's chilling and very well-documented discovery is yet another example of the "end justifies the means" policy of the United States during the Cold War—its willingness to do whatever it deemed "necessary" to defeat Communism. THE PLUTONIUM FILES is also further testimony to the willingness of the United States government to harm its own citizens in service of its political objectives.

Details of the U.S. government program of experimenting with humans with radioactive materials can be read in the Advisory Committee On Human Radiation Experiments at: http://www.eh.doe.gov/ohre/roadmap/achre/

I make available to my students a detailed report entitled "Secret U.S. Human Biological Experimentation" which outlines experiments on humans by the U.S. government from 1931 through 1999. This is available on the worldwide web at: http://www.apfn.org/apfn/experiment.htm

COVERT OPERATIONS ABROAD: OVERTHROWING REGIMES

As Fletcher Prouty has explained, the possession of the atomic bomb by the United States, the Soviet Union, and China made another world war unthinkable because world war would have ultimately resulted in the annihilation of the planet. Operating on the premise of the "domino theory" and realizing that all-out war must be a last resort, the U.S. government, through the CIA, operated undercover around the world to subvert and overthrow nations which did not fully capitulate to U.S. corporate interests or whose relationship with the communist bloc was discomforting the United States.

Of this, Prouty states:

> The Cold War, along with its various politically managed "battlegrounds" has ended, but the mystery lives on. What was going on? Increasingly, we have all begun to realize that the legislative creation of the CIA, the Korean War, the Vietnam War, the Bay of Pigs, the Cuban Missile Crisis, the development of rockets and missiles along with the space program and the moon landings, as well as with the assassination of John F. Kennedy, were craftily orchestrated events designed to fill the gap between what mankind has known as conventional warfare and the incalculable impact of all-out warfare. In terms of the military-industrial interests there had to be a demand for their products and there had to be attrition of that materiel. Thus preparation for warfare and some form of warfare had to continue. All this was done while carefully avoiding a nuclear exchange.[64]

Throughout the Cold War, the CIA operated covertly around the world to "orchestrate events" so that the United States would maintain economic and military superiority, and the "balance" between the capitalist and communist empires would not be tipped against the West.

The template for decades of this orchestration was first launched in Iran in 1953 when the non-communist Muhammad Mossadegh was democratically elected the Premier of Iran. One of the new leader's first acts was to demand that British and American oil companies importing oil from Iran would now pay their fair share of taxes to Iran, and when they refused to do so, Mossadegh nationalized Iran's oil supply.

Kermit Roosevelt, grandson of Theodore Roosevelt and Mideast agent for the CIA, was instrumental in managing the overthrow of Mossadegh and the installing of the Shah of Iran who was thoroughly compliant with Western capitalist interests.[65]

---

[64] Prouty, p.xxii.
[65] http://www.nytimes.com/library/world/mideast/041600iran-cia-index.html.

The CIA's efforts in Iran were wildly successful. Thus, using the same template, the CIA one year later overthrew the government of democratically-elected Jacobo Arbenz of Guatemala who began reforming his nation in ways that thwarted the economic agenda of the United Fruit Company's Guatemalan investments. Arbenz's goals were to make Guatemala economically independent from world coffee prices and United States corporations. Arbenz wanted to develop domestic industry and to raise the standard of living in the process. He was replaced by Castillo Armas, a CIA puppet ruler, and Guatemala was "saved" from becoming a communist satellite.

OPERATION NORTHWOODS

In 1962, the Joint Chiefs of Staff, worried about the presence of the Communist revolutionary, Fidel Castro, in the Western Hemisphere and his alliance with the Soviet Union, conspired to shoot down unmanned military planes disguised as commercial airliners as well as blow up ocean liners inflicting heavy casualties, then blame the tragedies on Castro in order to incite pro-war sentiments among the American public so that the U.S. military could wage war on Cuba. To their surprise, President John F. Kennedy did not condone this operation, and it was scrapped. The declassified Northwoods documents can be read at: http://www.picosearch.com/cgi-bin/ts.pl. Three specific pages from the documents detailing the plot to orchestrate a so-called attack by Cuba can be read below:

~~TOP SECRET SPECIAL HANDLING NOFORN~~

THE JOINT CHIEFS OF STAFF
WASHINGTON 25, D.C.

UNCLASSIFIED　　　13 March 1962

MEMORANDUM FOR THE SECRETARY OF DEFENSE

Subject: Justification for US Military Intervention in Cuba (TS)

1. The Joint Chiefs of Staff have considered the attached Memorandum for the Chief of Operations, Cuba Project, which responds to a request of that office for brief but precise description of pretexts which would provide justification for US military intervention in Cuba.

2. The Joint Chiefs of Staff recommend that the proposed memorandum be forwarded as a preliminary submission suitable for planning purposes. It is assumed that there will be similar submissions from other agencies and that these inputs will be used as a basis for developing a time-phased plan. Individual projects can then be considered on a case-by-case basis.

3. Further, it is assumed that a single agency will be given the primary responsibility for developing military and para-military aspects of the basic plan. It is recommended that this responsibility for both overt and covert military operations be assigned the Joint Chiefs of Staff.

For the Joint Chiefs of Staff:

L. L. Lemnitzer
Chairman
Joint Chiefs of Staff

1 Enclosure
  Memo for Chief of Operations, Cuba Project　　EXCLUDED FROM GDS

EXCLUDED FROM AUTOMATIC
REGRADING; DOD DIR 5200.10
DOES NOT APPLY

~~TOP SECRET SPECIAL HANDLING NOFORN~~

SECRET SPECIAL HANDLING NOFORN
ANNEX TO APPENDIX TO ENCLOSURE A
PRETEXTS TO JUSTIFY US MILITARY INTERVENTION IN CUBA

(Note: The courses of action which follow are a preliminary submission suitable only for planning purposes. They are arranged neither chronologically nor in ascending order. Together with similar inputs from other agencies, they are intended to provide a point of departure for the development of a single, integrated, time-phased plan. Such a plan would permit the evaluation of individual projects within the context of cumulative, correlated actions designed to lead inexorably to the objective of adequate justification for US military intervention in Cuba).

1. Since it would seem desirable to use legitimate provocation as the basis for US military intervention in Cuba a cover and deception plan, to include requisite preliminary actions such as has been developed in response to Task 33 c, could be executed as an initial effort to provoke Cuban reactions. Harassment plus deceptive actions to convince the Cubans of imminent invasion would be emphasized. Our military posture throughout execution of the plan will allow a rapid change from exercise to intervention if Cuban response justifies.

2. A series of well coordinated incidents will be planned to take place in and around Guantanamo to give genuine appearance of being done by hostile Cuban forces.

   a. Incidents to establish a credible attack (not in chronological order):

      (1) Start rumors (many). Use clandestine radio.

      (2) Land friendly Cubans in uniform "over-the-fence" to stage attack on base.

      (3) Capture Cuban (friendly) saboteurs inside the base.

      (4) Start riots near the base main gate (friendly Cubans).

Annex to Appendix
to Enclosure A

UNCLASSIFIED
TOP SECRET SPECIAL HANDLING NOFORN

(5) Blow up ammunition inside the base; start fires.

(6) Burn aircraft on air base (sabotage).

(7) Lob mortar shells from outside of base into base. Some damage to installations.

(8) Capture assault teams approaching from the sea or vicinity of Guantanamo City.

(9) Capture militia group which storms the base.

(10) Sabotage ship in harbor; large fires -- napthalene.

(11) Sink ship near harbor entrance. Conduct funerals for mock-victims (may be lieu of (10)).

b. United States would respond by executing offensive operations to secure water and power supplies, destroying artillery and mortar emplacements which threaten the base.

c. Commence large scale United States military operations.

3. A "Remember the Maine" incident could be arranged in several forms:

a. We could blow up a US ship in Guantanamo Bay and blame Cuba.

b. We could blow up a drone (unmanned) vessel anywhere in the Cuban waters. We could arrange to cause such incident in the vicinity of Havana or Santiago as a spectacular result of Cuban attack from the air or sea, or both. The presence of Cuban planes or ships merely investigating the intent of the vessel could be fairly compelling evidence that the ship was taken under attack. The nearness to Havana or Santiago would add credibility especially to those people that might have heard the blast or have seen the fire. The US could follow up with an air/sea rescue operation covered by US fighters to "evacuate" remaining members of the non-existent crew. Casualty lists in US newspapers would cause a helpful wave of national indignation.

4. We could develop a Communist Cuban terror campaign in the Miami area, in other Florida cities and even in Washington.

Annex to Appendix
to Enclosure A

Below is a list of interventions by the United States by country and date, compiled by Zoltan Grossman, published in the *Baltimore Chronicle and Sentinel* in 2002:[66]

U.S. Military "Interventions" From Wounded Knee to Afghanistan
Compiled by Zoltan Grossman

> *Editor's comment: Regrettably the numbers for military and civilian deaths for these 'interventions' are not readily knowable, but the total surely runs into the millions. Were the benefits achieved (if any) worth all of these violent deaths?*

The following is a partial list (revised on September 20, 2002) of U.S. military interventions from 1890 to 1999. This guide does NOT include demonstration duty by military police, mobilizations of the National Guard, offshore shows of naval strength, reinforcements of embassy personnel, the use of non-Defense Department personnel (such as the Drug Enforcement Agency), military exercises, non-combat mobilizations (such as replacing postal strikers), the permanent stationing of armed forces, covert actions where the U.S. did not play a command and control role, the use of small hostage rescue units, most uses of proxy troops, U.S. piloting of foreign warplanes, foreign disaster assistance, military training and advisory programs not involving direct combat, civic action programs, and many other military activities.

SOUTH DAKOTA, 1890 (-?) Troops: 300 Lakota Indians massacred at Wounded Knee.
ARGENTINA 1890 Troops Buenos Aires interests protected.
CHILE 1891 Troops Marines clash with nationalist rebels.
HAITI 1891 Troops Black workers revolt on U.S.-claimed Navassa Island defeated.
IDAHO 1892 Troops Army suppresses silver miners' strike.
HAWAII 1893 (-?) Naval, troops Independent kingdom overthrown, annexed.
CHICAGO 1894 Troops Breaking of rail strike, 34 killed.
NICARAGUA 1894 Troops Month-long occupation of Bluefields.
CHINA 1894-95 Naval, troops Marines land in Sino-Japanese War.
KOREA 1894-96 Troops Marines kept in Seoul during war.
PANAMA 1895 Troops, naval Marines land in Colombian province.
NICARAGUA 1896 Troops Marines land in port of Corinto.
CHINA 1898-1900 Troops Boxer Rebellion fought by foreign armies.
PHILIPPINES 1898-1910(-?) Naval, troops Seized from Spain, killed 600,000 Filipinos.
CUBA 1898-1902(-?) Naval, troops Seized from Spain, still hold Navy base.
PUERTO RICO 1898(-?) Naval, troops Seized from Spain, occupation continues.
GUAM 1898(-?) Naval, troops Seized from Spain, still use as base.
MINNESOTA 1898(-?) Troops Army battles Chippewa at Leech Lake.
NICARAGUA 1898 Troops Marines land at port of San Juan del Sur.
SAMOA 1899(-?) Troops Battle over succession to throne.
NICARAGUA 1899 Troops Marines land at port of Bluefields.

U.S. military spending ($343 billion in the year 2000) is 69 percent greater than that of the next five highest nations combined. Russia, which has the second largest military budget, spends less than one-sixth what the United States does. Iraq, Libya, North Korea, Cuba, Sudan, Iran, and Syria spend $14.4 billion combined; Iran accounts for 52 percent of this total. Here's what we've been buying with all that money. It's not being spent just for "national defense"—not by a long shot.

---

[66] http://www.zmag.org/list2.htm
    See also: http://www.angelfire.com/home/iran/1953coup.html

IDAHO 1899-1901 Troops Army occupies Coeur d'Alene mining region.
OKLAHOMA 1901 Troops Army battles Creek Indian revolt.
PANAMA 1901-14 Naval, troops Broke off from Colombia 1903, annexed Canal Zone 1914-99.
HONDURAS 1903 Troops Marines intervene in revolution.
DOMINICAN REP. 1903-04 Troops U.S. interests protected in Revolution.
KOREA 1904-05 Troops Marines land in Russo-Japanese War.
CUBA 1906-09 Troops Marines land in democratic election.
NICARAGUA 1907 Troops "Dollar Diplomacy" protectorate set up.
HONDURAS 1907 Troops Marines land during war with Nicaragua.
PANAMA 1908 Troops Marines intervene in election contest.
NICARAGUA 1910 Troops Marines land in Bluefields and Corinto.
HONDURAS 1911 Troops U.S. interests protected in civil war.
CHINA 1911-41 Naval, troops Continuous occupation with flare-ups.
CUBA 1912 Troops U.S. interests protected in Havana.
PANAMA 1912 Troops Marines land during heated election.
HONDURAS 1912 Troops Marines protect U.S. economic interests.
NICARAGUA 1912-33 Troops, bombing 20-year occupation, fought guerrillas.
MEXICO 1913 Naval Americans evacuated during revolution.
DOMINICAN REPUBLIC 1914 Naval Fight with rebels over Santo Domingo.
COLORADO 1914 Troops Breaking of miners' strike by Army.
MEXICO 1914-18 Naval, troops Series of interventions against nationalists.
HAITI 1914-34 Troops, bombing 19-year occupation after revolts.
DOMINICAN REPUBLIC 1916-24 Troops 8-year Marine occupation.
CUBA 1917-33 Troops Military occupation, economic protectorate.
WORLD WAR I 1917-18 Naval, troops Ships sunk, fought Germany
RUSSIA 1918-22 Naval, troops Five landings to fight Bolsheviks.
PANAMA 1918-20 Troops "Police duty" during unrest after elections.
YUGOSLAVIA 1919 Troops Marines intervene for Italy against Serbs in Dalmatia.
HONDURAS 1919 Troops Marines land during election campaign.
GUATEMALA 1920 Troops 2-week intervention against unionists.
WEST VIRGINIA 1920-21 Troops, bombing Army intervenes against mineworkers.
TURKEY 1922 Troops Fought nationalists in Smyrna (Izmir).
CHINA 1922-27 Naval, troops Deployment during nationalist revolt.
HONDURAS 1924-25 Troops Landed twice during election strife.
PANAMA 1925 Troops Marines suppress general strike.
CHINA 1927-34 Troops Marines stationed throughout the country.
EL SALVADOR 1932 Naval Warships sent during Faribundo Marti revolt.
WASHINGTON DC 1932 Troops Army stops WWI vet bonus protest.
WORLD WAR II 1941-45 Naval,troops, bombing, nuclear Fought Axis for 3 years; 1st nuclear war.
DETROIT 1943 Troops Army puts down Black rebellion.
IRAN 1946 Nuclear threat Soviet troops told to leave north (Iranian Azerbaijan).
YUGOSLAVIA 1946 Naval Response to shooting-down of U.S. plane.
URUGUAY 1947 Nuclear threat Bombers deployed as show of strength.
GREECE 1947-49 Command operation U.S. directs extreme-right in civil war.
CHINA 1948-49 Troops Marines evacuate Americans before Communist victory.
GERMANY 1948 Nuclear threat Atomic-capable bombers guard Berlin Airlift.
PHILIPPINES 1948-54 Command operation CIA directs war against Huk Rebellion.
PUERTO RICO 1950 Command operation Independence rebellion crushed in Ponce.
KOREA 1950-53 Troops, naval, bombing, nuclear threats U.S.& South Korea fight China & North Korea to stalemate; A-bomb threat in 1950, & vs. China in 1953. Still have bases.

IRAN 1953 Command operation CIA overthrows democracy, installs Shah.
VIETNAM 1954 Nuclear threat Bombs offered to French to use against siege.
GUATEMALA 1954 Command operation, bombing, nuclear threat CIA directs exile invasion after new gov't nationalizes U.S. company lands; bombers based in Nicaragua.
EGYPT 1956 Nuclear threat, troops Soviets told to keep out of Suez crisis; MArines evacuate foreigners
LEBANON 1958 Troops, naval Marine occupation against rebels.
IRAQ 1958 Nuclear threat Iraq warned against invading Kuwait.
CHINA 1958 Nuclear threat China told not to move on Taiwan isles.
PANAMA 1958 Troops Flag protests erupt into confrontation.
VIETNAM 1960-75 Troops, naval, bombing, nuclear threats Fought South Vietnam revolt & North Vietnam; 1-2 million killed in longest U.S. war; atomic bomb threats in 1968 and 1969.
CUBA 1961 Command operation CIA-directed exile invasion fails.
GERMANY 1961 Nuclear threat Alert during Berlin Wall crisis.
CUBA 1962 Nuclear threat Naval Blockade during missile crisis; near-war with USSR.
LAOS 1962 Command operation Military buildup during guerrilla war.
PANAMA 1964 Troops Panamanians shot for urging canal's return.
INDONESIA 1965 Command operation Million killed in CIA-assisted army coup.
DOMINICAN REPUBLIC 1965-66 Troops, bombing Marines land during election campaign.
GUATEMALA 1966-67 Command operation Green Berets intervene against rebels.
DETROIT 1967 Troops Army battles Blacks, 43 killed.
UNITED STATES 1968 Troops After King is shot; over 21,000 soldiers in cities.
CAMBODIA 1969-75 Bombing, troops, naval Up to 2 million killed in decade of bombing, starvation, and political chaos.
OMAN 1970 Command operation U.S. directs Iranian marine invasion.
LAOS 1971-73 Command operation, bombing U.S. directs South Vietnamese invasion; "carpet-bombs" countryside.
SOUTH DAKOTA 1973 Command operation Army directs Wounded Knee siege of Lakotas.
MIDEAST 1973 Nuclear threat World-wide alert during Mideast War.
CHILE 1973 Command operation CIA-backed coup ousts elected marxist president.
CAMBODIA 1975 Troops, bombing Gas captured ship, 28 die in copter crash.
ANGOLA 1976-92 Command operation CIA assists South African-backed rebels.
IRAN 1980 Troops, nuclear threat, aborted bombing Raid to rescue Embassy hostages; 8 troops die in copter-plane crash. Soviets warned not to get involved in revolution.
LIBYA 1981 Naval jets Two Libyan jets shot down in maneuvers.
EL SALVADOR 1981-92 Command operation, troops Advisors, overflights aid anti-rebel war, soldiers briefly involved in hostage clash.
NICARAGUA 1981-90 Command operation, naval CIA directs exile (Contra) invasions, plants harbor mines against revolution.
LEBANON 1982-84 Naval, bombing, troops Marines expel PLO and back Phalangists, Navy bombs and shells Muslim and Syrian positions.
HONDURAS 1983-89 Troops Maneuvers help build bases near borders.
GRENADA 1983-84 Troops, bombing Invasion four years after revolution.
IRAN 1984 Jets Two Iranian jets shot down over Persian Gulf.
LIBYA 1986 Bombing, naval Air strikes to topple nationalist gov't.
BOLIVIA 1986 Troops Army assists raids on cocaine region.
IRAN 1987-88 Naval, bombing US intervenes on side of Iraq in war.
LIBYA 1989 Naval jets Two Libyan jets shot down.
VIRGIN ISLANDS 1989 Troops St. Croix Black unrest after storm.
PHILIPPINES 1989 Jets Air cover provided for government against coup.
PANAMA 1989-90 Troops, bombing Nationalist government ousted by 27,000 soldiers, leaders arrested, 2000+ killed.
LIBERIA 1990 Troops Foreigners evacuated during civil war.

SAUDI ARABIA 1990-91 Troops, jets Iraq countered after invading Kuwait; 540,000 troops also stationed in Oman, Qatar, Bahrain, UAE, Israel.
IRAQ 1990-? Bombing, troops, naval Blockade of Iraqi and Jordanian ports, air strikes; 200,000+ killed in invasion of Iraq and Kuwait; no-fly zone over Kurdish north, Shiite south, large-scale destruction of Iraqi military.
KUWAIT 1991 Naval, bombing, troops Kuwait royal family returned to throne.
LOS ANGELES 1992 Troops Army, Marines deployed against anti-police uprising.
SOMALIA 1992-94 Troops, naval, bombing U.S.-led United Nations occupation during civil war; raids against one Mogadishu faction.
YUGOSLAVIA 1992-94 Naval Nato blockade of Serbia and Montenegro.
BOSNIA 1993-95 Jets, bombing No-fly zone patrolled in civil war; downed jets, bombed Serbs.
HAITI 1994-96 Troops, naval Blockade against military government; troops restore President Aristide to office three years after coup.
CROATIA 1995 Bombing Krajina Serb airfields attacked before Croatian offensive.
ZAIRE (CONGO) 1996-97 Troops Marines at Rwandan Hutu refuge camps, in area where Congo revolution begins.
LIBERIA 1997 Troops Soldiers under fire during evacuation of foreigners.
ALBANIA 1997 Troops Soldiers under fire during evacuation of foreigners.
SUDAN 1998 Missiles Attack on pharmaceutical plant alleged to be "terrorist" nerve gas plant.
AFGHANISTAN 1998 Missiles Attack on former CIA training camps used by Islamic fundamentalist groups alleged to have attacked embassies.
IRAQ 1998-? Bombing, Missiles Four days of intensive air strikes after weapons inspectors allege Iraqi obstructions.
YUGOSLAVIA 1999-? Bombing, Missiles Heavy NATO air strikes after Serbia declines to withdraw from Kosovo.
YEMEN 2000 Naval Suicide bomb attack on USS Cole.
MACEDONIA 2001 Troops NATO troops shift and partially disarm Albanian rebels.
UNITED STATES 2001 Jets, naval Response to hijacking attacks.
AFGHANISTAN 2001 Massive U.S. mobilization to attack Taliban, Bin Laden. War could expand to Iraq, Sudan, and beyond.

U.S. military spending ($343 billion in the year 2000) is 69 percent greater than that of the next five highest nations combined. Russia, which has the second largest military budget, spends less than one-sixth what the United States does. Iraq, Libya, North Korea, Cuba, Sudan, Iran, and Syria spend $14.4 billion combined; Iran accounts for 52 percent of this total.

Among sources used, besides news reports, are the *Congressional Record* (23 June 1969), "180 Landings by the U.S. Marine Corps History Division," Ege & Makhijani in *Counterspy* (July-Aug. 1982), and Daniel Ellsberg in *Protest & Survive*. Also used: "Instances of Use of United States Forces Abroad, 1798-1993" by Ellen C. Collier of the Library of Congress Congressional Research Service.

For more information or with comments and additions please contact: Zoltan Grossman at mtn@igc.apc.org

Permission to reproduce this list in its entirety is granted by the author. Please notify of publication via email to above address.

Copyright © 2003 The Baltimore Chronicle and The Sentinel. All rights reserved. We invite your comments, criticisms and suggestions.

Republication or redistribution of Baltimore Chronicle and Sentinel content is expressly prohibited without their prior written consent.

This story was published on October 2, 2002.

An updated list of U.S. interventions may be viewed at:
http://academic.evergreen.edu/g/grossmaz/interventions.html

What was America's "justification" for all these interventions? During the era in which we are currently focusing, the rationale was a policy of **containment** toward communism. That is, the U.S. realized that it could not wage an all-out war to defeat communism, so the best it could hope for and the foundation on which it built its foreign policy was *containment* of the dominoes that would fall toward communism.

17

FALLING DOMINOES IN SOUTHEAST ASIA

The origins of the Vietnam War

On the same day that Japan officially surrendered to the United States, September 2, 1945, a Declaration of Independence was signed in a small city in Indochina, Hanoi, by the President of a new nation, the Democratic Republic of Vietnam. The man who signed it was named Ho Chi Minh. Ho had lived in Paris as a young man and became a member of the Communist Party, but at the same time, he greatly admired the American Declaration of Independence.

Indochina had been dominated by the French since 1887. When Ho signed the declaration in September, 1945, he stated that "A people who have courageously opposed French domination for more than eighty years, a people who have fought side by side with the Allies against the Fascists during these last years—such a people must be free and independent."[67]

A communist revolution in China was completed in 1949. China, at that point, the largest Asian nation, was solidly in the communist bloc. In 1950, the United States had responded to the movement of North Korea's armies across the 38th parallel into South Korea. North Korea was a communist country and an ally of China. Local communist movements had sprung up throughout Southeast Asia, seeming to validate the domino theory and fanning the flames of anti-communist hysteria within the United States. Four years after the beginning of the Korean War, another event in Southeast Asia struck fear into the hearts of American policy makers.

In 1954, the French were defeated in Indochina in the Battle of Dien Bien Phu. However, since the Chinese revolution, the U.S. had begun giving large amounts of military aid and weapons to equip the French in Indochina, believing that if the French lost, communism would triumph. Moreover, the U.S. had a long chain of military bases along the coast of China, the Philippines, Taiwan, Japan and South Korea.

Ho Chi Minh was intent on uniting all of Indochina—the northern and southern regions which had been one nation before the French controlled Indochina. After Dien Bien Phu, it was agreed that the French would withdraw to the southern part of the region, and that the Vietminh, that is, the communist population, would live in the north.

---

[67] Prouty, p. 44.

Indochina was from that time referred to as North Vietnam and South Vietnam, Vietnam being the traditional name the people gave themselves.

It was also agreed that within two years (1956) an election would take place which would allow the Indochinese people to choose their own government. The United States quickly intervened to prevent unification by setting up South Vietnam as its own sphere, installing as President of South Vietnam one of its own anti-communist puppets, Ngo Dinh Diem. In other words, South Vietnam was a creation of the United States.

While it is true that the U.S. had been financing the French against the Vietnamese, **we now know from hindsight that the U.S. had also been financing the communist Vietnamese.**[68] Such is the nature of the Military Industrial Complex. As Prouty concludes: "War is the best business in town."

President Eisenhower spoke forcefully in public and in private against involvement in Vietnam. Yet top-level government policy makers went about the business of getting increasingly involved, principally through the efforts of the CIA. Of this Prouty writes:

> Lest there are still some among us who believe that the President runs the country, that the Congress participates effectively in determining the course of its destiny, and that the Supreme Court assures compliance with the Constitution and all federal laws, let them witness this action, and the results of this blatant disregard for all elements of government, as we find it on the record....Nothing whatsoever has ever deterred them from the essential business of making war. These are incredible men, these defiers of Presidents.[69]

> THE VIETNAM WAR TAKES ON NEW MEANING WHEN WE UNDERSTAND THAT THE U.S. HAD BEEN ARMING BOTH SIDES FROM 1945 ON, AND THAT THE COVERT WAR CONTINUED IN OPPOSITION TO A PRESIDENT. THROUGHOUT THE COLD WAR, AND ESPECIALLY AFTER THE DEATH OF JOHN F. KENNEDY, THE CENTRAL INTELLIGENCE AGENCY AND U.S. PENTAGON CONTINUED TO ORCHESTRATE WARS AROUND THE WORLD IN THE NAME OF "CONTAINING COMMUNISM." OFTEN, THE MILITARY INDUSTRIAL COMPLEX SECRETLY FINANCED BOTH SIDES OF THE WARS BECAUSE IN SO DOING, THE PROFITS OF WAR WERE DOUBLED.

The Crimes of The Vietnam War

- **The Phoenix Program**

The CIA even had an official program of state terrorism in Vietnam, known as "Operation Phoenix". Through the Phoenix Program, hundreds of thousands of people were tortured to death in provincial "interrogation centers" all

---

[68] Prouty, P. 58.
[69] *Ibid.*, p.56.

over Vietnam. These torture centers were built specifically for that purpose by the United States. Women were always raped as part of the torture before being murdered. The large-scale terrorism, rape and mass-murder throughout the countryside was the collective policy of the CIA, the U.S. Army, the U.S. Air Force, the U.S. Marines and the U.S. Navy. The My Lai massacre itself was an operation of the Phoenix Program.

- **The My Lai Massacre** (pronounced *"Me Lie"*) was a massacre by American soldiers of hundreds of unarmed Vietnamese civilians, mostly women and children, on March 16, 1968, during the Vietnam War. It prompted widespread outrage around the world and reduced public support for the war in the United States.

For further reading and analysis of the Phoenix and My Lai incidents, please see:

http://www.angelfire.com/rnb/y/phoenix.htm

http://en.wikipedia.org/wiki/My_Lai_massacre

http://www.pbs.org/wgbh/amex/vietnam/trenches/mylai.html

The Geneva Conventions, first signed in 1864 and revised in 1949, is an international agreement regarding the protocols of war. This agreement defines what are legitimate acts of war and what are war crimes in terms of the treatment of civilians, the treatment of soldiers, and the treatment of prisoners of war.

For further information see: http://www.genevaconventions.org/

- **The Politics of Heroin**

It has now been documented that the Central Intelligence Agency was heavily involved in opium and heroin trafficking during the Vietnam War. The CIA Inspector General's Report of 1972 confirms this complicity: http://ciadrugs.homestead.com/files/cia-ig-heroin-complicity.html

In addition, Alfred McCoy, Professor of Southeast Asian History at the University of Wisconsin, has written extensively on the issue in numerous articles and most notably in his book, *The Politics of Heroin*.

Although the North American market was closed, several thousand American military personnel were inhabiting Southeast Asia, and as we know, many of them became heroin addicts. Their return to the U.S. as heroin addicts: 1) created a new market for the drug, and 2) opened new connections within the U.S. that had previously been unavailable.

- **The Killing of U.S. Prisoners of War In Laos**
  In 1998, CNN aired a story by two courageous journalists, April Oliver and Peter Arnett, regarding the CIA's use of Sarin gas to kill American military defectors in Southeast Asia, specifically in Laos. CNN later retracted the story, and Oliver and Arnett were fired. However, both journalists have stood by their story. A summary of the story may be read at:
  http://users.westnet.gr/~cgian/sarin.htm

For additional information, see:

- U.S. Used Nerve Gas During Vietnam War,
  www.reformation.org/poison.html

- The POW's, CIA and Drugs: Uglier Truths Behind The Sarin Gas Stories, by Mike Ruppert at: http://www.fromthewilderness.com/free/pandora/POW.html
- *KISS THE BOYS GOODBYE: How the United States Betrayed Its Own POWs in Vietnam*, by Monika Jensen-Stevenson, New York: Dutton (Penguin Books), 1990.

In her superbly-documented book, Jensen-Stevenson, a former Emmy award-winning producer for CBS News' *Sixty Minutes*, reveals countless eyewitness statements, documents, and even admissions from Ronald Reagan and other White House officials and intelligence experts in the Pentagon and National Security Council showing that the U.S. knowingly left POW's behind in Southeast Asia in 1973. The evidence reveals that the U.S. government sabotaged at least a half-dozen rescue attempts with high probabilities for success and that the U.S. government ordered the liquidation of live POW's if sighted.

As we have seen, on numerous occasions, the United States government has sanctioned or permitted the harming of its own citizens, and on other occasions, such as the attack on Pearl Harbor, mind control experiments, and plutonium research on unknowing subjects, directly harmed innocent Americans.

THE LEGACY OF THE VIETNAM WAR

We cannot understand the Vietnam War unless we understand Low Intensity Conflict and the military strategy following the use of the atomic bomb in Japan to avoid nuclear war at all costs by relying on conventional weapons. Low Intensity Conflict (LIC) necessarily means "long-term duration." This was and is especially true in fighting indigenous and tribal populations as the United States did in Southeast Asia. It is also the strategy for fighting wars in Iraq and Afghanistan which are being fought at the time of this writing and are likely to continue for decades to come.

While such populations do not have sophisticated weaponry at their disposal, they have numbers and an indomitable will to win. Hence, the stories told in the Vietnam War of groups of hundreds of Vietnamese people working together to pull up railroads with their bare hands. These stories were not exaggerations but fact. Ultimately, this kind of tenacity and the Pentagon's determination to keep the war going as long as possible in service of the Military Industrial Complex and positioning itself as a daunting enemy of China and the Soviet Union during the Cold war, brought about America's loss in Vietnam.

Americans during the sixties grew increasingly weary of and angry about the Vietnam War. In 1968, powder kegs of protest exploded throughout the nation. Americans, particularly those who had served in Vietnam, were growing progressively more aware of the war's futility. Many military personnel themselves became protestors.

Some of the consequences of the Vietnam War were:

- 58,156 Americans were killed in the war
- Over 300,000 were wounded
- Nearly 3,000 were missing in action
- Three presidents told the American people that the war was ending or "winding down" when, in fact, they had no intention of ending it, thus producing unprecedented distrust of government and polticians among the American people.
- While the majority of Vietnam Veterans became productive members of peace time society after returning home, a generation of alcoholics and heroin addicts returned to the United States from Southeast Asia and became homeless, committed violent crimes, or became dependent for survival on public assistance.
- American society was torn asunder by opposition to the war, as well cultural issues such as racial justice, women's equality, and confrontation with post-World War II values.

I strongly recommend the following movies on the Vietnam War:

- "Platoon", Directed by Oliver Stone
- "Apocalypse Now", Directed by Francis Ford Copola
- "Born On The Fourth of July", Directed by Oliver Stone
- "Coming Home", Directed by Hal Ashby

18

THE ASSASSINATION OF JOHN F. KENNEDY

In January, 1961, John F. Kennedy, a young Democrat from Massachusetts, was inaugurated following the eight-year Republican administration of Dwight Eisenhower.

First Mention Of The Military Industrial Complex

Although Eisenhower was a Republican and had been a five-star general hero of World War II, he gave a remarkable speech upon leaving office. One paragraph in particular is worth closer examination:

> Our military organization today bears little relation to that known by any of my predecessors in peacetime, or indeed by the fighting men of World War II or Korea.
>
> Until the latest of our world conflicts, the United States had no armaments industry. American makers of plowshares could, with time and as required, make swords as well. But now we can no longer risk emergency improvisation of national defense; we have been compelled to create a permanent armaments industry of vast proportions. Added to this, three and a half million men and women are directly engaged in the defense establishment. We annually spend on military security more than the net income of all United States corporations.
>
> This conjunction of an immense military establishment and a large arms industry is new in the American experience. The total influence—economic, political, even spiritual—is felt in every city, every State house, every office of the Federal government. We recognize the imperative need for this development. Yet we must not fail to comprehend its grave implications. Our toil, resources and livelihood are all involved; so is the very structure of our society.
>
> **In the councils of government, we must guard against the acquisition of unwarranted influence, whether sought or unsought, by the military-industrial complex. The potential for the disastrous rise of misplaced power exists and will persist.**

> We must never let the weight of this combination endanger our liberties or democratic processes. We should take nothing for granted. Only an alert and knowledgeable citizenry can compel the proper meshing of the huge industrial and military machinery of defense with our peaceful methods and goals, so that security and liberty may prosper together.[70]

In the section above, "Falling Dominoes In Southeast Asia", Fletcher Prouty refers to the military industrial complex, but he does not define it as specifically as does Eisenhower in the above passage from his Farewell Address. Specifically, what did Eisenhower mean by "military industrial complex"? Perhaps he foresaw the symbiosis of two gargantuan entities: "the conjunction of an immense military establishment and a large arms industry."

Clearly, as we noted in the above section on the lasting outcomes of World War II, a confluence of the military establishment, that is, the Pentagon, and the manufacturers of weapons, i.e., Lockheed-Martin, General Dynamics, Raytheon, and other transnational arms corporations, have throughout the twentieth century, formed an increasingly impenetrable alliance with the legislative branch of the American government. Unequivocally, Congressional appropriations for the Pentagon are inextricably connected with each legislator's personal and political connections with the weapons industry, as well as the Pentagon.

The Center For Responsive Politics has documented contributions during Fiscal Year 1997 from the weapons industry to both political parties:[71]

This is only one example of the Military-Industrial Complex. Additional examples will be documented subsequently. At this point, our focus is on the burgeoning Military Industrial Complex warned about by President Eisenhower as he left office and as John F. Kennedy became President in 1961.

At that time, the ruling elite of U.S. corporations and of the U.S. military were counting on a victory by Kennedy's opponent, Vice-President Richard Nixon. Significant evidence exists that Joseph P. Kennedy, father of John Kennedy, had close ties with organized crime, particularly in the Chicago area. Allegedly, mob boss, Sam Giancana's ties with the Chicago political machine guaranteed that JFK would win in the Chicago area, barely putting him ahead in the popular vote over Nixon in an extremely close election. The elder Kennedy's ties with organized crime might have been a minor detail in the life of his son, were it not for the fact that during his presidency, JFK and his brother Robert, targeted organized crime and sought to bring convictions against several of its members. It is likely that the mob was part of the assassination of JFK and that it was motivated, in part, by what it perceived as betrayal by the Kennedy brothers.

Fletcher Prouty (www.prouty.org) has written the most comprehensive, firsthand analysis of the JFK assassination, and I strongly recommend both his books: *THE SECRET TEAM* and *JFK: THE CIA, VIETNAM, AND THE PLOT TO ASSASSINATE JOHN F. KENNEDY* parts of which can be read or downloaded at the Prouty website.

Prouty provides a detailed explanation of motives on the part of a variety of players for the removal of Kennedy. One of those entities was the weapons industry to whom Kennedy had shown indifference, particularly with respect to the Tactical Fighter Experimental (TFX) jet fighter for which Boeing, General Dynamics, and Grumman were competing to build. The Kennedy inner circle began to talk seriously of ending the Cold War in the second term, and as Prouty concludes:

> Nothing, absolutely nothing, could have had a greater impact on the enormous military machine of this nation than the specter of peace. The Kennedy plan jeopardized not hundreds of millions, not

---

[70] Eisenhower Farwell Address,
(http://www.yale.edu/lawweb/avalon/presiden/speeches/eisenhower001.htm)

[71] (http://www.fpif.org/papers/micr/companies_body.html)

even billions, but trillions of dollars. (The Cold War has cost no less than $6 trillion.) It shook the very foundation upon which our society has been built over the past two thousand years.[72]

In the first one thousand days of the administration, Kennedy created the Peace Corps, a space program, and a war on poverty, touting his agenda as a New Frontier. The youthful president and his close allies were not the old guard of a former generation of backward-looking, World War II, ruling-elite dinosaurs who had assumed they would be working with one of their own, Richard Nixon, and not the innovative Kennedy.

The Bay Of Pigs

Only one year after Kennedy took office, Fidel Castro led a Communist revolution in Cuba, ninety miles from Miami. The CIA planned a counter-revolutionary attack on Cuba for April, 1961 at the Bay of Pigs, and the attack was then approved by Kennedy. The attack would be two-pronged: First ground forces would secure the beach head, then air forces would eliminate Castro's aircraft capabilities. At the last moment, however, air support for the invasion was cancelled, most likely by McGeorge Bundy, the President's special assistant for national security or General Charles Cabell, or Secretary of State, Dean Rusk. As a result of the loss of air support, the invasion was an abysmal failure, and according to Prouty, the cancellation of air support was probably an act of sabotage by someone in Kennedy's inner circle.[73] Kennedy could have told the truth to the American people—he could have disclosed the fact that he was sabotaged, but he did not do so and took full responsibility for the debacle. He was seriously damaged politically and attacked by rabid Cold Warriors as "soft on Communism."

One year later in March, 1962, the Joint Chiefs of Staff would devise Operation Northwoods, mentioned above, as a strategy for evoking support from the American public for attacking Cuba.[74] In October, 1962, Kennedy would be faced with the Cuban Missile Crisis which would politically compensate for the fallout from the Bay of Pigs.

The Cuban Missile Crisis

Individuals not living through the Cold War and having no experiental memory of it usually have difficulty comprending the significance of the Cuban Missile Crisis. On October 28, 1962 as John F. Kennedy and Nikita Krushchev, Prime Minister of the Soviet Union, played "nuclear chicken", the world came closer to nuclear war than at any moment prior to that time. Fidel Castro was strongly allied with the Soviet Union, and agreed to allow the Soviets to install nuclear missiles in Cuba—missiles pointed at the United States. Kennedy had demanded that Russia remove the missiles from Cuba, but Krushchev refused. For thirteen days, it appeared that Russia would not remove the missiles and that a nuclear attack on Cuba and Russia by the United States was inevitable. However, at the last moment, Krushchev capitulated and agreed to remove the missiles, thereby averting nuclear war.

National Security Action Memorandum #263

Both President Kennedy and his brother, Attorney General Robert Kennedy, were intent upon curtailing, if not destroying, the power of the CIA. They had openly declared their determination to "break it into a thousand pieces".[75] In front of the nation, President Kennedy supported the CIA, in spite of the Bay of Pigs fiasco. Nevertheless, his and his brother's actions revealed a very different reality. Prouty asserts that his personal vendetta against the CIA essentially signed his own death warrant:

---

[72] Prouty, L. Fletcher, *JFK, The CIA, Vietnam And The Plot To Assassinate John F. Kennedy*, Kensington Edition, 2003, p. 151.
[73] *Ibid*, pp.118-135.
[74] Operation Northwoods: (http://www.fromthewilderness.com/free/ww3/11_20_01_op_nwoods.html)
[75] "CIA: Marker of Policy or Tool? survey finds widely feared agency is tightly controlled" *New York Times*. April 25, 1966.

He did not get to the root of the disaster of the Bay of Pigs invasion, and as a result, he, too, became a victim of the sinister power of those agencies of the government that operate in total secrecy, knowing that they do not have to account to anyone for their actions and expenditures…he was up against impossible odds.[76]

Throughout Kennedy's Presidency, he signed several National Security Action Memoranda which increasingly curtailed the power of the Central Intelligence Agency, divesting the agency of policy-making powers and investing those powers instead in the Joint Chiefs of Staff and the Presidency. Additionally, those memos designed a dramatic, protracted shrinkage of the military industrial complex and American military intervention in other countries around the world.

Most momentous, however, was National Security Action Memo #263, signed by Kennedy one month before his death. According to Prouty, it "ordered that 1,000 U.S. military personnel be brought home [from Southeast Asia] by the end of 1963, and that the bulk of U.S. personnel be withdrawn by the end of 1965. NSAM #263 and its accompanying policy became the 'straw that broke the camel's back'."[77]

Fletcher Prouty, James Marrs, and Peter Dale Scott, all of whom have researched the JFK assassination in depth, concur that Kennedy had to be eliminated because his policies were in direct opposition to the agenda of the ruling elite. In addition to Prouty's work on the assassination, please see:

- *Deep Politics And The Death Of JFK*, by Peter Dale Scott, University of California Press, 1993

and

- *Crossfire: The Plot That Killed Kennedy*, by Jim Marrs, Carroll & Graf Publishers, 1989.

Prouty has given us an extraordinary analysis of the JFK assassination from the perspective of an insider. He was also chief advisor to Oliver Stone in the making of Stone's 1992 film, *JFK*, the story of New Orleans District Attorney Jim Garrison's attempt to re-open the Kennedy assassination case in 1968.

Near the movie's end, Garrison is summoned to Washington, D.C. to meet with an anonymous "Mr X", played by Donald Sutherland. The Mr X character is none other than Fletcher Prouty. Their conversation, lasting about fifteen minutes, is a central feature of the movie, and I regularly show that particular conversation to students after I have explained the above points regarding the assassination. I have found this to be a powerful culmination of all the information I teach regarding the assassination as students hear in Prouty's own words, how the assassination was devised, carried out, and covered up.

Garrison's efforts were thwarted, and he lost his case against Clay Shaw of New Orleans, who was clearly involved in the plot to kill Kennedy. Lee Harvey Oswald was closely tied to and worked with the CIA all of his adult life. Over 200 witnesses, either those who were present or who had substantial information regarding the assassination, died "mysteriously" within a few months or years after the event.

Throughout human history, we notice momentous "tipping points" in which life is never the same after the event as before. Today's generation of students have experienced the events of September 11, 2001 and is familiar with the concept of tipping point as applied to that moment in time. In my opinion, the assassination of John F. Kennedy was such a tipping point because to fully understand it is to understand that it was nothing less than a *coup d' etat*—not the overthrow of the republic by armies with bullets, bombs, or bayonets, but rather, the removal from power of a chief

---

[76] Prouty, JFK, The CIA, Vietnam, And the Plot To Assassinate John F. Kennedy, p.161.
[77] *Ibid*, pp. 350-351.

executive who could have and most likely would have radically altered the agenda of the ruling elite, and therefore, the course of the twentieth century. As you will understand by the end of this course, November 22, 1963 and September 11, 2001 are not unrelated

On November 22, 1963, the various interests involved in the assassination—some in government, some in organized crime, and some in corporate America and all other participating players, won. AND, because the American people as a whole were never strong enough or determined enough to get to the bottom of that assassination, we had another ten years of the Vietnam War, the assassinations of Martin Luther King, Jr., Robert Kennedy, Jr., and Watergate. The assassination coverup was gargantuan and extraordinarily intimidating. I have mentioned above the fate of some two hundred witnesses, in addition to which was the Jim Garrison case which exemplifed what would happen when impeccably-researched evidence by fiercely resolute individuals was unveiled in a court of law: essentially nothing. Add to the squelching of Garrison the assassinations of Martin Luther King and Robert Kennedy, and the coverup was virtually sealed.

I spent most of my college years asking, and often today, still ask: "What *might* have been had we been able to uncover the truth about the assassination of John F. Kennedy?" I can only conclude that today, we might be a very different nation than we have become.

19

THE CIVIL RIGHTS MOVEMENT: THE SECOND RECONSTRUCTION

At the beginning of this course, we noted that from the African American historian's perspective, there were two Reconstructions, not *the* Reconstruction. We recall from the First Reconstruction period that African American efforts to attain full equality with whites and to create an equal-opportunity society were egregiously sabotaged by a white backlash in the South and a loss of will on the part of slavery's foes in the North.

We recall that in 1896, the Supreme Court ruled in the *Plessy vs. Ferguson* case that blacks and whites would have separate facilities throughout the nation, but that those facilities were "equal." In no way, however, were facilities and services for African Americans even remotely equal. Nowhere was this more evident than in the public school system of America.

Brown vs. Board of Education

In the early 1950's, racial segregation in public schools was the norm across America. Although all the schools in a given district were supposed to be equal, most black schools were far inferior to their white counterparts.

In Topeka, Kansas, a black third-grader named Linda Brown had to walk one mile through a railroad switchyard to get to her black elementary school, even though a white elementary school was only seven blocks away. Linda's father, Oliver Brown, tried to enroll her in the white elementary school, but the principal of the school refused. Brown went to McKinley Burnett, the head of Topeka's branch of the National Association for the Advancement of Colored People (NAACP) and asked for help. The NAACP was eager to assist the Browns, as it had long wanted to challenge segregation in public schools. With Brown's complaint, it had "the right plaintiff at the right time." Other black parents joined Brown, and, in 1951, the NAACP requested an injunction that would forbid the segregation of Topeka's public schools.

The U.S. District Court for the District of Kansas heard Brown's case from June 25-26, 1951. At the trial, the NAACP argued that segregated schools sent the message to black children that they were inferior to whites; therefore, the schools were inherently unequal.[78]

---

[78] Early Civl Rights History: http://www.watson.org/~lisa/blackhistory/early-civilrights/brown.html

Brown and the NAACP appealed to the Supreme Court on October 1,1951, and their case was combined with other cases that challenged school segregation in South Carolina, Virginia, and Delaware. The Supreme Court first heard the case on December 9, 1952, but failed to reach a decision. In the re-argument, heard from December 7-8, 1953, the Court requested that both sides discuss "the circumstances surrounding the adoption of the Fourteenth Amendment in 1868." The re-argument shed very little additional light on the issue. The Court had to make its decision based not on whether or not the authors of the Fourteenth Amendment had desegregated schools in mind when they wrote the Amendment in 1865, but based on whether or not desegregated schools deprived black children of equal protection of the law when the case was decided, in 1954.

The Supreme Court struck down the "separate but equal" doctrine of *Plessy* for public education, ruled in favor of the plaintiffs, and required the desegregation of schools across America.[79]

School Integration Struggles In Little Rock

In 1957, a group of black students attempted to integrate Central High School in Little Rock, Arkansas where Governor Orville Faubus proclaimed that he would not allow it and had called out the Arkansas National Guard to prevent integration. However, President Eisenhower sent the 101st Airborne Division to Little Rock where black students were escorted by federal troops into the school. In 1958, the Supreme Court upheld the principle of integration, whereupon Governor Faubus shut down four of Little Rock's public schools, using a package of new segregation laws passed by the state legislature. In the summer of 1959, the segregation laws were declared unconstitutional.

The crisis in Little Rock had a profound impact on America and the rest of the world. It provided indelible proof of the lengths to which some Southerners would go to prevent integration. It also showed African Americans that they *could* attain the rights guaranteed to them by the Constitution if they made themselves heard, on the street and in the courtroom.[80]

Freedom Rides

In 1947, the Congress of Racial Equality (CORE) planned a "Journey of Reconciliation," designed to test the Supreme Court's 1946 decision in the Irene Morgan case, which declared segregated seating of interstate passengers unconstitutional. An interracial group of passengers met with heavy resistance in the upper South, and some members of the group served on a chain gang after their arrest in North Carolina. The Journey of Reconciliation quickly broke down. Clearly the South, even the more moderate upper South, was not ready for integration.

Nearly a decade and a half later, John F. Kennedy was elected president, in large part due to widespread support among blacks, who believed that Kennedy was more sympathetic to the civil rights movement than his opponent, Richard Nixon. Once in office, however, Kennedy proved less committed to the movement than he had appeared during the campaign. To test the president's commitment to civil rights, CORE proposed a new Journey of Reconciliation, dubbed the "Freedom Ride." The strategy was the same: an interracial group would board buses destined for the South. The whites would sit in the back and the blacks in the front. At rest stops, the whites would go into blacks-only areas and vice versa. "This was not civil disobedience, really," explained CORE Director James Farmer, "because we [were] merely doing what the Supreme Court said we had a right to do." But the Freedom Riders *expected* to meet resistance. "We felt we could count on the racists of the South to create a crisis so that the federal government would be compelled to enforce the law," said Farmer. "When we began the ride I think all of us were prepared for as much violence as could be thrown at us. We were prepared for the possibility of death."

The Freedom Ride left Washington, D.C. on May 4, 1961. It was scheduled to arrive in New Orleans on May 17, the seventh anniversary of the *Brown* decision. Unlike the original Journey of Reconciliation, the Freedom Ride met little resistance in the upper South.

---

[79] *Ibid.*
[80] School Integration, (http://www.watson.org/~lisa/blackhistory/school-integration/lilrock/shutdown.html)

On Mother's Day, May 14, the Freedom Riders split up into two groups to travel through Alabama. The first group was met by a mob of about 200 angry people in Anniston. The mob stoned the bus and slashed the tires. The bus managed to get away, but when it stopped about six miles out of town to change the tires, it was firebombed. The other group did not fare any better. It was greeted by a mob in Birmingham, and the Riders were severely beaten. Birmingham's Public Safety Commissioner, Bull Conner, claimed he posted no officers at the bus depot because of the holiday; however, it was later discovered that the FBI knew of the planned attack and that the city police stayed away on purpose. Alabama governor John Patterson offered no apologies, explaining, "When you go somewhere looking for trouble, you usually find it....You just can't guarantee the safety of a fool and that's what these folks are, just fools."

Despite the violence, the Freedom Riders were determined to continue. Jim Peck, a white who had fifty stitches from the beatings he received, insisted, "I think it is particularly important at this time when it has become national news that we continue and show that nonviolence can prevail over violence." The bus company, however, did not want to risk losing another bus to a bombing, and its drivers, who were all white, did not want to risk their lives. After two days of unsuccessful negotiations, the Freedom Riders, fearing for their safety, flew to New Orleans. It appeared that the Freedom Ride was over.

The Freedom Riders went on to Montgomery, Alabama where police protection, disappeared as they entered the city limits. The bus terminal was quiet. "And then, all of a sudden, just like magic, white people everywhere," said Freedom Rider Frederick Leonard. The Riders considered leaving by the back of the bus in hopes that the mob would not be quite as vicious. But Jim Zwerg, a white rider, bravely marched off the bus first. The other riders slipped off while the mob focused on pummeling Zwerg. Floyd Mann tried to stop the mob, but it continued to beat the Riders and those who came to their aid, such as Justice Department official John Seigenthaler, who was beaten unconscious and left in the street for nearly a half an hour after he stopped to help two Freedom Riders. Mann finally ordered in state troopers, but the damage was already done. When news of the Montgomery attack reached Washington, Robert Kennedy was not happy. He decided to send federal marshals to the city.

Martin Luther King, Jr., flew to Montgomery and held a mass meeting, surrounded by federal marshals, in support of the Freedom Riders. As night fell, a mob of several thousand whites surrounded the church. The blacks could not leave safely. At 3 AM, King called Robert Kennedy, and Kennedy called Governor Patterson. Patterson declared martial law and sent in state police and the National Guard. The mob dispersed, and the blacks left safely.

More Freedom Riders arrived in Jackson, Mississippi, and they were arrested too. Freedom Riders continued to arrive in the South, and by the end of the summer, more than 300 had been arrested.

The Freedom Riders never made it to New Orleans. Many spent their summer in jail. Some were scarred for life from the beatings they received. But their efforts were not in vain. They forced the Kennedy administration to take a stand on civil rights, which was the intent of the Freedom Ride in the first place. In addition, the Interstate Commerce Commission, at the request of Robert Kennedy, outlawed segregation in interstate bus travel in a ruling, more specific than the original Supreme Court mandate, that took effect in September, 1961. The Freedom Riders may not have finished their trip, but they made an important and lasting contribution to the civil rights movement.[81]

The Civil Rights Act of 1964

President Kennedy's support of civil rights had been patchy, but increasingly, he realized that the federal government must take action to end racial strife in the South and throughout the nation. Kennedy was faced with facts that were indisputable and came from the organization created in the 1960 Civil Rights Act to analyse civil rights issue in America-the Civil Rights Commission. They found that:

- 57% of African American housing was judged to be unacceptable
- African American life expectancy was 7 years less than whites
- African American infant mortality was twice as great as whites

---

[81] Freedom Rides, (http://www.watson.org/~lisa/blackhistory/civilrights-55-65/freeride.html)

- African Americans found it all but impossible to get mortgages from mortgage lenders
- Property values would dropped a great deal if an African American family moved into a neighborhood that was not a ghetto.

Although the seeds of the 1964 Civil Rights Act were sown during Kennedy's presidency, he did not live to see them come to fruition, and after his assassination, Lyndon Johnson used Kennedy's death and the country's veneration of him to pass push the act through Congress. The new law was sweeping and dramatic:

- It gave the federal government the right to end segregation in the South.
- It prohibited segregation in public places. A public place was anywhere that received any form of federal (tax) funding (most places). This act tried to cover every aspect that some lawyer might use to avoid implementing this act.
- An Equal Employment Commission was created.
- Federal funding would not be given to segregated schools (note that these had been banned in 1954, ten years previous).
- Any company that wanted federal business (the biggest spender of money in American business) had to have a pro-civil rights charter. Any segregationist company that applied for a federal contact would not get it.[82]

The Voting Rights Act of 1965

Following on the heels of the Civil Rights Act of 1964 was the Voting Rights Act of 1965 which outlawed literacy tests and poll taxes as a way of assessing whether anyone was fit or unfit to vote. As far as Johnson was concerned, the only voting requirement was American citizenship and the registration of one's name on an electoral list. No form of hindrance to this would be tolerated by the law courts.

The impact of this act was dramatic. By the end of 1966, only 4 out of the traditional 13 Southern states, had less than 50% of African Americans registered to vote. By 1968, even hard-line Mississippi had 59% of African Americans registered. In the longer term, far more African Americans were elected into public office. The Act was the boost that the civil rights cause needed to move it swiftly along, and Johnson has to be given full credit for this. As Martin Luther King had predicted in earlier years, demonstrations served a good purpose, but real change would only come through the power of Federal government.[83]

Assassinations

Despite the Civil Rights Act of 1964 and the Voting Rights Act of 1965, the nation's African-American community was extremely volatile in the mid-sixties. The past decade had been one of racial strife, white backlash, and tireless activism by Martin Luther King and other civil rights activists. A momentous incident ignited a powder keg of race war in America, even as it appeared that the nation was advancing toward a more egalitarian society. In February, 1965, militant black Muslim leader Malcom X was assassinated in New York.

Six months later, on August 11, 1965, a routine traffic stop in South Central Los Angeles provided the spark that lit the fire of seething feelings in what became known as the Watts Riots. The riots lasted for six days, leaving 34 dead, over a thousand people injured, nearly 4,000 arrested, and hundreds of buildings destroyed.

After the riots, then Governor Pat Brown named John McCone to head a commission to study the riots. The report issued by the Commission concluded that the riots weren't the act of thugs, but rather symptomatic of much deeper problems: the high jobless rate in the inner city, poor housing, bad schools. Although the problems were clearly pointed out in the report, no great effort was made to address them, or to rebuild what had been destroyed in the riots.[84]

---

[82] Civil Rights Act, 1964, (http://www.historylearningsite.co.uk/1964_civil_rights_act.htm)
[83] Voting Rights Act, 1965, (http://www.historylearningsite.co.uk/1965_voting_rights_act.htm)
[84] Watts Riots, (http://www.usc.edu/isd/archives/la/watts.html)

For the next two summers, particularly "the long, hot summer" of 1967, rioting erupted throughout black communities nationwide. Moreover, in 1967, Martin Luther King began to speak out against the Vietnam War. On April 4, 1967 at Riverside Church in New York City, King gave his infamous "A Time To Break Silence" speech opposing the Vietnam War in which he said:

> Somehow this madness must cease. We must stop now. I speak as a child of God and brother to the suffering poor of Vietnam. I speak for those whose land is being laid waste, whose homes are being destroyed, whose culture is being subverted. I speak for the poor of America who are paying the double price of smashed hopes at home and death and corruption in Vietnam. I speak as a citizen of the world, for the world as it stands aghast at the path we have taken. I speak as an American to the leaders of my own nation. The great initiative in this war is ours. The initiative to stop it must be ours.[85]

(The speech may be read in its entirety at: http://www.hartford-hwp.com/archives/45a/058.html or listened to at various locations online.)

One year to the day after the Riverside Church speech, Martin Luther King was assassinated in Memphis. As with the assassination of John Kennedy, King was not indiscriminately eliminated by a lone nut, but rather by a carefully-orchestrated plan constructed by those members of the ruling elite who feared the power King was gathering in the United States among the black community and how threatening his stand against the Vietnam War had become.

King's assassination must be understood in the context of the events surrounding it, not only the Vietnam War, but massive protest against the war by the predominantly white anti-war movement, the upheaval in the black community in reaction to poverty, police brutality, and the ghetto-izing of its citizens.

William Pepper, attorney for King's alleged assassin, James Earl Ray, and associate of King during the last years of King's life, has written two remarkable books on the assassination of King. *Orders To Kill*, (1995) and *An Act Of State*, (2003) expose the motive, means, and opportunity for the United States government to eliminate King. Pepper states that as long as King remained focused on issues of civil rights, he was tolerated:

> When, however, Dr. King began to assert his moral leadership on issues of peace and economic justice, he became intolerable. Then the massive weight of the American government came down on him. As we have seen he and his followers were subjected to harassment, infiltration, surveillance, and wiretapping. Finally he was killed—and for what? For seeking peace and justice in his native land which had rejected one and denied the other.[86]

Pepper emphasizes that it is important to understand that civil disobedience and unrest were so pervasive during the late sixties that government security forces were gravely concerned that civil war might erupt within the United States. In late 1967 and early 1968, an election year, in addition to the pervasive violence within urban black communities, Martin Luther King, Eugene McCarthy, and Robert Kennedy, Jr. were experiencing a groundswell of support from Americans opposed to the Vietnam War who were hopeful that they might find in King, McCarthy, or Kennedy, a viable Presidential candidate who could topple the pro-war Johnson Administration.

Two months after the King assassination, June 5, Robert Kennedy was murdered in Los Angeles moments after winning the California Democratic primary. He was bound for the Chicago Democratic Convention where he would have faced his only feasible rival, Eugene McCarthy, and very likely would have won the nomination to run against Richard Nixon in November, 1968.

---

[85] "A Time To Break Silence" Speech, (http://www.hartford-hwp.com/archives/45a/058.html)
[86] Pepper, William, *Orders To Kill*, (New York: Warner Books, 1995), p. 494.

A close friend of Martin Luther King, Jr. and adamantly opposed to the Vietnam War, Robert Kennedy as president would have gravely jeopardized the military industrial complex and the continuation of the Vietnam War. A second Kennedy would be opposing Richard Nixon in one decade, and to make matters worse, Robert Kennedy openly vowed that as President, he would investigate the deeper truths of his brother's assassination.

COINTELPRO (Counter-Intelligence Program)

COINTELPRO was a program of the Federal Bureau of Investigation aimed at investigating and disrupting dissident political organizations in the United States from 1956-1971. According to the Select Committee to Study Governmental Operations of the United States (1976):

> For fifteen years from 1956 until 1971, the FBI carried out a series of covert action programs **directed against American citizens**. These "counterintelligence programs" (shortened to the acronym COINTELPRO) resulted in part from frustration with Supreme Court rulings limiting the Government's power to proceed overtly against dissident groups.
>
> They ended formally in 1971 with the threat of public exposure. Some of the findings discussed herein are related to the findings on lawlessness, overbreadth, and intrusive techniques previously set forth. Some of the most offensive actions in the FBI's COINTELPRO programs (anonymous letters intended to break up marriages, or efforts to deprive people of their jobs, for example) were based upon the covert use of information obtained through overly-broad investigations and intrusive techniques. Similarly, as noted above, COINTELPRO involved specific violations of law, and the law and the Constitution were "not [given] a thought" under the FBI's policies.
>
> But COINTELPRO was more than simply violating the law or the Constitution. In COINTELPRO the Bureau secretly took the law into its own hands, going beyond the collection of intelligence and beyond its law enforcement function to act outside the legal process altogether and to covertly disrupt, discredit and harass groups and individuals. A law enforcement agency must not secretly usurp the functions of judge and jury, even when the investigation reveals criminal activity. But in COINTELPRO, the Bureau imposed summary punishment, not only on the allegedly violent, but also on the nonviolent advocates of change. Such action is the hallmark of the vigilante and has no place in a democratic society.
>
> Under COINTELPRO, certain techniques the Bureau had used against hostile foreign agents were adopted for use against perceived domestic threats to the established political and social order.
>
> Some of the targets of COINTELPRO were law-abiding citizens merely advocating change in our society. Other targets were members of groups that had been involved in violence, such as the Ku Klux Klan or the Black Panther Party. Some victims did nothing more than associate with targets.[87]

Moreover, specific persons and groups, we now know, were targeted by COINTELPRO. Among them were: The Communist Party, the Socialist Workers Party, the New Left (students and other individuals protesting the Vietnam War), Martin Luther King, Malcom X, and the Black Panthers. The Senate Select Committee Report states that:

---

[87] Senate Select Committee To Study Government Operations, 1976,
(http://www.icdc.com/~paulwolf/cointelpro/churchfinalreportIIa.htm)

The Committee devoted substantial attention to the FBI's covert action campaign against Dr. Martin Luther King because it demonstrates just how far the Government could go in a secret war against one citizen. In focusing upon Dr. King, however, it should not be forgotten that the Bureau carried out disruptive activities against hundreds of lesser known American citizens. It should also be borne in mind that positive action on the part of high Government officials outside the FBI might have prevented what occurred in this case.

The FBI's claimed justification for targeting Dr. King—alleged Communist influence on him and the civil rights movement—is examined elsewhere in this report. The FBI's campaign against Dr. Martin Luther King, Jr. began in December 1963, four months after the famous civil rights March on Washington, when a nine-hour meeting was convened at FBI Headquarters to discuss various "avenues of approach aimed at neutralizing King as an effective Negro leader." Following the meeting, agents in the field were instructed to "continue to gather information concerning King's personal activities…in order that we may consider using this information at an opportune time in a counterintelligence move to discredit him.[88]

The disruptive and undercover surveillance techniques of COINTELPRO are explained at: http://www.icdc.com/~paulwolf/cointelpro/churchfinalreportIIIa.htm. The 1976 Senate Select Committee hearings reveal that COINTELPRO egregiously violated the First Amendment rights of countless innocent citizens based on the supposition that dissent and protest in the United States were caused by Communist and Socialist influences.

While official U.S. history teaches that COINTELPRO activities came to an end in 1976, there is compelling evidence to suggest that it has been revived post-September 11 and is again functioning in the United States to scrutinize individuals who criticize the current administration and its domestic and foreign policies. As we shall see in our consideration of September 11, 2001, the USA Patriot Act and other measures utilized by the federal government in its so-called War on Terrorism, have re-invigorated domestic spying, attended by unprecedented violations of the civil liberties of American citizens.

---

[88] *Ibid.,*

20

THE END OF THE VIETNAM WAR AND WATERGATE

In November, 1968, Richard Nixon won the Presidency against Hubert Humphrey who had been Lyndon Johnson's Vice-President and a Democratic moderate in support of the war. Nixon came to power reassuring the American people that he and his administration "had a plan" for ending the war in Vietnam.

The antiwar movement, especially students, continued to protest the war, and in the spring of 1970, an enormous wave of antiwar demonstrations swept across college campuses as Richard Nixon ordered an invasion of Cambodia.

Kent State

A 1969 survey of college students revealed that at least 215,000 students had participated in campus protests. The culmination of the protests occurred on May 4, 1970, and at Kent State University in Ohio the protests were fatal when four students were shot and killed, and another paralyzed for life, by National Guardsmen.

The events at Kent State did not halt protest in the United States, but in my opinion, the horror of the establishment's slaying its own children left the student movement subdued. Shortly thereafter, it seemed that activists increasingly looked away from the outside world and more perceptively into themselves. It would be another three years before the end of the Vietnam War and another five before all U.S. troops would leave Vietnam.

The Pentagon Papers

One cannot deny that unlike blacks had been for generations, white students were not accustomed to being shot at. But even as a chill descended on the children of privilege, a Harvard-trained economist, ex-Marine, and former RAND Corporation executive, then working in the Pentagon, duplicated 7,000 pages of classified documents exposing the history of the Vietnam War and the appalling reality that throughout five presidential administrations, the United States government had no intention of winning the war, but rather, perpetuating it for as long as possible. These explosive documents were published in the *New York Times* and came to be known as *The Pentagon Papers*. The man who brought them to light, Daniel Ellsberg, was quite certain that he would spend the rest of his life in prison, but as a result of criminal efforts by the White House to silence and incapacitate him, his charges were dismissed. *The Pentagon Papers* and

Secrets[89], Ellsberg's more recent autobiographical account of his decision to publish the documents, are fascinating reading and have distinguished Ellsberg as a stellar American hero of the twentieth century.

By the time the Vietnam War ended in 1973, the U.S. had stepped up its covert operations in other countries because waging an overt war had damaged the establishment severely in terms of public opinion.

Bringing The War Home

As the war drew to a close and America endeavored to process the loss of 58,000 troops, an entire generation of physically and psychologically wounded soldiers returned to America where the demons of their horrors in Southeast Asia erupted in families and on the streets of America. Many who fought in Laos did not return home. Some experts have speculated that they could not be allowed to return because of what they knew about the secret war in Laos, the Phoenix Program, and CIA drug trafficking in Laos.[90] (See reference above to *Kiss The Boys Goodbye*, by Monika Jensen-Stevenson)

As antiwar protest diminished and black militancy waned in the early 1970s, other groups such as women, Native Americans, and gay and lesbian people began protesting and demanding equal rights.

WATERGATE

In 1972, Richard Nixon was planning his second term in the White House. On June 17, 1972, the Democratic National Headquarters, located in the Watergate Hotel in Washington, D.C. was burglarized. Records of the Democratic Party and its campaign strategy were stolen. The burglars were arrested, and evidence began pointing to the White House's influence in the crime. Although Nixon was re-elected, storm clouds were gathering over his administration.

In February, 1973, a Congressional investigation of the Watergate incident began and ran through the summer of 1974. As the investigation proceeded, it became increasingly clear from testimony of those in the White House close to Nixon that he had been deeply involved in the crime. Not only had he been behind the Watergate burglary, but a number of other crimes of spying on groups and individuals. One of the most egregious was the break-in, ordered by Nixon, into the office of the psychiatrist of Daniel Ellsberg in order to portray him as mentally ill and therefore discredit the *Pentagon Papers*.

Some individuals close to Nixon in the White House, and then Deputy Director of the FBI, Mark Felt, began leaking information to the press. Most notably, Felt who for decades has been known as "Deep Throat", began disclosing secret information regarding the Nixon's criminal activities to *Washington Post* reporters, Bob Woodward and Carl Bernstein. "Deep Throat" is the name Woodward called his source, Felt, who did not reveal his identity until 2005. Woodward and Bernstein authored a detailed account of their investigative reporting of Watergate entitled, *All The President's Men*.

Nixon resigned from the presidency on August 8, 1974 and left office the following day. However, before leaving, he was pardoned by his Vice-President, Gerald Ford, which assured Nixon that he would never be charged with any crimes in relation to the Watergate incident.

Watergate represents a reprehensible violation of trust and integrity by a president, demonstrating that he would do whatever it took to win a second term. As a result of Watergate and the Vietnam War, Americans lost faith in their government, and from Watergate onward, fewer and fewer numbers of Americans voted in national elections.

---

[89] Daniel Ellsberg, *Secrets: A Memoir of Vietnam and the Pentagon Papers* (NewYork: Penguin, 2003).
[90] Chaos In Laos, (http://www.peacemagazine.org/archive/v04n2p09.htm)

21

THE CARTER PRESIDENCY

In 1977, Jimmy Carter, a Democrat, began his one term as President. As Howard Zinn concludes Carter:

> ...despite a few gestures toward black people and the poor, despite talk of 'human rights' abroad, remained within the historic public boundaries of the American system, protecting corporate wealth and power, maintaining a huge military machine that drained the national wealth, allying the United States with right-wing tyrannies abroad....Carter's job as President, from the point of view of the Establishment, was to halt the rushing disappointment of the American people with the government, with the economic system, with disastrous military ventures abroad.[91]

The Iran Hostage Crisis

As noted earlier in the course, in 1953, the CIA orchestrated an overthrow of the democratically-elected leader of Iran, Mohammed Mossadeq, replacing him with Shah Pahlavi. One reason for the overthrow was that Mossadeq was in the process of nationalizing Iran's oil supply which would have limited America's access to it. The Shah, however, was strongly allied with U.S. oil companies and promised to give them full access to Iranian oil.

The Shah ruled oppressively, using torture and massive human rights violations, from 1953 to 1979 when a revolution, led largely by Iranian students swept him from power and replaced him with a Shia Muslim cleric, Ayatollah Khomeni. As part of the overthrow of the Shah, the revolutionaries kidnapped and held fifty-two hostages from the American embassy in Tehran for 444 days.

The U.S. Energy Crisis

The Iranian oil sector was shattered by the revolution, and oil prices were driven up. As a result, the United States, principal enemy of the Iranian Revolution, faced enormous increases in oil prices, creating in 1979, a huge energy crisis in America.

---

[91] Zinn, *The Twentieth Century*, pp.330-331.

Carter made symbolic efforts to curtail America's energy consumption by telling Americans to keep thermostats at sixty-eight degrees in the winter, by installing solar panels on the roof of the White House, and by lowering the speed limit to fifty-five miles per hour. As well as being only symbolic, these efforts were non-agessive in relation to Iran and the rest of the world. This would change, however, as a result of Carter's 1980 State of the Union address.

The Carter Doctrine

In his State of the Union message in 1980, Jimmy Carter articulated a policy which has come to be known as the Carter Doctrine. One particular portion is extremely significant:

> An attempt by an outside force to gain control of the Persian Gulf region will be regarded as an assault on the vital interests of the United States of America, and such an assault will be repelled by any means necessary, including military force.

In an excellent article by Michael Klare on the connection between the Carter Doctrine and U.S. oil supply, Klare states that:

> Enunciated by then-President Jimmy Carter in his State of the Union speech in January 1980, the doctrine defines Persian Gulf oil as a "vital interest" of the United States that must be defended "by any means necessary, including military force."[92]

Klare further notes that the Carter Doctrine now covers much of the planet. In addition to protecting the oil of the Gulf, the United States has also assumed responsibility for the protection of energy supplies in Central Asia and the Caspian region. At the same time, U.S. forces in Europe are helping to protect oil pipelines in the Republic of Georgia and oil-rich waters off the coast of Africa. American forces in the Pacific guard the oil lanes of the South China Sea. And troops from the Southern Command are helping to protect pipelines in Colombia.[93]

The Soviet Invasion of Afghanistan

In 1979, the Soviet Union invaded Afghanistan. We now know that the Soviets were drawn into a trap set by the U.S. in order to embroil them in a "Soviet Vietnam" which would deplete and debilitate their economy and ultimately lead to the fall of the Soviet Union. This has been verified by Jimmy Carter's former Secretary of State, Zbigniew Brzezinski, in a 1998 interview.[94]

The Afghan forces fighting the Soviet invasion were the Mujahadeen. Their leader, trained, financed, and supported by the United States was Osama bin Laden. As documented by Economics Professor Michel Chossudovsky of the University of Ottawa and host of the website Global Research, Osama bin Laden has been a CIA intelligence asset for decades.[95] Chossudovsky's evidence will be examined below as we discuss the events of September 11, 2001.

---

[92] Michael Klare On The Carter Doctrine, (http://www.thirdworldtraveler.com/Oil_watch/Carter_Doctrine_Global_Oil.html)
[93] *Ibid.*
[94] Interview With Brzezinski, (http://www.globalresearch.ca/articles/BRZ110A.html)
[95] "Fabricating An Enemy", (http://www.globalresearch.ca/articles/CHO301B.html)

22

THE REAGAN-BUSH PRESIDENCY

The October Surprise

The Reagan-Bush era marks the beginning of a new level of corruption and unprecedented sovereignty of corporations and the military-industrial complex. Even before Reagan took office, George Bush, Sr. and Inspector General of the CIA, William Casey, then Reagan's campaign manager, were working behind the scenes to orchestrate a surreptitious political triumph for Reagan.

In the fall of 1980, Carter was marginally leading Reagan in the polls with the election right around the corner. The release of hostages before election day presumably would have insured the election for Carter. The Reagan team conspired to negotiate a deal with Ayatollah Khomeini of Iran. Campaign manager William Casey and George Bush met with Iranian Prime Minister Bani-sadr in Paris in October, only weeks before the election, Carter then having a slight lead over Reagan.

Part of the deal cut between the Reagan team and Iran was to provide military weapons which Iran desperately needed in its war with Iraq. As it turned out, the 52 American hostages remained captive in Teheran. Carter's popularity continued to plummet, enabling Reagan to be elected in November, and ironically the hostages were returned at 12 o'clock noon on January 21, 1981 when Reagan was inaugurated.

The first meeting regarding arms-to-Iran occurred in July, 1980 in Barcelona, Spain and not in Madrid as was initially reported. The Republican team met at the Hotel Princess Sofia and at the Pepsico International headquarters. The American team was led by Republican campaign director William Casey, who months later was to be named CIA chief by Reagan, and by Robert McFarlane, who later became National Security adviser under Reagan. Three months after Barcelona, a more important meeting took place in Paris. CIA agent Richard Brenneke testified that George H.W. Bush, who would become Reagan's Vice-President, was in Paris on Sunday, October 19, 1980 when he met with members of the Khomeini regime to consummate an arms package to Iran. Bush, along with Casey and other government officials, flew to Paris on Saturday evening, October 18. The plane arrived in Paris on Sunday morning October 19 at 8:40 A.M. European time.

While in Paris, the Republican team gave $40 million to the Iranian government as a gesture of good faith that the Reagan team was serious in dealing with the terrorist Khomeini government—and that the 52 American hostages should remain captive until after the November election. After the meeting, Bush had to quickly return to the United States in order to deliver a speech at the Washington Hilton Hotel. He departed France in an SR-71 reconnaissance plane, piloted by Gunther Russbacher. The plane was refueled by an Air Force tanker nearly 2,000 miles out of Paris. The entire return flight to the United States was less than two hours.

When news of the Paris meeting leaked out, the CIA moved quickly to cover-up Bush's meeting. CIA agent Frank Snepp wrote an article in the *Village Voice,* stating that the pilot, Gunther Russbacher, was not capable of flying an SR-71 and, therefore, his allegations were false. However, in an interview between government whistle-blower Rodney Stich and Russbacher, it was very clear that Russbacher had been trained in flying the SR-71.

Several other witnesses corroborated the story that Bush was present in Paris. Ari Ben-Menashea, a member of Israel's Mossad and involved in the transfer of arms to Iran, stated that Bush was at the meeting. Also, Iranian Prime Minister Bani-sadr produced documents indicating that Bush was present. On the other hand, CIA agent Donald Gregg, who was on the flight to Paris, failed a polygraph test when asked about Bush's presence.

The Secret Service unequivocally denied the fact that Bush was in Paris. Yet, the agency refused to allow any of its agents who were assigned to Bush at that time, to testify. Justice Department prosecutors called two Secret Service agents who swore that Bush was in Washington, D.C. on that weekend. The Secret Service claimed that Bush was in Pennsylvania on Saturday, October 18; however, the agency did not produce any evidence to indicate Bush's activities on the following day.

Congress refused to investigate the October Surprise. However, eventually in 1991, the Senate Foreign Relations Committee made a token gesture and superficially did begin an investigation. Under pressure by the Republicans, both the House and the Senate initially looked into allegations of improprieties. The investigation was virtually blocked, since the committee prevented investigators from traveling to Europe to interview witnesses; denied subpoena power to investigators; limited the time frame of the investigation; and limited the funds to investigate alleged illegalities.[96]

A series of mainstream newspaper stories written about the October Surprise from various perspectives can be read at: http://www.fas.org/irp/congress/1992_cr/h920205-october-clips.htm

Vice-President In Charge Of Corruption

George Herbert Walker Bush, son of Prescott Bush, had been the Director of Central Intelligence in the mid-seventies. We know that the Bush family had been involved in the intelligence community and had close ties with the weapons industry throughout the twentieth century. These connections are superbly documented as mentioned above in Webster Tarpley's *The Unauthorized Biography of George Bush, Sr.* (www.tarpley.net) and more recently by Kevin Phillips in *American Dynasty: Aristocracy, Fortune And The Politics Of Deceit.*

Two monumentally significant events were implemented by Bush during the Reagan presidency.

- In 1981 **National Security Decision Directive 1 (NSDD 1)** was signed by Reagan which would **re-organize the National Security Council (NSC)** which is the arm of the CIA in the White House. Subsequently, a second document called NSDD 2 would be signed, formalizing the establishment of a Special Situation Group (SSG) crisis management staff chaired by Bush.

  On Sunday, March 22, 1981, the *Washington Post* published the headline "WHITE HOUSE REVAMPS TOP POLICY ROLES; Bush to Head Crisis Management". The *Post* continued:

  Partly in an effort to bring harmony to the Reagan high command, it has been decided that Vice President George Bush will be placed in charge of a new structure for national security crisis management, according to senior presidential assistants. This assignment will amount to an unprecedented role for a vice president in modern times. In the Carter administration, the crisis management structure was chaired by Zbigniew Brzezinski, the national security adviser. [...]

---

[96] The October Surprise: http://www.angelfire.com/ca3/jphuck/BOOK3Ch7.html

On a broader, policy-making level, senior White House officials were unhappy with what they felt to be ill-timed and ill-considered actions by Secretary of State Alexander M. Haig Jr. that placed the brightest spotlight on El Salvador at a time when the administration was trying to focus maximum attention on Reagan's economic proposals. […]

Bush's stature, by virtue of job title and experience, was cited as the reason that he was chosen to chair meetings in the Situation Room in time of crisis. Principal officials involved in crisis management will be the secretaries of state and defense, the Central Intelligence Agency director, the national security adviser, Meese, and Baker, officials said, adding that the structure has not been fully devised nor the presidential directive written.

Reagan officials emphasized that Bush, a former director of the CIA and former United Nations Ambassador, would be able to preserve White House control over crisis management without irritating Haig, who they stressed was probably the most experienced and able of all other officials who could serve in that function.

"The reason for this [choice of Bush] is that the secretary of state might wish he were chairing the crisis management structure," said one Reagan official, "but it is pretty hard to argue with the vice president being in charge." [fn 7]

Tarpley concludes: George Bush had seized control of the Special Situation Group, which would take control of the Executive Branch in time of crisis or national emergency. In Tarpley's opinion, "It was a superb starting point for a *coup d'etat*."[97]

- In 1986, in an effort to overcome traditional agency reluctance, President Reagan issued **Executive Order 12615 requiring departments and agencies to establish and fulfill ambitious privatization goals**. The order also created the Office of Privatization within the Office of Management and Budget to oversee the program, and established an independent Commission on Privatization to study and recommend opportunities for privatization within the federal government. Although few, if any, of the recommendations that emerged from this effort were enacted at the time, several of the programs first proposed, developed, and advocated by the Reagan Administration (the Alaska Power Marketing Administration, the U.S. Enrichment Corporation, the National Helium Reserve, and the Naval Petroleum Reserve at Elk Hills, California) eventually were approved for privatization by the 104th Congress and the Clinton White House. When completed, these privatization divestitures yielded more than $3 billion in revenues to the federal government.[98]

As we will examine in further detail subsequently, constructing a closer relationship between the Presidency and the Central Intelligence Agency than had existed since the creation of the CIA in 1947, and the use of private corporate contractors to do government work secretly (ostensibly for reasons of national security) creates two very negative realities:

- Private contractors do not have to be accountable for the work they do or how they use the money allocated to them and
- A black budget is created in which government money is being spent without the oversight of Congress and the American people. THIS IS A RECIPE FOR FRAUD AND CORRUPTION TO BECOME STANDARD OPERATING PROCEDURE IN THE FEDERAL GOVERNMENT.

The Iran-Contra Scandal—Falling Dominoes in Central America

In 1979 the Sandinista revolutionary movement of Nicaragua overthrew a brutal dictator and puppet of the United States, Anastasio Somoza. The Sandinistas proceeded to institute unprecedented changes in the country such as

---

[97] Tarpley, The Unauthorized Biography of George Bush, Sr., (www.tarpley.net, Chapter 17)
[98] *Improving Government Performance Through Competitive Contracting*, Donald Utt, 2001
http://www.heritage.org/Research/GovernmentReform/BG1452.cfm

throwing out U.S. corporations, creating jobs, health care, housing, and reforming education. Their elected leader, Daniel Ortega, had been exiled to Cuba by Somoza, and while in Cuba, learned about revolution from Fidel Castro. Ortega was sympathetic with Cuba and Castro, but he was also distrustful of the Soviet Union. Nevertheless, as a result of his ties to Castro, the U.S. decided that the Sandinista regime must be eliminated.

In 1981 Reagan signed an executive order to begin covert operations in Central America against the Sandinistas. However, in 1982, Congress passed the Boland Amendment which barred the use of federal money to overthrow the government of Nicaragua.[99]

The Reagan Administration responded, not by abiding by the amendment, but by circumventing it illegally. **Marine Lt. Colonel, Oliver North**, working for the National Security Council was secretly put in charge of raising money from private corporations to support the CIA-created **Contra** forces fighting the Sandinistas in Central America. Using the Domino Theory, President Reagan publicly addressed the nation regarding the imminent threat of Communism in Central America:

> Central America is a region of great importance to the United States. And it is so close: San Salvador is closer to Houston, Texas, than Houston is to Washington, DC. Central America is America. It's at our doorstep, and it's become the stage for a bold attempt by the Soviet Union, Cuba, and Nicaragua to install communism by force throughout the hemisphere.
>
> We can and must help Central America. It's in our national interest to do so, and morally, it's the only right thing to do. But helping means doing enough—enough to protect our security and enough to protect the lives of our neighbors so that they may live in peace and democracy without the threat of Communist aggression and subversion. This has been the policy of our administration for more than 3 years.[100]

Reagan called the Contras "freedom fighters" and "the moral equivalent of the Founding Fathers," portraying them as part of what he called the "Evil Empire" of the global Communist conspiracy.

John Stockwell, the highest-ranking CIA official ever to leave the agency and go public, has a very different perception of the Contras:

> They use terror. This is a technique that they're using to traumatize the society so that it can't function. I don't mean to abuse you with verbal violence, but you have to understand what your government and its agents are doing. They go into villages, they haul out families. With the children forced to watch they castrate the father, they peel the skin off his face, they put a grenade in his mouth and pull the pin. With the children forced to watch they gang-rape the mother, and slash her breasts off. And sometimes for variety, they make the parents watch while they do these things to the children. This is nobody's propaganda. There have been over 100,000 American witnesses for peace who have gone down there and they have filmed and photographed and witnessed these atrocities immediately after they've happened, and documented 13,000 people killed this way, mostly women and children. These are the activities done by these contras. The contras are the people president Reagan calls 'freedom fighters'. He says they're the moral equivalent of our founding fathers. And the whole world gasps at this confession of his family traditions. Read *Contra Terror* by Reed Brodie, former assistant Attorney General of New York State. Read *The Contras* by Dieter Eich. Read *With the Contras* by Christopher Dickey.[101]

---

[99] Boland Amendment, (http://www.nationmaster.com/encyclopedia/Boland-Amendment)
[100] Address To Nation, Ronald Reagan, May 9, 1984 (http://www.reagan.utexas.edu/resource/speeches/1984/50984h.htm)
[101] Addresss by John Stockwell, 1987, (http://www.stratmag.com/issueDec-15/kargil.htm)

Arms For Hostages

What was disclosed in the Iran-Contra Hearings of 1987 was that the Reagan administration secretly sold arms to Iran in exchange for the release of the American hostages, and then diverted the profits from the arms sales to the Contras. Both transactions were violations of acts of Congress which prohibited the funding of the Contras and the sale of weapons to Iran. Moreover, both activities violated UN sanctions.

Financing The Contras With Cocaine

In 1997, the *San Jose Mercury News* released a series of stories by investigative reporter, Gary Webb, revealing the CIA's involvement in drug trafficking in South Central Los Angeles to finance the Contras. Webb later compiled his series into a best-selling book, *Dark Alliance*.

Below is a brief synopsis by Webb of the 1998 Report of the Inspector General of the Central Intelligence Agency:

By GARY WEBB

The sale of missiles to the Ayatollah Khomeini, it seems, wasn't the real scandal of the Iran-contra affair. It was the sale of cocaine to American citizens.

This we know thanks to a recently declassified CIA inspector general's report.

Though hacked and shredded to about half its original length for alleged national security reasons, the 361-page CIA report paints a damning picture of official malfeasance.

Had these secret cables surfaced during the firestorm of controversy then raging over Iran-contra, it is likely neither the CIA nor the Reagan administration would have survived the conflagration.

By 1987, the CIA report shows, the agency was sitting on six years' worth of reports from field agents, station chiefs, informants, private citizens and some of the contras themselves, all indicating that Ronald Reagan's "freedom fighters" were shipping planeloads of cocaine and marijuana into the U.S.

The justice department's files likewise bulged with evidence of contra drug-running, including eyewitness testimony from inside informants. Ditto for the state department. The CIA had briefed vice-president George Bush personally.

"Allegations of drug trafficking continue to plague our operations," CIA headquarters grumbled in a July 1986 cable to its agents in Costa Rica.

Prime example

A prime example was international drug kingpin Norwin Meneses, a California-based contra who supplied the South-Central L.A. crack market with cocaine powder during the 80s and early 90s.

A 1988 FBI cable shows that the bureau knew Meneses was working for the drug enforcement agency (DEA) and believed he "was, and may still be, an informant for the Central Intelligence Agency." At the time, the FBI was unsuccessfully seeking his indictment on federal cocaine-trafficking charges.

According to the report, the CIA not only failed to act against the contra traffickers, but also, deliberately or otherwise, misled others who were investigating them.

The agency repeatedly sent false reports to U.S. attorneys, U.S. customs and other federal agencies assuring them that the CIA had no record of men and companies who were plainly listed in CIA files as being involved with drugs.

Most important, the declassified cables show that the CIA knew exactly what it was doing and was fully aware of how the American public would react if word of its shenanigans ever surfaced.

"There is a very real risk that news of our relationship with (Alan Hyde), whose reputation as an alleged drug trafficker is widely known to various agencies, will hit the public domain—something that could bring our program to a full stop," CIA headquarters nervously cabled its agents in Honduras in July 1987.

Six years later, the CIA report says, the agency was still protecting Honduran trafficker Hyde in an effort to keep the CIA's relationship with drug dealers during the contra war under wraps.

A March 11, 1993, cable discouraged counter-narcotics efforts against Hyde because "his connection to the CIA is well documented and could prove difficult in the prosecution stage," says the report, which was posted on the CIA's Web site in early October.

The CIA knew from the very beginning of the war that the men it had hired to run its main contra army were narco-terrorists, but it continued to finance and protect them.

Contra army

In September 1981—to take just one example—as the CIA was becoming formally involved with the contras, the agency learned that a faction called the Legion of September 15 "had made a decision to engage in drug smuggling to the United States in order to finance its anti-Sandinista operations."

A few months after discovering the Legion's involvement with drugs, the CIA put the group's senior commanders in charge of the agency's newly formed contra organization, the Nicaraguan Democratic Force (FDN).

According to the testimony of former L.A. drug kingpin Danilo Blandon, the contra middleman who sold Meneses' cocaine to South-Central's crack dealers, it was the Legion's commander in chief, Enrique Bermudez, who recruited him and Meneses in late 1981 to raise money for the contras in California.

As part of their fundraising efforts, they began selling cocaine to the street gangs of South-Central and, in the process, helped touch off the crack-cocaine explosion there.

The inspector general's report should put to rest the long-simmering historical debate over what the CIA as an institution knew about the contras' drug trafficking. The answer? It knew everything, despite its best efforts to remain ignorant.

So where was the watchdog press while the Reagan administration, Congress and the CIA were scrambling to keep a lid on the contra drug connection? Dishing out the official story as fast as possible.

Only now—nearly 12 years later—can we fully appreciate what an astounding lie that was and how eagerly it was swallowed by a gullible Washington, DC, press corps.

While the press was dismissing the issue as the combined fantasies of dopers and contra-haters, the DEA was sitting on information from several reliable informants—eyewitnesses on the U.S. government's payroll—who reported that the contras were selling drugs in Los Angeles and San Francisco with the CIA's connivance.

DEA operative

In one case, Ivan Torres, a contra official who was part of Blandon's South Central drug ring, told an undercover DEA operative that "CIA representatives are aware of his drug-related activities and that they don't mind. He said they have gone so far as to as to encourage cocaine trafficking by members of the contras because they know it is a good source of income."

That 1987 DEA report corroborated information the drug agency had received two years earlier from Renato Pena, another member of the Blandon/Meneses cocaine ring and the FDN's military representative in San Francisco.

In 1985, Pena told the DEA that "the CIA was allowing the contras to fly drugs into the United States, sell them and keep the proceeds." Pena told CIA inspectors that "Norwin Meneses and Danilo Blandon told him they were raising money for the contras through drug-dealing and that Blandon stated that the contras would not have been able to operate without drug proceeds."

Ironically, these recently declassified reports are still secret to most Americans.[102]

Copyright 1998 Gary Webb

**At this point in the course, I show the second part of "Fifty Years Of The CIA And Drug Dealing" with Mike Ruppert (1997), or "The CIA And Drugs: The Confession And The Impeachment" with Mike Ruppert (1999).

**I also strongly recommend Gary Webb's superbly documented work, *Dark Alliance*, for an in-depth account of the CIA's involvement in drug trafficking in South Central Los Angeles in the late 1980s in order to finance the Contras.

---

[102] Webb on CIA Report: (http://ciadrugs.homestead.com/files/cia-ig-rpt-gw.html)

The Iran-Contra (Cover Up) Hearings, 1987

During the summer of 1987, Congress investigated the illegal selling of arms to Iran by the Reagan Administration. The principal focus was on Oliver North. Other players involved in the scandal were Elliot Abrams, Robert MacFarlane, Richard Secord, and John Poindexter. Most of the convictions were overturned or vacated, and Oliver North went on to run for the Senate in Virginia in the 1990s.

During the hearings, the issue of the CIA and drug trafficking and the involvement of North, Abrams, MacFarlane, Secord, or Poindexter in it was never discussed in open sessions. Each time the discussion approached the issue, a recess was called, and the investigation went into a private, closed-door session.

**The entire Inspector General's Report of 1998 may be read online at: http://ciadrugs.homestead.com/files/index-cia-ig-rpt.html Clearly, in the report, the agency admits involvement in drug trafficking during the Contra war.

Mediation by other Central American governments under Costa Rican leadership led finally to a ceasefire agreement of March 23, 1988, which with additional agreements (February, August 1989) provided for the Contras' disarmament and re-integration into Nicaraguan society and politics, and internationally-monitored elections which were subsequently won (February 25, 1990) by an anti-Sandinista centre-right coalition.[103]

The question naturally arises, is the United States government still participating in drug trafficking? The evidence overwhelmingly suggests that it is. I refer the reader to the website of Michael Ruppert at www.fromthewilderness.com and Ruppert's book *Crossing The Rubicon: The Decline Of The American Empire At The End Of The Age Of Oil* for further information not only on U.S. government involvement in drug trafficking but also how drug money is laundered through the U.S. stock market. In addition, at Ruppert's website, his video lecture "Wall Street's War For Drug Money", a one-hour lecture at the University of Southern California in 2000, is available for purchase.

The Savings And Loan Scandal

Early in the Reagan Administration which began in January, 1981, savings and loan institutions (S&L's) were de-regulated, putting them on an equal footing with commercial banks. Before that time, unlike commercial banks, S&L's could not pay higher market rates for deposits, borrow money from the Federal Reserve, make commercial loans, or issue credit cards. With de-regulation, they could now do all of these.

One of the best researchers on the savings and loan scandal is author and researcher, Peter Brewton. Below is the introduction to his book, *The Mafia, CIA, and George Bush* [Sr.]

Brewton's book documents the intricate connections between organized crime, the intelligence community, and the Bush and other prominent Texas families in the savings and loan scandal. The book is currently out of print, but the introduction can be accessed on the internet where links to other relevant facts can also be obtained.

---

[103] "The Contra War" (http://en.wikipedia.org/wiki/Contra_War)

INTRODUCTION
The Mafia, CIA and George Bush
Pete Brewton
(New York: S.P.I. Books, 1992)
http://www.freerepublic.com/forum/a389b6a173e33.htm

Something very significant happened during our country's savings-and-loan crisis, the greatest financial disaster since the Great Depression. It happened quietly, secretly, without any fanfare and attention. It happened before our very eyes, yet we knew it not.

What we all missed was the massive transfer of wealth from the American taxpayers to a select group of extremely rich, powerful people. What these people had in common—unknown to the American public—were their symbiotic relationships to the Mafia and the CIA, and to the two most prominent, powerful politicians from Texas, President George Bush and Senator Lloyd Bentsen.

This small cabal of businessmen realized that the S&Ls were going the way of the dinosaurs. They recognized that S&Ls couldn't survive under rapid inflation and high interest rates. So they decided to exploit the situation for their own purposes, with help from, and rewards for, the Mafia, the CIA and their favorite politicians. They probably figured that the insulation and protection these powerful institutions and individuals conferred upon them, in addition to all the endemic protections with the financial, judicial, political and journalistic systems, made them invulnerable. They were probably right.

For unlike Watergate and Iran-Contra, this was a bipartisan scandal. There was no opposition party to push for an independent investigation. In fact, the same group of wealthy, powerful businessmen, centered in Houston, that encircle Republicans like George Bush and James A. Baker III, also encircle Democrats like Jim Wright and Lloyd Bentsen.

This information enables one to view the 1988 elections, in which not one cross word was ever spoken about the savings-and-loan debacle, in a whole new perspective. It was not merely a fortuitous coincidence that both Bush, the Republican nominee for President, and Bentsen, the Democratic nominee for Vice President, were part of, and beholden to, the same group of Houston businessmen. Even if the Democrats lost that presidential election, as they did, Bentsen could still win re-election to his Senate seat under the so-called "LBJ rule." The Houston boys, as usual, had their bets covered.

(If the Democrats had won in 1988, this book would be entitled "The Mafia, the CIA and Lloyd Bentsen," for Bentsen and Bush are two interchangeable peas in a pod. They have many friends, business associates and campaign donors in common. The story of the most important one they share begins this book.)

But Bush won in 1988, and one of the reasons he did was his ability to keep the S&L scandal out of the political debate. He was assisted in this by none other than Bentsen, as we shall see. They both had much to hid, Bush in particular. Not only were many of the President-to-be's friends involved—along with two of his sons—but Bush himself, as Vice President, had personally intervened in the federal regulation of a dirty Florida savings and loan that was being looted by people with connections to the Mafia and the CIA. This S&L ultimately failed, costing taxpayers nearly $700 million.

The S&L scandal is the vehicle for telling the story about these leading American politicians and businessmen. But the relationships between these individuals and how they control and manipulate public and private institutions is the bigger story. Unless we know who these people are and understand how they operate, we can all look forward to more S&L-type debacles to come.

The S&L scandal was almost the perfect crime. The layers of protection and insulation between what the public discovered was going on at the savings and loans and what actually happened with the money were so many and so thick that the crimes and theft would never be completely figured out. And even if the truth were ultimately unearthed, there were additional layers between that revelation and the bringing of those responsible to the bar of justice and recovering the money.

The first and foremost layer of protection is the difficulty in tracking the money from the savings and loans to its ultimate destination. That is why almost no FBI agent, federal prosecutor, S&L regulator, congressional committee or journalist has been able to track the money. Yet where the money went is really the only thing that matters. The rest of the "facts" that, typically, got investigated, prosecuted and written about were mostly smoke and mirrors, set up to shield who really got the hundreds of billions of dollars that taxpayers must pay back and to hide what the money was used for.[1]

---

[1]—A notable exception is the book *Inside Job*, by Stephen Pizzo, Mary Fricker and Paul Muolo, which nailed down the fact that the savings-and-loan debacle was caused primarily by fraud.

The five years that went into this book represent my efforts to peel back all the layers of insulation and protection to get to the real culprits. I have organized this book with that process in mind, to help the reader understand a complicated and confusing subject.

In general, the bulk of the money lost in the S&L crisis that American citizens must now pay for went to the owners of the property and assets that the more notorious borrowers purchased with money from S&Ls run by equally infamous owners. This seems to be obvious, yet it somehow got lost in all the hype and hysteria. While Congress, the Justice Department and the press concentrated on the flamboyant borrowers and managers of the S&Ls, the big recipients of the money—the wealthy, powerful landowners and property owners—crept off quietly with their profits.

In the second half of this book, a number of examples will be detailed to show how this happened, and who got the money. For example, one later chapter deals with a $200 million, 21,000-acre land transaction in Florida in which much of the borrowed S&L money went to a paper company owned by the Du Pont empire, one of the oldest, richest, most powerful bastions of wealth in this country.

We know this because many of the lending documents were pursued by a lone, shrewd, tenacious federal regulator named Kenneth Cureton. However, the unraveling of this transaction was a rare and exceptional event. But even it could not be called a complete victory. The Department of Justice's International Division, the government body through which subpoenas to offshore banks must pass, inexplicably became a brick wall for Cureton's efforts to obtain records on the Isle of Jersey in the English Channel, where a big chunk of the money went—possibly to buy weapons for Iraq.

Since so many of the crucial documents in this scandal are not available, we are left with the second-best avenue of investigation: finding out who the original property owners were and everything we can about them, and then doing the same thing for the S&L proprietors and borrowers. The bulk of this book consists of that enterprise.

The evidence uncovered is clear, convincing, and compelling: Members and associates of the Mafia and the United States Central Intelligence Agency were key participants in our nation's savings-and-loan debacle, and some of the richest, most powerful people in the country did business with these participants and profited from the S&L crisis.

That members of the Mafia and the CIA, two organizations that operate in secrecy and whose members take sacred oaths—one supposedly dedicated to national security, the other simply to their organizations' security—may have been working together is not unprecedented in this country. But that fact doesn't make their cooperation any less outrageous.

It is well known that members of the Mafia and the CIA conspired to try to assassinate Fidel Castro. There are other, less substantiated, although credible, allegations regarding the two groups' involvement together in drug smuggling and money laundering in Southeast Asia, Australia and the Caribbean.[2]

---

[2]—*The Politics of Heroin in Southeast Asia*, by Alfred W. McCoy (New York: Harper and Row, 1972); *The Crimes of Patriots*, by Jonathan Kwimy (New York: Norton, 1987); and *In Banks We Trust*, by Penny Lernoux (Penguin Books, 1986).

There are also some curious, ominous connections between members of these groups and JFK-assassination figures Lee Harvey Oswald and Jack Ruby.

Drawing a straight, direct line from the CIA operatives discussed in this book to the top officials of the CIA and on to the President is extremely difficult because of the way the CIA works. Most of the characters in this book are not the card-carrying bureaucrats and bean counters at CIA headquarters in Langley, Virginia. They are what are called CIA "assets," who can be someone who turns over an occasional piece of information to the CIA, without even knowing it is for the CIA, all the way up to someone who is continually working for the CIA in covert operations.

A similar and, likewise, important cog in CIA operations is what is known as a cutout. A cutout is a front man or middle man set up to protect the identities of the primary participants. Like an asset, a cutout may or may not know for whom he is working and the actual purpose of his work. (The Mafia also makes use of such cutouts, except they call them "mustaches" or "beards.")

The CIA uses assets and cutouts to maintain one of its prime directives: plausible deniability, or, in other words, "Don't get caught embarrassing the President." (The CIA is the intelligence-gathering and covert-action arm of the President. Perhaps that is the definition journalists should always refer to, rather than just throwing the general term "CIA" around as if it were some sort of independently run mythical loose cannon.) So…if an asset or cutout is caught breaking the law, the CIA can deny that its operative was working for it at that particular time.

This leads to one difference between the Mafia and the CIA, particularly in this story. Once it is established that members and associates of the Mafia are involved in a failed savings and loan, that is usually enough to establish, prima facie, the involvement of the Mafia. Members and associates of the Mafia don't do such things without the knowledge, permission and the sharing of the spoils, with their superiors.

The destruction of the savings and loan industry in Texas, and in some other parts of the country, worked basically like an organized-crime bustout or burnout. This is a mob scam in which a failing company is taken over, built up on credit, then drained of all its assets and purposely put into bankruptcy, leaving the creditors holding the bag.

In the case of savings and loans, the credit was federally insured deposits injected by money brokers, like mob associate Mario Renda, and the creditors are the taxpayers. The front men, the cutouts and the "mustaches," like Don Dixon, Tyrell Barker, Ed McBirney, Jarrett Woods, Roy Dailey, Mike Adkinson and Robert Corson, are left to take the blame. But don't feel sorry for them, for they have usually skimmed enough off to offshore bank accounts to make it well worth a couple of years in jail, keeping their mouths shut.

However, because of the CIA's doctrine of plausible deniability, the involvement of a CIA asset in a failed savings and loan does not make a prima facie case for the involvement of the CIA. In fact, I know of no independent test a journalist can conduct to determine whether the involvement of a CIA asset means the CIA has sanctioned it or whether the asset is just freelancing for his own gain. Both possibilities would look the same to an outside observer.

The only way to tell would be if the CIA admitted its involvement or if there were unassailable, documented evidence showing S&L money going from an asset to a CIA operation. This is attainable only by subpoena, if at all. Even in such a case the CIA might deny that it knew the asset was pumping money into the operation or that it knew money came from an S&L. But if the CIA admitted that, it would be admitting that it is both incompetent and stupid.

In the case of the failed S&Ls, the CIA has categorically denied its involvement. The CIA did admit to a congressional committee that it had a relationship to five individuals connected to failed savings and loans, and that it had also done business with four savings and loans that later failed. But the spy agency claimed that its business with these S&Ls was legitimate. however, there are several cases in which there are clear indications that S&L money went directly to operations that the CIA took part in, even if it didn't overtly control them—for example, the cases of Iran-Contra and of weapons shipments to the Middle East.

But one thing we can say, categorically: The CIA either knew or didn't know what its operatives were doing at S&Ls. If it knew, why didn't it stop them or alert the proper authorities? If it didn't know, how effective an intelligence agency could it really be?

Finally, a word about the circumstantial evidence in this book. Circumstantial evidence must necessarily be used because of the secretive nature of the CIA and the unavailability of S&L documents. The evidence appears many times in *this* way: A failed S&L was owned and controlled by people who have done business with Mafia associates and CIA operatives; many of the borrowers were Mafia and CIA associates; many of the original property owners have done business with Mafia and CIA operatives and some of the money disappears in foreign accounts controlled by Mafia and CIA associates.

What does such evidence prove? Based on my research and knowledge of the CIA, I believe it makes it more likely than not that someone in the CIA hierarchy knew about and approved, if not instigated, the S&L actions of its operatives. In any event, journalists are not in the proof business, we are in the information business. Proof is for mathematicians and courts of law, and even in those arenas, there are great disputes about what constitutes proof. The readers of this book, and the American public, can evaluate the evidence and information in this book for themselves and decide whether it should be acted upon or ignored.

There is nothing intrinsically wrong with circumstantial evidence. In our country's courts of law, fortunes and lives can be won or lost, fairly and squarely, on the basis of circumstantial evidence. Juries, as well as readers of this book, may infer facts and conclusions from circumstantial evidence. I have attempted to set out all the facts and circumstantial evidence that I know. In some cases the meanings are clear and conclusions can be drawn. In other places the going gets a little tough, because there is not enough data and evidence to draw meanings and reach conclusions. For this I apologize; i wish I had found more information.

In all, I have tried to follow the injunction of our forefathers, who in proclaiming their thesis in the Declaration of Independence, stated: "…let facts be submitted to a candid world."

Admittedly, it is easy to be cynical and discouraged about the situation presented in the following chapters. One question I am constantly asked is: "What can we, the American people, do about this?" There are no quick-and-easy solutions or panaceas. However, like our founding fathers, we should have faith in the liberating power of knowledge and information. If we know how and why something happened, and who benefitted by it, then we will know the right thing to do.

In summary, the savings and loan scandal involved the lending of money for home loans to people at high interest rates, and the savings and loan industry knew that many of these individuals could not repay the loans. However, the loans were guaranteed by the federal government through the Federal Housing Administration. Therefore, if the loans were not repaid, the savings and loan entity could collect reimbursement from the FHA plus interest, which at that time, was quite high. Thus, certain S&L inside players made a great deal of money, and when the repossessed houses were auctioned off, these same players bought them back for pennies on the dollar, making money at both ends of the transaction.

The total loss of money to U.S. taxpayers was $1.4 trillion.

Two very famous players were Neil Bush of Silverado Savings and Loan in Colorado and Jeb Bush in Florida. Neither were ever charged or even investigated.[104] Both are brothers of President George W. Bush, Jr.

---

[104] The Bush Family and The S&L Scandal: (http://www.rationalrevolution.net/war/bush_family_and_the_s.htm)

23

HUD, HAMILTON, AND SOLARI: THE STORY OF CATHERINE AUSTIN FITTS

In 1989, George Herbert Walker Bush, former Vice-President of Ronald Reagan, was inaugurated as President of the United States. That same year, Catherine Austin Fitts resigned her position as investment banker with Dillon Read on Wall St. in order to become Assistant Secretary of Housing and Urban Development (HUD) for the Bush Administration.

The HUD Awakening

Very soon, Fitts discovered what she first believed was massive financial mismanagement and waste at HUD. She brought these issues to the attention of her immediate supervisor, Jack Kemp, a former Congressman who would later become Chairman of the National Commission on Economic Growth and Tax Reform, working closely with Senator Bob Dole and House Speaker Newt Gingrich. What most troubled Fitts was the lack of place-based financing in HUD which meant that financial accounting for local HUD offices was non-existent because all financial accounting for the agency was centralized out of Washington. Consequently, it was virtually impossible to ascertain the status of HUD's finances at the local level. Kemp's response to Fitts' concerns was at first indifferent, then hostile, then ultimately quite candid as he boasted that he and other administrators at HUD were not there to worry about place-based financing, but rather, to get government contracts for their friends in the private sector.

The Birth of Hamilton Securities, The Death Of The Rule of Law

Fitts left HUD in 1990 and went on to start a private company, Hamilton Securities which secured a government contract to serve HUD under the Clinton Adminstration. One facet of Hamilton was its development of a software program called Community Wizard which had the capacity to monitor public and private sector finances in any place in the U.S. and sort out which funds were being appropriated and spent legitimately and which were not.

In the course of researching specific communities, Fitts began focusing on South Central Los Angeles and the repossession of HUD homes in that area as a result of the massive influx of crack/cocaine during the Iran-Contra era. What she discovered was that thousands of homes had dramatically depreciated in value, forcing homeowners to walk away whereupon the houses were repossessed and bought back by HUD for pennies on the dollar. When Fitts began to disclose her findings, her offices were broken into and HUD froze all assets that were owed to her for work Hamilton had performed for the agency. The Department of Justice (DOJ) began litigation against Hamilton on charges which have since been dismissed as completely false. Currently, DOJ is in the process of settling with Fitts, the current assets owed to her now in excess of $3 million.

Fitts Fights For Government Financial Accountability

During her term at HUD, Catherine Austin Fitts was instrumental in the passage of the HUD Reform Act of 1989. The purpose of the Reform Act was to help prevent waste, fraud, abuse, and political favoritism in HUD programs. Among other things, it required HUD to publish in the Federal Register information on funding availability, selection criteria, and funding decisions. It also required that most housing program funds be distributed geographically on the basis of a needs-based fair-share formula and awarded to localities through open competition.[105]

In 1990 the Chief Financial Officer's Act was passed which required that "Not later than March 31 of 1992 and each year thereafter, the head of each executive agency identified in section 901(b) of this title shall prepare and submit to the Director of the Office of Management and Budget a financial statement."[106]

This act required that all federal agencies produce an annual audited financial statement.

Subsequently, the Government Management Reform Act of 1994 stated that: "Not later than March 31 of 1998 and each year thereafter, the Secretary of the Treasury, in coordination with the Director of the Office of Management and Budget, shall

1. Annually prepare and submit to the President and the Congress an audited financial statement for the preceding fiscal year, covering all accounts and associated activities of the executive branch of the United States Government. The financial statement shall reflect the overall financial position, including assets and liabilities, and results of operations of the executive branch of the United States Government, and shall be prepared in accordance with the form and content requirements set forth by the Director of the Office of Management and Budget.
2. The Comptroller General of the United States shall audit the financial statement required by this section."[107]

To date, virtually no audited financial statements have been produced by U.S. Government agencies. As Catherine Austin Fitts states:

> To date, Congress has not held them accountable, but instead has given them even more money and guarantees without making it conditional on minimal standards of financial performance and compliance with the law.[108]

As a result of the insights gained while working at HUD and Hamilton, Fitts is now actively exposing government corruption and assisting individuals and communities in transforming how the money works at the local level. In 2000, one of Hamilton's creditors wrote on behalf of Hamilton to Senator Kit Bond, then Chairman of the HUD Senate Appropriations Subcommittee. Fitts met with Bond's chief of staff who expressed concern to her that HUD was being run as a "criminal enterprise."[109]

---

[105] HUD Reform Act, (http://www.gao.gov/new.items/rc00091.pdf)
[106] Chief Financial Officer's Act, (http://wwwoirm.nih.gov/itmra/cfoact.html)
[107] Government Management Reform Act, 1994, (http://govinfo.library.unt.edu/npr/library/misc/s2170.html)
[108] Catherine Austin Fitts, Frequently Asked Questions: (http://www.whereisthemoney.org)
[109] Solari Litigation: (http://www.solari.com/media/summary.html)

> NATURALLY, THE QUESTIONS MUST BE ASKED: ARE OTHER GOVERNMENT AGENCIES BEING RUN AS "CRIMINAL ENTERPRISES"? MOREOVER, IS THE ENTIRE UNITED STATES GOVERNMENT BEING RUN AS A CRIMINAL ENTERPRISE?

** Catherine Austin Fitts' series, *Dillion Read And Company, Inc. And The Aristocracy Of Prison Profits* is a must-read account of her discoveries of corruption and fraud at the highest levels of the United States government. It may be read at: www.dunwalke.com. Equally crucial reading is Fitts' website, www.solari.com which includes numerous articles documenting trillions of dollars currently "missing" from a number of federal government agencies, including $59 billion from HUD and $2.3 trillion from the Department of Defence.

Summarizing the importance of financial transparency at both the national and local levels, Catherine Austin Fitts states:

> The supremacy of the central banking-warfare investment model that has ruled our planet for the last 500 years depends on being able to combine the high margin profits of organized crime with the low cost of capital and liquidity that comes with governmental authority and popular faith in the rule of law. Our economy depends on insiders having their cake and eating it too and subsidizing a free lunch by stealing from someone else. This works well when the general population shares in some of the subsidy, grows complacent and does not see the "real deal" on how the system works. However, liquidity and governmental authority will erode if the general population becomes aware of how things really work. As this happens, they begin to understand the power of innovative technology and re-engineering of government resources to create greater abundance both for themselves and other people. As this happens, they lose faith in the myth that the current system is fundamentally legitimate. This jeopardizes the financial markets that depend on fraudulent collateral and practices to continue to work. It also jeopardizes the wealth and power of the people who are winning with financial fraud.
>
> In short, transparency blows the game and cannot be allowed. No expense will be spared to insure that the insiders—at the expense of the outsiders—control financial data. As Nicholas Negroponte, founding Chairman of the MIT Media Lab, once said, "In a digital age, data about money is worth more than money"...[110]

---

[110] Dillon Read & Co., Inc. And The Aristocracy Of Prison Profits, (http://www.dunwalke.com)

24

THE "IRAQGATE" SCANDAL

In September, 1980, the nation of Iraq invaded Iran. Although the Iran-Iraq war of 1980-1988 was fundamentally a war over dominance of the Persian Gulf region, the roots of the war go back many centuries. There has always been rivalry between various kingdoms of Mesopotamia (modern Iraq) and the Persian Empire (Iran).

U.S. involvement with Iraq dates back to the 1950s Cold War era when Iraq was perceived by the United States as a key buffer against the Soviet Union. At that time, as we have seen, the CIA was involved in many Middle Eastern nations besides Iran as discussed above. According to the U.S. State Department, Saddam Hussein was then in his early twenties and became part of a U.S. plot to eliminate the left-leaning dictator, Qasim.

By the 1980s, Saddam had become dictator of Iraq, and the CIA's relationship with him intensified. During the 1980s, Iran was the enemy of the United States subsequent to the Iran Hostage Crisis discussed above. During the administration of George Bush, Sr., the United States backed and financed Saddam's military campaigns against Iran, but did so secretly.

A 1993 *Harpers Magazine* series of stories on "Iraqgate" asks: "Why would U.S. officials conceal such a scheme? The U.S. government's stake in the case turns out to be considerable: about $2 billion of the money loaned to Iraq was backed by guarantees from the Department of Agriculture, and now must be paid by American taxpayers. In October, 1989, when it began to be suspected that Iraq was diverting the agricultural credits to arms purchases, the Department of Agriculture considered withdrawing the loan guarantees. The consideration was dropped on the advice of the State Department—after a persuasive phone call from then Secretary of State James Baker to then Secretary of Agriculture Clayton Yeutter. The State Department's strategy—to use the loan guarantees as a carrot to keep Iraq in line—proved misguided when, on August 2, 1990, Saddam Hussein invaded Kuwait."[111]

In an investigative report, "Crude Vision: How Oil Interests Obscured US Government Focus on Chemical Weapons Use by Saddam Hussein," Jim Vallette, Steve Kretzmann, and Daphne Wysham trace an intense effort by Reagan officials in the mid-1980s to win Hussein's approval for a $2-billion oil pipeline to be built by the Bechtel Corporation, running from the Euphrates oilfields in southern Iraq westward to Jordan and the Gulf of Aqaba.[112]

---

[111] Iraqgate: The Making Of An Investigation, (http://www.24hourscholar.com/p/articles/mi_m1111/is_n1712_v286/ai_13309316)

[112] "Crude Vision: How Oil Interests Obscured U.S. Government Focus On Chemical Weapons Use By Saddam Hussein," (http://www.globalpolicy.org/security/oil/2003/03crudevision.pdf)

Commenting on the report, journalist Dave Lindorff in his 2003 *Counterpunch* article "Yes, It's About Oil", discloses the intimate links between the Bechtel Corporation, Bechtel executives, and U.S. policy towards Iraq. Lindorff also shows that some key players in the push for America's 2003 war against Iraq, including Rumsfeld, Vice-President Dick Cheney, and other former Reagan Administration officials may have been intimately involved in issues relating to Iraqi oil as far back as the early 1980s.[113]

Texas Congressman, Henry Gonzalez, attempted to investigate the Iraqgate affair, and in a speech on the floor of the House documented how pre-Gulf War policy helped Iraq develop weapons of mass destruction. However, President George Bush, Sr. enlisted the CIA to derail Gonzalez' investigation. Subsequently, Gonzalez was investigated for receiving allegedly secret intelligence information which supposedly would harm U.S. national security interests.

An excellent Iraqgate website at http://www.apfn.org/apfn/iraqgate.htm provides details of the scandal with links to relevant documents.

Understanding the above history of U.S. involvement with Iraq provides necessary background for understanding the Persian Gulf War and the current occupation of Iraq by U.S. forces. Moreover, this history will become more meaningful when the concept of Peak Oil is explained below.

---

[113] "Yes, It's About Oil", Dave Lindorff, April 9, 2003 (http://www.counterpunch.org/lindorff04092003.html)

25

THE END OF THE COLD WAR AND THE LOOTING OF THE SOVIET UNION

In 1989, the Soviet Union and the European Communist bloc collapsed. While Ronald Reagan and the Republicans attribute the collapse to their foreign policy and maintaining a strong military, the most devastating evisceration of the Soviet Union occurred economically from within. The U.S. banking and financial industries were instrumental in looting Russia financially even before the time of the fall of Communism. A fascinating and detailed account of this is "The Rape of Russia", by Anne Williamson and can be read at:
http://www.russians.org/williamson_testimony.htm

An additional article by Williamson, "Why Russia Is Not A Market For U.S. Goods" (http://www.freerepublic.com/forum/a3924de1174e0.htm) explains America's fascination with China and abandonment of Russia as a trading partner. The article sheds light on U.S.-Chinese relations during the 1990s and into the twenty-first century.

Harkening back to Fletcher Prouty's assertion that since the advent of nuclear weapons, super-power warfare must now be conducted with Low Intensity Conflict, we will increasingly witness throughout the remainder of the twentieth century and into the twenty-first, America's use of economic warfare, with or without the use of conventional weapons, to subdue other nations and achieve the economic goals of the United States.

Students frequently ask, "What can we do?" regarding the state of our communities and our world at this time in history. One answer I am giving more frequently is simply, "Get to know how the money works." Over the years, I have found that many people who know that we desperately need social and economic justice (activists) are quite illiterate regarding economics. At the same time, many people who do know a lot about economics (such as accountants) are uninformed about the social and economic injustice in their community and in their world. Therefore, I have written the following article with the intention of helping to join those two worlds:

Opinion
Activists and accountants: Absolute allies
By Carolyn Baker
Online Journal Contributing Writer

> *As soon as we see money as an object in its own right, it can be stolen, hoarded, and worshipped. Greed depends on money being experienced as a noun—a thing that sits in stacks and stays there. But prosperity consciousness, in its best form, is seeing money as a verb—an energy that flows continuously from hand to hand in support of transformation, growth, and love.*—Julia Mossbridge, author of *Money Is Love*

March 26, 2005—Traditionally, activists and business management majors have seen each other as enemies. MBA graduates perceive activists as financially clueless retreads from the '60s—philosophy majors clad in tie-dye—while activists typically shun accountants with their buttoned-down, Brooks Brothers, Rotary Club, 401K banter.

To mention the word "investment" among activists is to invite accusations of "materialistic" or "elitist" at best and "money-grubbing" at worst. Among the management set, one dare not refer to "quality of life issues" or "environmentally hazardous criteria" lest one risk epithets of "naiveté" or "bleeding-heart liberal."

While such binary worldviews may have been applicable in the mid-twentieth century, they are no longer useful in a world where both progressives and small business entrepreneurs are being equally defrauded by federal, state, and local governments and where both have something profoundly constructive to offer the other.

In order to inform my argument, I refer to three basic terms: *sustainability*, *investment*, and *equity*.

Sustainability refers to duration—creating sustainable (lasting) communities or infrastructures which meet the needs of both the current and future generations.

Investment means the time, money, or energy that one puts forth in pursuit of a particular outcome, be it financial, political, social, environmental, physical, or spiritual. Hence, everyone is an investor, not just individuals who own mutual funds or trade on the New York Stock Exchange.

Equity refers to the wealth one has after obligations have been met. This wealth can be financial, but more often, it is living equity—natural resources, human resources, and knowledge or life experience.

Accountants often overlook living equity in favor of financial equity, whereas activists often overlook financial equity in favor of quality of life issues. Each may accuse the other of erroneously valuing one kind of equity over the other, but the pivotal criteria must always be *sustainability*. What happens when the accountant blithely devotes herself to a life of balance sheets, numbers, and audited financial statements while minimizing living equity, and when the activist passionately commits himself to struggling for social and political justice while discounting the fact that his personal and community prosperity could (or perhaps even should) be enhanced by way of, not in spite of, his altruism? When one disparages financial equity or living equity, one devalues both and implements an unsustainable path. The accuracy of this assertion is more obvious when we examine the common enemies and common alliances of both the activist and the accountant.

First, I want to emphasize that when I speak of the world of finance and commerce of which the accountant is symbolic, I am not referring to transnational corporations and their centralized, globalized systems, but rather to the local merchant, entrepreneur, or investor. The worlds of both the account and the activist are compromised, exploited, and drained by the predatory economics of centralization and globalization. Both suffer the consequences of a predatory economic system that relies on drug trafficking, debt, and in the very near future, the reinstatement of the draft in order to maintain its rapacious supremacy.

Unless they are accurately informed, both the anti-war marcher and the marketing major are casualties of the public relations-dominated American media in which journalists serve as stenographers for the current administration or lose their jobs—or their lives. Both are generally dependent on fossil fuels and public utilities for transportation, home heating, cooling, and water supply. Both must purchase food and necessities either from locally-owned businesses or from superstores where "always low prices" are available because corporate monstrosities have purchased land by using the local pension funds to which they have access and provide no health care benefits—a liability which both the accountant and activist must pay for with state and local taxes.

Likewise, the activist and the accountant have spectacular potential for forming common alliances. Both benefit from banking with local banks, which keep funds in the local community rather than funneling them to other geographical areas. Moreover, if the activist and the accountant are willing to focus on the electoral politics of their own community and avoid being dazzled by rigged national elections, they can join hands to create financial transparency among their local politicians. I do not wish to imply that state and local elections are never rigged, but since corporations and fraudulently-managed federal and local government agencies have the capacity to steal local resources, one neighborhood at a time, it behooves every American to watch his/her back by keeping the focus local. In fact, the activist, as much as the accountant, has an obligation, indeed, a duty, to demand audited financial statements from state and local governments annually.

Both the activist and the accountant risk having their local resources and infrastructure privatized (piratized) as federal and state treasuries are intentionally bankrupted in order to "justify" privatization. Both can invest small or large amounts of money in local land, water, and alternative energy concerns and unite on the common ground of protecting these resources from corporate resource looters.

One does not have to be an accountant to understand the "if-you-don't-have-it-don't-spend-it" maxim. All citizens can commit to freeing themselves as soon as possible from credit card debt and living a cash-based lifestyle.

When the accountant understands that war increases the deficit and destroys living equity, he/she can join with the activist in shining the light on military conscription and slick recruiters who have been rigorously trained to seduce minorities and poor whites into the infinitely-expanding U.S. Oil Protection Service, otherwise known as the United States military establishment.

Both the accountant and the activist must understand that the increasingly precarious, illusive, and treacherous American economy has been and continues to be propped up by $500 billion to $1 trillion that are annually laundered through the US banking system and public trading and that the majority of these funds are acquired in the neighborhoods of the activist and the accountant as illegal drugs are sold to their children.

Investment is an economic term that superbly describes how the activist and the accountant can join worlds and forces to create healthier lives and communities. While the accountant may be preoccupied with financial investments, the activist, along with all humans must make choices moment-to-moment, about things in which he wishes to invest his time, energy, and, yes, money. While the accountant needs to be educated in how a poor quality of life in her own home or community is a poor financial investment, the activist needs to understand that banking with large branch banks, many of whom are documented money launderers, investing time and money in corporate media, and maintaining a limited concept of "investment," as if it only applied to people who own publicly-traded stocks, is draining him—emotionally, spiritually, physically, and financially.

When the accountant, marketing major, or local entrepreneur begins to focus on greed rather than sustainability, transnational corporations and all their attendant evils are born. Unequivocally and without exception, quality of life deteriorates. Contrary to the worldview of many activists, individuals engaged in commercial endeavors and seeking to generate income and invest in successful opportunities are not inherently amoral, clueless human beings. Unquestionably clueless, in my opinion, is the activist who prides him/herself in "the righteousness of austerity" and who has never considered that prosperity can be created for oneself and one's community by way of creating sustainability. Not all of our ancestors walked 10 miles a day, barefoot in the snow to attend school, living on $500 a year. Some actually created abundance for their families and communities by improving the quality of life.

Economic injustice only results when people sacrifice sustainability for profit. Economic means that people create prosperity, not at the expense of others, but for and with others in order to enhance the overall abundance of everyone.

Former Wall Street investment banker and undersecretary of Housing and Urban Development (and activist), Catherine Austin Fitts, speaks of the Popsicle Index which is the percentage of people in a neighborhood who believe that a child can leave their home and go to the nearest place to get a Popsicle and come back safely. In other words, the Popsicle Index is a quality of life index. The Dow Jones Index, as we know, is supposedly a guide to the financial well being of the American economy. Fifty years ago, the Popsicle Index was very high, and the Dow very low. Today, the Dow fluctuates above and below 10,000 while the Popsicle Index appears to diminish daily. The truly visionary activist comprehends that these two very different indices need each other, and that the ultimate challenge of the current century is not to destroy the Dow, but to work with the accountant to make the Dow and the Popsicle best friends.

The polarization of the world's of the activist and the accountant is very useful for the predators, but it is not useful for individuals who wish to create a better world for themselves, their families, and their communities. When, not if, the American economy collapses, a great leveling is inevitable. Perhaps when gas is $10 per gallon and weeds are growing in what used to be the parking lot of Wal-Mart because the U.S. is at war with China, our current binary perceptions of *sustainability, equity,* and *investment* will not serve us and will jeopardize our very survival. At that point, the activist and the accountant will appreciate the extent to which they need each other's perspective, expertise, and values.

Money, (as well as time and energy), as Julia Mossbridge writes, *is* a verb, but these resources cannot flow freely for growth, transformation, and love, unless we expand its meaning in our lives and open our eyes to discover that our assumed enemies may be automatic allies.

The views expressed herein are the writers' own and do not necessarily reflect those of Online Journal.

Email editor@onlinejournal.com
Copyright © 1998-2005 Online Journal™. All rights reserved.

***Catherine Austin Fitts maintains an extensive website at www.solari.com where many articles by and about her can be read, as well as audio interviews and seminars which can be downloaded or purchased. I highly recommend the use of one or more of her audio CD's in class.

**As mentioned above, Fitts' extensive personal insider account of U.S. government corruption and violations of the rule of law, can be read at www.dunwalke.com where footnotes and photos are available. I am now integrating much of her material from the series, *Dillion Read And Company, Inc. And The Aristocracy Of Prison Profits* into my courses.

2 6

CLINTON, MENA, NAFTA, AND THE DISSOLUTION OF THE TWO-PARTY SYSTEM

The Harriman Connection

It is very important to understand that as the politician's politician, William Jefferson Clinton never had any interest in maintaining a position distinct from the Republican Party except in name only. We have only to consider his connection with the ruling elite to understand this.

As we have considered earlier in the course, the ties between the Bush and Harriman families are very old. Traditionally, the Harrimans were Democrats; nevertheless, their associations with the Bush family were deeply convoluted. Recall the above comments on E.H. Harriman, one of the famous Robber Barons, railroad tycoon, and proponent of eugenics.

It is common knowledge that Clinton was introduced to the Washington, D.C. political scene by Pamela Harriman, wife of then deceased Averell Harriman, son of E.H. Harriman, and that Mrs. Harriman contributed handsomely to Clinton's election in 1991. In addition, a major contributor to the Clinton campaign was chairman of the nation's largest investment bank off Wall Street, Jackson Stephens, a very close friend of George Bush, Sr. Stephens was well-known for playing both sides of the fence. In 1991, he contributed $100,000 to Bush's presidential campaign, and his wife was the Arkansas co-chair for the George Bush, Sr. presidential campaign[114] Stephens and his wife hosted the Inaugural party for Bush in 1989; additionally, Stephens brokered a deal that allowed the Union Bank of Switzerland to rescue the failing Harken Energy project of George Bush, Jr. in 1987, obtaining a $25 million cash infusion for Harken from Union Bank which rarely invested in small companies.[115]

Clinton had been cozy, but became increasingly so during his administration, with the banking, financial, and corporate worlds—more so than any Democratic president in modern history. Moreover, twenty-first century, mainstream media

---

[114] What's Up In Jakarta?, (http://www.freerepublic.com/forum/a388e6d515014.htm)
[115] Jackson Stephens, The Father Of WTI [Waste Technologies Incorporated], (http://www.freerepublic.com/forum/a37d95a0809ce.htm)

is now replete with photos and stories of Bill Clinton and the Bush family drowning in gushing conviviality as if their political differences never existed. Off camera, they never have.

The Arkansas Cocaine Connection

In 1972, during Richard Nixon's term, the CIA established an airstrip outside a small town not far from Little Rock—Mena, Arkansas. Its most active period was during the Contra wars of the 1980s when massive quantities of cocaine were being landed there to help finance the Contras. While Mena was not the only place where drugs were being landed in the United States at that time, it was a very significant location because it could not have existed or been maintained without the knowledge and cooperation of then Governor Clinton.

"The Crimes of Mena", by Sally Denton and Roger Morris, was a story about the Mena airstrip and a particular CIA pilot, Barry Seal, who often flew drugs into Mena and who had ties with Clinton. This story was going to be published in the *New York Times* in 1995 but was cancelled by the *Times* at the last minute. It was then published in *Penthouse Magazine* in July, 1995.[116] I strongly recommend it for information regarding the Clinton-Mena connection.

Making Corporations Sovereign Around The World

In 1993 the North American Free Trade Agreement (NAFTA) was championed by the Clinton Administration as a triumph for the American economy and as a mechanism for creating more jobs within the United States and throughout the third world. In reality, however, NAFTA has resulted in a massive trade deficit for the United States, the loss of millions of American jobs, and economic devastation in Latin America.

George Herbert Walker Bush was the first government official to publicly use the term **New World Order** which is synonymous with globalization and its international control of people, profits, and the environment.[117]

Below is an article by David Morris documenting the failure of NAFTA

NAFTA: A Clear Failure of Public Policy,
by David Morris, March 11, 1996

A little over two years ago the North American Free Trade Agreement (NAFTA) went into effect. NAFTA constituted an unprecedented experiment in social and economic policy. Never before had two nations with such unequal economies been so forcibly integrated.

NAFTA opponents forecast disaster. The public believed them. Public opinion polls in both the U.S. and Mexico consistently found a majority of people opposed to NAFTA. Arrayed against the people were the White House, the leaders of the Republican Party, big business, virtually all economists and 99 percent of the country's media.

President Clinton won a come from behind victory. "I courted some of these congressmen longer than I courted my wife," boasted Treasury Secretary Lloyd M. Bentsen. Yet it was not Democrats that put NAFTA over the top. Sixty percent of the Democrats in the House voted against Clinton. It was Newt Gingrich's aggressive intervention and Republican votes that made the difference.

Two years later the results are in. The people were right. The pundits, the business leaders, the economists, the White House and Newt Gingrich were wrong.

---

[116] "The Crimes Of Mena", (http://www.serendipity.li/cia/c_o_mena.html)
[117] State Of The Union Speech, January 29, 1991 (http://www.infoplease.com/ipa/A0900156.html)

Let's look at the facts. Bill Clinton promised 200,000 additional jobs because of NAFTA "by 1995 alone". In fact, over 200,000 jobs have been lost because of NAFTA. The Global Trade Watch project of Public Citizen reviewed the job creation promises of dozens of corporations and found that every one of those companies has already "laid off workers because of NAFTA". In 1993 a vice president of Mattel Corporation assured a Congressional subcommittee that NAFTA would have "a very positive effect" on that company's 2,000 U.S. employees. Two years later 520 workers in Mattel's Medina, New York plant were laid off. Why? Because of "increased company imports from Mexico" that resulted from NAFTA.

In 1993 NAFTA supporters used sophisticated statistical models to prove that the $1.7 billion U.S. trade surplus with Mexico in that year would soar to $9 billion by the end of 1995. In fact, in 1995 the U.S. had a trade deficit with Mexico of about $15 billion.

In 1993 Clinton administration officials promised that NAFTA would slow the move of U.S. factories to the Mexican side of the border. In fact, Mexico approved 300 new such branch plants in 1995, an 80 percent increase over 1994.

The impact of NAFTA north of the border has been disturbing. The impact of NAFTA south of the border has been shocking. A million people have lost their jobs. Mexico's Secretary of Social Development estimates that 2.5 million Mexicans have crossed the line from poverty to extreme poverty. They cannot satisfy their daily nutritional needs. The daily wage in Mexican factories in the border area has dropped by 50 percent since 1993. Whole industries such as truck making and construction have virtually shut down.

The social fabric of Mexico is disintegrating, a phenomenon law professor Raphael Ruiz calls "the pulverization of a society". The crime rate in Mexico City, which had declined from 1930 through the 1970s, has doubled since 1990 and increased by about 50 percent in 1995. Mexico has had more cholera cases the past year than in the whole century. Drug trafficking is rampant.

NAFTA, far from being forgotten, may become a major issue in this year's election. Pat Buchanan's surprising victories in the early primaries reminded us of the widespread anger about NAFTA. Clinton is already taking actions to avoid possible flash points in an election year. In December, citing safety concerns, Clinton announced an indefinite delay in the NAFTA provision that would have allowed Mexican trucks to travel freely in southwestern border states, including politically important California and Texas. U.S. trade representative Mickey Kantor recently tightened restrictions on Mexico tomato imports to placate tomato growers in Florida, another key election state.

In the House, Marcie Kaptur (D-Ohio) has introduced HR 2651, a bill that would force the U.S. to withdraw from NAFTA if targets in such areas as job growth, public health and the trade deficit are not met. Fifteen Republicans have signed on as co-sponsors. The bill may have 80 supporters in the House.

The NAFTA experiment has failed. The evidence is overwhelming. The challenge now before us is how to withdraw from NAFTA and design a new relationship between Mexico, Canada and the United States. A relationship that can truly strengthen communities and economies on both sides of the border.

David Morris is Vice-President for the Institute For Self-Reliance at: http://www.ilsr.org/columns/

Bill Clinton's chummy relationship with transnational corporations and the financial and banking systems place him in the company of what Catherine Austin Fitts calls "the real economic hit men."[118] Fitts continues, "The fact that the Bushes and the Clintons are on the same team-and have been since their alleged Iran-Contra partnership in an airport operation in Mena, Arkansas involving the transshipment of cocaine destined for the streets of America-is not something that most Americans have yet incorporated into our political equation.[119]

The Clinton Impeachment That Wasn't

In 1998, the U.S. House of Representatives voted to impeach Bill Clinton for lying regarding an inappropriate relationship he had with a White House intern, Monica Lewinsky. However, when the Senate was faced on February 11, 1999 with the impeachment question, it refused to give the house the majority of votes it wanted for impeachment, and Clinton was essentially acquitted and allowed to serve out the rest of his term in office.

I have chosen to include the aforementioned events in relation to the Clinton presidency in order to introduce a little-known reality related to the Clinton impeachment. That reality was introduced in 1999 by investigative journalist, Mike Ruppert, former Los Angeles Police Narcotics investigator and publisher of the *From The Wilderness* newsletter (http://www.fromthewilderness.com).

In 1999 Ruppert published an article in his newsletter entitled "How The CIA-Drug Controversy Was Clinton's Hole Card In The Impeachment"[120] In that article, and in greater detail in a video presentation entitled "The CIA And Drugs: The Confession And The Impeachment", Ruppert explains the significance of the CIA Inspector General's Report of 1998 on the findings regarding the CIA's involvement in drug trafficking during the Iran-Contra scandal—and its connection with the impeachment of President Clinton. The report was published in two volumes. On March 16, 1998, the House Permanent Select Committee held a hearing on Volume I of the Inspector General's report which examined allegations of CIA drug ties during the Contra era, focusing specifically on Southern California connections.[121] The contents of the report firmly coroborrated the information reported by Gary Webb in his *San Jose Mercury* series and his subsequent book, *Dark Alliance*.

The report was clearly a major embarrassment to the Central Intelligence Agency, and Los Angeles Congresswoman, Maxine Waters, incensed by the report's contents, demanded a full investigation of the allegations against the CIA. However, on March 16, Waters and Congress had only Volume I of the report. Volume II was, at that point, expected to be unveiled in May,1998. Until that time, it would remain classified. However, the report ultimately remained classified for another seven months.

The summer of 1998 passed with the nation obsessed with further revelations regarding President Clinton's relationship with Monica Lewinsky, culminating in a confession by Clinton and a nationally televised testimony by the President. Events were coming to a head, and the topic of impeachment was on everyone's mind.

Impeachment proceedings were conducted in October,1998. Extraordinarily significant, according to Mike Ruppert, is the fact that Volume II of the Inspector General's Report was released one hour after the House of Representatives voted for impeachment. Ruppert contends that this was a clear message sent by President Clinton to the Republican majority in the House and those in the Senate who sought to impeach him, that if they succeeded in doing so, he would adopt a scorched-earth policy by revealing, via the released report and the investigations that he would invariably implement as a result of it, the extent of involvement of Republicans in drug trafficking during the Contra era.

---

[118] "Will The Real Economic Hit Men Please Stand Up?"
(http://www.fromthewilderness.com/free/ww3/010705_economic_hitmen.shtml)
[119] *Ibid.*
[120] How The CIA-Drug Controversy Was Clinton's Hole Card In The Impeachment"
(http://www.fromthewilderness.com/free/politics/alert_Jan.1.html)
[121] "Surprise Hearings In House Intelligence Committee Backfire on CIA", by Mike Ruppert, *From The Wilderness*, March, 1998 (http://www.fromthewilderness.com/free/ciadrugs/news1.html).

Clinton was almost certainly guilty of illegal fundraising while president, illegal transfers of technology to China, and involvement in the narcotics trafficking that took place in Mena, Arkansas before he became president. However, the timing of the release of Volume II of the Inspector General's Report on October 8, 1998, one hour after the House voted for impeachment, was an unmistakeable signal that if the Congress took him down, he would take a swarm of politicians with him in a veritable political bloodbath.

With the Clinton presidency, we see the virtual erasure of distinctions between the two parties. In fact, some would argue that Clinton succeeded in destroying the liberal wing of the Democratic Party, if not the party itself. What is clear from Clinton's connections with the Bush family, both before and after his presidency, is that he and the Bush dynasty[122], as historian Kevin Phillips has named it, are two sides of the same coin of political expediency.

Enron

Although the Enron scandal did not take place during the Clinton Administration, it exemplifies the sovereignty of corporations in the early-twenty-first century. Enron was an energy trading, natural gas, and electric utilities company based in Houston, Texas, employing some 21,000 people until it went bankrupt in 2001.

Fraudulent accounting techniques allowed it to be listed as the seventh-largest company in the United States. As a result of massive fraud, Enron became the largest corporate failure in history and became symbolic of institutionalized corporate greed and white-collar crime. While only a handful of Enron executives were convicted of any crime, thousand of Enron employees lost their pensions and life savings in the debacle. Enron's CEO, Ken Lay, was convicted in 2006 of all counts of fraud and conspiracy against him, but died just two months later. Enron's now bankrupt and fradulent accounting firm, Arthur Andersen, which served Enron by "cooking" its books and destroying Enron documents, had its conviction for document destruction overturned by the Supreme Court in May, 2005.

Furthermore, a close personal relationship between Ken Lay and President George W. Bush raises further suspicions about why prosecution of Lay took so long to bring about. In addition, Enron was the largest contributor to the Bush campaign of 2000.

**I highly recommend the viewing of the documentary *Enron: The Smartest Guys In The Room* for a deeply insightful, breath-taking examination of the Enron debacle.

While George W. Bush insists that he and Ken Lay did not know each other personally, numerous personal notes between the two are readily available for reading at: http://www.thesmokinggun.com/archive/0708042lay1.html. One of these may be read below:

---

[122] Phillips, Kevin, *American Dynasty: Aristocracy, Fortune, And The Politics of Deceit In The House Of Bush*, New York: Viking, 2003.

```
RECEIVED
NOV 16 1998 0363
ROUTE TO: GWB
CC TO: Bill Brown
utilities/Gen
```

Kenneth L. Lay
Chairman and
Chief Executive Officer

Enron Corp.
P.O. Box 1188
Houston, TX 77251-1188
(713) 853-6773
Fax (713) 853-5313

November 11, 1998

The Honorable George W. Bush,
Governor
State Capitol, Room 2S.1
Austin, Texas 78711

GOVERNOR HAS SEEN

Dear George:

Congratulations! What a fabulous victory for you and the entire Republican slate in Texas. While the rest of the Republican ticket was clearly strong in its own merit, your leadership and ability no doubt had much to do with the unprecedented sweep of statewide offices that the Republican party enjoyed.

Your focus on opportunity and responsibility was one that I believe resonates around the country as well as in Texas. As one of those opportunities, we hope that you will again actively support efforts to pass a bill restructuring the electric industry in Texas. By passing such a bill, your administration would be responsible for providing the citizens of Texas with the equivalent of a tax cut which could immediately amount to $1.7 billion or more annually.

Texans spent $17.7 billion on electricity in 1997. Even a 10 percent reduction in bills will yield significant savings for Texas homeowners and businesses. Historically, deregulated industries see savings in the 20 to 40 percent ranges over time. There is no reason to expect this industry to behave differently.

Enron has worked during the last year with interested parties from all segments of the electric industry in Texas - legislators, IOUs, coops, munis, consumer advocates, large customers, small customers, marketers, and independent power producers, to name a few - to forge a better understanding of the others' positions and to try to craft a consensus bill. While we have not yet achieved consensus on all topics, it appears that all parties accept that there will be legislation bringing retail competition to Texas passed by the 76th Legislature. Enron looks forward to participating in these deliberations and has confidence that Texas can pass the best piece of restructuring legislation yet in the United States. Please have your team let me know what Enron can do to be helpful in not only passing electricity restructuring legislation but also in pursuing the rest of your legislative agenda.

Again, Linda and I extend our heartiest congratulations! We look forward to working with you and your team as you bring Texas into the 21st century.

Sincerely,

Ken

George—
Linda and I are
incredibly proud of
you and Laura

Natural gas. Electricity. Endless possibilities.

27

PREPARING FOR WORLD DOMINATION

The Global Chessboard And Its Players

In 1997, Zbigniew Brzezinski published his little-known book, *The Grand Chessboard*. Brzezinski had been Secretary of State under President Jimmy Carter and a member of Ronald Reagan's National Security Commission, as well as a member of Reagan's Foreign Intelligence Advisory. He is currently a Professor of American Foreign Policy at Johns Hopkins University.

In *The Grand Chessboard*, Brzezinski lays out a strategy for world domination by the United States in conquest of natural resources, principally oil—a campaign that involves the United States in Eurasia, essentially Central Asia. The key to controlling the oil-rich republics of Central Asia is to control Uzbekistan where the U.S. Army and the Central Intelligence Agency have been active for several years.

Brzezinski writes that "...the Eurasian Balkans are infinitely more important as a potential economic prize: an enormous concentration of natural gas and oil reserves is located in the region, in addition to important minerals, including gold."[123]

"Without sustained and directed American involvement," Brzezinski writes, "before long the forces of global disorder could come to dominate the world scene."[124] Therefore, "That puts a premium on maneuver and manipulation in order to prevent the emergence of a hostile coalition that could eventually seek to challenge America's primacy."[125] Without reservation, Brzezinski speaks adamantly about the necessity for United States hegemony (domination) of global politics: "Hence, America is not only the first, as well as the only, truly global superpower, but it is also likely to be the very last."[126]

Brzezinski calls for world domination by the United States, not specifically military domination, but certainly economic and political. Although, he speaks of the ambivalence historically of the American people toward "the external projection of American power." He then explains what we have discussed above—that ultimately, the American people

---

[123] Brzezinski, Zbigniew, *The Grand Chessboard*, New York: Basic Books, 1997, p. 124.
[124] *Ibid.*, p. 194
[125] Ibid., p. 198
[126] *Ibid.*, p. 209

supported the United States' involvement in World War II "because of the shock effect of the Japanese attack on Pearl Harbor."[127]

In other words, Brezezinski's frightening book outlines a blueprint for geostrategic hegemony (world domination) by the United States and notes that the American people would not support such an endeavor without the shock effect of the proportion of Pearl Harbor.

Project For A New American Century (PNAC)

In the same year as the publication of *The Grand Chessboard*, 1997, a group of ultra-conservatives, very far on the right side of the political spectrum and very friendly with and financially invested in the weapons and energy industries, formed an organization called The Project For A New American Century (PNAC).

Their position was that although the United States had won the Cold War, its defenses were not as strong as they should be, and these individuals composed a lengthy document called "Rebuilding America's Defenses"[128] later published in 2000 in which they outlined what should be done to strengthen America's military might. What was needed, they concluded, was massive rebuilding and upgrading of U.S. weapons, rebuilding old and constructing new military bases all over the world, and an all-out effort to recast America's defense establishment—in other words, a colossal revamping of the military industrial complex.

The extent to which the neo-conservative think tank, PNAC, collaborated with Brzezinski, a member of the Democratic Party[129], is unknown. However, the similarities in perspective and content between "Rebuilding America's Defenses" and *The Grand Chessboard* are glaring, including the following statement regarding the prodigious upgrading of America's defense systems:

> Further, the process of transformation, even if it brings revolutionary change, is likely to be a long one, absent some catastrophic and catalyzing event—like a new Pearl Harbor.[130]

One unique aspect of the PNAC document not emphasized by Brzezinski is the authors' insistence on the strategic supremacy of Israel in America's global hegemony. While they seek economic, political, and military domination of the world by the United States, they are also committed to defending Israel at all costs and supplanting the strategic influence in the Middle East of any and all other nations with the primacy of Israel. This may be more easily understood after reading the article below, "Who Are The Neocons?", by Richard Heinberg.

An in-depth analysis of the PNAC document by Bette Stockbauer (2003) may be read at: (http://www.antiwar.com/orig/stockbauer1.html). Summarizing the document, Stockbauer writes:

> "Many PNAC members now hold key positions in the White House, Defense and State Departments, among them Dick Cheney, Donald Rumsfeld, Paul Wolfowitz, Richard Perle, Elliot Abrams, Lewis Libby, and John Bolton, along with others in lesser positions. William Kristol, writer for the conservative magazine, the *Weekly Standard*, is chairman of the group.

---

[127] *Ibid.*, pp. 24-25.
[128] "Rebuilding America's Defenses", 2000, (http://www.newamericancentury.org/RebuildingAmericasDefenses.pdf)
[129] Wikipedia Online Encyclopedia, (en.wikipedia.org/wiki/Zbigniew_Brzezinski)
[130] *Ibid.*, p.52.

Some of these men have been advocating for a strong military posture since the ending of cold war hostilities with the Soviet Union. Wishing to capitalize on the fact that the US had emerged as the world's pre-eminent superpower, they have lobbied for increases in military spending in order to establish what they call a Pax Americana that will reap the rewards of complete military and commercial control of land, sea, air, space, and cyberspace. This, they said, would be accomplished by the waging of "multiple simultaneous large-scale wars" and one of their first orders of business was always the removal of Saddam Hussein, thereby giving the US a toehold in the oil-rich Middle East.

During the Clinton presidency, when the Republicans were out of power, this militaristic wing in American politics became highly organized and efficient. They formed the PNAC in 1997 And published "RAD" in September 2000. Determined to have their world empire, they offered an eerie prophecy on page 52 of that document about how it might be accomplished, "Further, the process of transformation, even if it brings revolutionary change, is likely to be a long one, absent some catastrophic and catalyzing event—like a new Pearl Harbor." Their dream of a catalyzing event could not have been better actualized than in the events of 9/11."[131]

During the Clinton Presidency, the Project sent a letter to the President requesting that before he leave office, he do whatever was necessary to eliminate Saddam Hussein. Clinton declined their request.

An excellent resource for understanding PNAC and its history entitled "PNAC 101", can be read at: http://www.911truth.org/article.php?story=20050518223342591

Even as Clinton refused to eliminate Saddam, PNAC continued to lay the groundwork for electing a candidate who would be friendly with their agenda. Given the deep and lifelong involvement of George Herbert Walker Bush in the weapons and intelligence domains, they did not have to look far. As a result, their careers would flourish in a George W. Bush, Jr. administration.

> ABOVE ALL, IT IS MONUMENTALLY IMPORTANT TO UNDERSTAND THAT THE "REBUILDING AMERICA'S DEFENSES", AS WELL AS *THE GRAND CHESSBOARD*, ARE BLUEPRINTS FOR EMPIRE. THEY ARE NOT MERE OPINIONS ON FOREIGN POLICY BUT POLITICAL "MAPS" FOR ECONOMIC, POLITICAL, AND MILITARY DOMINATION OF THE PLANET BY THE UNITED STATES.

Additionally important to understand is that many PNAC members, including now Vice-President Dick Cheney, are very closely tied with the oil and natural gas industries.

The individual members of PNAC are often referred to as *neo-conservatives*.
The following article by Richard Heinberg, author of *The Party's Over* and *Power Down*, explains the neo-conservative political position its philosophical roots:

---

[131] Bette Stockbauer on Project For A New American Century, (http://www.antiwar.com/orig/stockbauer1.html)

WHO ARE THE NEOCONS?

By Richard Heinberg, From *POWER DOWN*, 2004

Neoconservatism is the intellectual offspring of Leo Strauss (1899-1973), a Jewish scholar who fled Hitler's Germany and taught political science at the University of Chicago. According to Shadia Drury in *LeoStrauss and the American Right,* (Griffin, 1999), Strauss advocated an essentially Machiavellian approach to governance.

He believed that:

- A leader must perpetually deceive those being ruled. Those who lead are accountable to no overarching system of morals, only to the right of the superior to rule the inferior.
- Religion is the force that binds society together, and is therefore the tool by which the ruler can manipulate the masses (any religion will do).
- Secularism in society is to be supressed, because it leads to critical thinking and dissent.
- A political system can be stable only if it is united against an external threat, and that if no real threat exists, one should be manufactured.

Drury writes that:

"In Strauss's view, the trouble with liberal society is that it dispenses with noble lies and pious frauds. It tries to found society on secular rational foundations."

Among Strauss's students was Paul Wolfowitz, one of the lead. Leading hawks in the US Defense Department, who urged the invasion of Iraq; second-generation students include Newt Gingrich, Clarence Thomas, Irving Kristol, William Bennett, John Ashcroft, and Michael Ledeen. Ledeen, a fellow at the American Enterprise Institute and author of Machiavelli on Modern Leadership: Why Machiavelli's Iron Rulesare as Timely and Important Today as Five Centuries Ago (1999), is a policy advisor (via Karl Rove) to the Bush administration. His fascination with Machiavelli seems to be deep and abiding, and appears to be shared by his fellow neocons. "In order to achieve the most noble accomplishments," writes Ledeen, "the leader may have to 'enter into evil.' This is the chilling insight that has made Machiavelli so feared, admired, and challenging. It is why we are drawn to him still."

Machiavelli's books, *The Prince* and *The Discourses,* constituted manuals on amassing political power; they have inspired kings and tyrants, including Mussolini, Hitler, Lenin, and Stalin. The leader, according to Machiavelli, must pretend to do good even as he is actually doing the opposite. "Everybody sees what you appear to be, few feel what you are, and those few will not dare to oppose themselves to the many, who have the majest of the state to defend them. Let a prince therefore aim at conquering and maintaining the state, and the means will always be judged honourable and praised by everyone, for the vulgar is always taken by appearances." It is to Machiavelli that we owe the dictum that "the end justifies the means."

In her essay "The Despoiling of America," investigative reporter Katherine Yurica explains how a dominant faction of the Christian Right, which she calls **dominionism,** has found common cause with the neoconservative movement. Dominionism arose in the 1970s as a politicized religious reaction to communism and secular humanism. One of its foremost spokespersons, Pat Robertson (religious broadcaster, former presidential candidate, and founder of the Christian Coalition), has for decades patiently and relentlessly put forward the view to his millions of daily television viewers that God intends His followers to rule the world on His behalf. Yurica describes dominionism as a Machiavellian perversion of Christianity. For the Christian right, neoconservatives like George W. Bush and John Ashcroft can do no wrong, because they are among God's elect. All is fair in the holy war against atheists, secular humanists, Muslims, and liberals.

"THIS IS TOTAL WAR. WE ARE FIGHTING A VARIETY OF ENEMIES. THERE ARE LOTS OF THEM OUT THERE. ALL THIS TALK ABOUT FIRST WE ARE GOING TO DO AFGHANISTAN, THEN WE WILL DO IRAQ, THIS IS ENTIRELY THE WRONG WAY TO GO ABOUT IT. IF WE JUST LET OUR VISION OF THE WORLD GO FORTH, AND WE EMBRACE IT ENTIRELY AND WE DON'T TRY TO PIECE TOGETHER CLEVER DIPLOMACY, BUT JUST WAGE A TOTAL WAR, OUR CHILDREN WILL SING GREAT SONGS ABOUT US YEARS FROM NOW."

RICHARD PERLE, Former Chairman, Bush Administration's Defense Policy Board and nicknamed by Beltway insiders as "the Prince of Darkness." He was also a key member of the Project For The New American Century and was instrumental in the authorship of "Rebuilding America's Defenses."

C. The Year 2000 Election

In November, 2000, former Clinton Administration Vice-President, Al Gore, ran on the Democratic ticket against George W. Bush, Jr., the Republican Governor of Texas. This unprecedented election ultimately was decided in favor of George Bush by the Supreme Court of the United States. The election was unprecedented because Bush won by only 537 popular votes, and in the election of 2000, electronic voting machines were used in the United States on a wider scale than ever before.

The state which proved pivotal in giving Bush the majority of electoral votes was Florida where Bush's brother, Jeb, was governor, and where the Secretary Of State, Katherine Harris, the person officially in charge of the voting process, was also the chair person of Bush's election campaign in Florida. In December, 2000, in a 5-4 decision, the Supreme Court ruled Bush the winner of the election.

When one reads the research of BBC Investigative Journalist, Greg Palast (www.gregpalast.com) and electronic voting machine researcher, Bev Harris, author of *Black Box Voting*, which can be downloaded at www.blackboxvoting.org, it is clear that a plethora of unanswered questions and suspicious events surrounded the 2000 election.

Some glaring irregularites were:

- The scrubbing of some 90,000 names from the list of eligible voters in Florida, the majority of whom were Democratic voters
- The questionable ties of the Bush Administration with Choice Point, the corporation that gave the Florida Secretary of State the list of scrubbed names.
- The questionable ties of the Bush Administration to electronic voting machine manufacturers such as: Diebold, Elections Systems and Software (ES&S), and Sequoia

**I further suggest two documentaries on the 2000 election:

- "Counting On Democracy" (http://www.globalvision.org/sample/sample.html)
- "Unprecedented: The 2000 Election" (http://www.unprecedented.org/#purchaseinformation)

George Bush, Jr. came into office in January, 2001 without a mandate, having lost the popular vote and having been "selected" by the Supreme Court. Shortly before the September 11, 2001 attacks, Bush's popularity was at an all-time low, and he had spent more time on vacation in the first nine months of his presidency than any other Chief Executive in American history.

28

THE NEW PEARL HARBOR

On a warm, sunny autumn morning, September 11, 2001, four commercial airliners were hijacked from Boston's Logan Airport. Allegedly, two were flown into the World Trade Center Towers in New York City. Another, allegedly flew into the Pentagon in Washington, D.C., and yet another allegedly crashed in an open field in Pennsylvania. The word "allegedly" is used here carefully and intentionally.

Everything contained in this abstract has been written with the intention of revealing and pondering profoundly significant aspects of American history which are almost never addressed in traditional U.S. history textbooks. We are now entering a chapter in American history which, like the assassination of John F. Kennedy, was a tipping point, a watershed, a point-of-no-return in all that transpired from 1865 to the present moment.

This abstract will not attempt to prove that the September 11 attacks were orchestrated, financed, and abetted by the United States government, but that indeed is my position, based on the overwhelmingly compelling evidence gathered and analyzed by diligent, devoted, and discriminating researchers such as:

- Investigative journalist, Mike Ruppert in his scholarly and superbly-documented book *Crossing The Rubicon: The Decline Of The American Empire At The End Of The Age of Oil*
- The dispassionate critical thinker, David Ray Griffin, Professor Emeritus of Religion and Philosophy at Claremont College in his two monumental works, *The New Pearl Harbor*, and *The 9-11 Commission Report: Ommissions And Distortions*
- Nafeez Ahmed, British author and human rights activist, in his impeccably-researched book, *War On Freedom: Why And How America Was Attacked On September 11, 2001*
- Paul Thompson, a computer analyst, who has given us the most thorough timeline of the events of September 11 in his book *Terror Timeline*.
- Voluminous research done by Michel Chossudovsky, Professor of Economics, University of Ottawa, mentioned above, and host of the website, Global Research at www.globalresearch.ca.

In addition, it is crucial to view Mike Ruppert's video lecture "The Truth And Lies Of 9-11", recorded at Portland State University, November 28, 2001 (www.fromthewilderness.com) ; Barry Zwicker's documentary "The Great Conspiracy" (www.septembereleventh.org), and the documentary "Hijacking Catastrophe: 9/11, Fear, And The Selling Of The American Empire" (www.hijackingcatastrophe.org).

When we become aware of and analyze the events which transpired in America from 1865 to the present moment, both those which are "acceptable" to include in traditional textbooks and those that are not, the likelihood of the United States government orchestrating a treasonous and savage event such as September 11, 2001, is hardly implausible. What is imperative to understand, however, is that the significance of September 11 cannot be grasped nor its perpetrators brought to justice without being informed by the historical context in which it occurred.

One of the principle arguments of disbelief raised by those who are unwilling to consider that the September 11 attacks were orchestrated by the U.S. government is the claim that "our government would not harm its own citizens." In this abstract, we have witnessed numerous occasions on which the United States government was willing to harm or considered harming its own citizens. For example, we have seen the suspicious circumstances under which the Spanish-American War commenced in "response" to the bombing of the battleship, *Maine*, in Havana Harbor. We have discussed the Tuskegee Experiments, conducted by the U.S. government in which hundreds of African American males were left untreated for syphillis, resulting in their deaths and those of their loved one; we have considered the extraordinarily well-documented evidence for U.S. government foreknowledge regarding the Pearl Harbor attacks; we have witnessed the protracted, lethal use of plutonium against American citizens, and we have seen the documents from Operation Northwoods which considered perpetrating the deaths of American citizens in order to blame those casualties on Cuba in order to justify an attack on that country.

Attacking Afghanistan

In early October, 2001, the United States attacked Afghanistan, ostensibly because it had concluded that the 9-11 attacks were carried out by Osama Bin Laden and his terrorist organization, Al Qaeda. Bin Laden's base of operations was known to be in Afghanistan, and the objective of the invasion of the country was to destroy Al Qaeda and capture Bin Laden. The operation was called "Enduring Freedom", and its targets were not only Al Qaeda and Bin Laden, but the Taliban government in Afghanistan which supported and protected Al Qaeda.

It should be understood that some months earlier, the U.S. had threatened to attack Afghanistan because of the Taliban's lack of cooperation in establishing a strategic oil pipeline across the country which petroleum giant, Unocal, had been trying to secure for years. As we have seen in our discussion above of *The Grand Chessboard* by Brzezinski, it was believed that a large quantity of oil in the Caspian Basin was waiting to be claimed by the United States. Subsequent to the U.S. occupation of Afghanistan, it was determined that much less oil than was thought existed in that region.

Essentially, attacking Afghanistan was about oil; however, the amount of oil in the region was greatly overestimated. At the completion of this abstract, 2006, Osama Bin Laden remains at large. U.S. forces remain in Afghanistan, but for the Bush Administration, the ultimate prize lay not in Afghanistan, but in the Middle East, specifically in Iraq.

The Creation Of Osama Bin Laden

As mentioned above in our discussion of the invasion of Afghanistan in the late seventies by the Soviet Union, the United States financed and created Osama Bin Laden. That is to say that Bin Laden has been an intelligence asset of the United States. An intelligence asset is someone or some organization that can be manipulated by a more powerful entity for political, economic, or military purposes. In a 1998 interview with Zbigniew Brzezinski, he defended the economic and military support of militant Islamic fundamentalism by the United States to combat the Soviet invasion of Afghanistan. When asked if he regretted the support given to Islamic fundamentalism at that time, he replied:

> **Interviewer**: When the Soviets justified their intervention by asserting that they intended to fight against a secret involvement of the United States in Afghanistan, people didn't believe them. However, there was a basis of truth. You don't regret anything today?

Brzezinski: Regret what? That secret operation was an excellent idea. It had the effect of drawing the Russians into the Afghan trap and you want me to regret it? The day that the Soviets officially crossed the border, I wrote to President Carter. We now have the opportunity of giving to the USSR its Vietnam war. Indeed, for almost 10 years, Moscow had to carry on a war unsupportable by the government, a conflict that brought about the demoralization and finally the breakup of the Soviet empire.

Interviewer: And neither do you regret having supported the Islamic fundamentalism, having given arms and advice to future terrorists?

Brzezinski: What is most important to the history of the world? The Taliban or the collapse of the Soviet empire? Some stirred-up Moslems or the liberation of Central Europe and the end of the cold war?

Interviewer: Some stirred-up Moslems? But it has been said and repeated Islamic fundamentalism represents a world menace today.

Brzezinski: Nonsense! It is said that the West had a global policy in regard to Islam. That is stupid. There isn't a global Islam. Look at Islam in a rational manner and without demagoguery or emotion. It is the leading religion of the world with 1.5 billion followers. But what is there in common among Saudi Arabian fundamentalism, moderate Morocco, Pakistan militarism, Egyptian pro-Western or Central Asian secularism? Nothing more than what unites the Christian countries.[132]

In 1978, the Cold War was drawing to a close, but American policy makers, still employing the Domino Theory, perceived all other nations, organizations, leaders, or entities as secondary threats in relation to the Soviet Union. As Brzezinski states, the United States drew the Soviet Union into invading Afghanistan, and therefore, into a conflict that would become "its Vietnam." As discussed above in the article by Anne Williamson, the Russian economy was looted into extinction by the United States, and the conflict in Afghanistan with U.S.-trained and financed Mujahadeen forces under the leadership of Osama Bin Laden, served to further deplete the resources of the Soviet Union.

How Governments Use Terrorism To Control Citizens

Two excellent studies of state sponsorship of terrorism by western governments, targeting their own populations are *NATO's Secret Armies, Operation Gladio and Terrorism in Western Europe* by Daniele Ganser (http://www.globalresearch.ca/articles/GAN412A.html) and *The War On Truth, 9/11, Disinformation, and the Anatomy of Terrorism* by Nafeez Mosaddeq Ahmed (www.mediamonitors.net). Both researchers document a 40-year history of the United States and other governments fostering and manipulating terrorism for their own political, social, and economic ends. The de-stablization of other governments and the sowing of chaos serve as pretexts for military intervention which sustain the military industrial complex indefinitely. Additional documentation of the use of terrorism by western governments can be obtained at Chossudovsky's website: www.globalresearch.ca.

Shock and Awe: The Invasion and Occupation of Iraq

As discussed above, one of the principal objectives of the Project For The New American Century (PNAC) was the removal from power of Saddam Hussein. Immediately following the September 11 attacks, the United States publicly declared a war on terror, both domestically and internationally. Key U.S. government officials, such as Vice-President Dick Cheney, emphasized that it would be a long and protracted war, and that as Cheney stated to the press shortly after 9-11, "it may never end, at least not in our lifetime." He also stated that "The American way of life is not negotiable."

---

[132] Interview With Zbigniew Brzezinski, Le Nouvel Observateur, Paris, 15-21 January 1998,

It is not the intention of this abstract to trace the timeline of events from the 9-11 attacks, to the invasion of Afghanistan, to the invasion of Iraq in March, 2003. What is more important, in my opinion, than tracing the chronology of events, is the compelling evidence for the reality that the Bush Administration took office in January, 2001 with a specific agenda for the removal of Saddam Hussein and the occupation of Iraq.

The following pieces of evidence substantiate the theory of a pre-September 11 agenda for attacking Iraq:

- **The Neil Mackay, *Sunday Herald* story of September 15, 2002:**
  (http://www.sundayherald.com/print27735)

- <u>O'Neill: Bush planned Iraq invasion before 9/11</u>[133]
  (http://www.cnn.com/2004/ALLPOLITICS/01/10/oneill.bush/index.html)

- **Remarks by Condoleeza Rice and Donald Rumsfeld:**

Secretary of State, Condoleeza Rice, testified at the 9-11 Commission Hearings in 2004 in relation to the tragic events of September 11 that:

> Now, we have an opportunity and an obligation to move forward together. Bold and comprehensive changes are sometimes only possible in the wake of catastrophic events…Just as World War II led to a fundamental reorganization of our national defense structure, so has September 11th made possible sweeping changes in the ways we protect our homeland.[134]

In addition, Secretary of Defense, Donald Rumsfeld, on the afternoon of September 11 at the National Military Command Center instructed U.S. military commanders to:

> Go massive. Sweep it all up. Things related and not. Judge whether good enough hit S.H."—meaning Saddam Hussein—at same time. Not only UBL—the initials used to identify Osama bin Laden.[135]

- **The New Pentagon Papers**
  http://www.salon.com/opinion/feature/2004/03/10/osp_moveon/

Another incriminating piece of evidence is the Downing Street Memo of July 23, 2002:

---

[133] (http://www.cnn.com/2004/ALLPOLITICS/01/10/oneill.bush/index.html)
[134] Condoleeza Rice Testimony Before 9-11 Commission: (http://www.nationalreview.com/document/rice200404080930.asp)
[135] CBS News: "Plans For Iraq Attack Began On 9-11"
(http://www.cbsnews.com/stories/2002/09/04/september11/main520830.shtml)

THE DOWNING STREET MEMO

Facts of the Memo: July 23, 2002	Words of the Bush Administration leading up to War in Iraq
"There was a perceptible shift in attitude. **Military action** was now seen as **inevitable**. Bush wanted to remove Saddam, through **military action**, justified by the conjunction of **terrorism and WMD**" "No decisions had been taken, but he thought the most likely timing in US minds for **military action** to begin was January, with the timeline beginning **30 days before the US Congressional elections.**"	"**We are doing everything we can to avoid war in Iraq.** But if Saddam Hussein does not disarm peacefully, he will be disarmed by force" —George W. Bush, <u>Radio Address Mar. 8, 2003</u> "I think that that presumes there's some kind of **imminent war plan**. As I said, I have **no timetable**." —George W. Bush, <u>Aug. 10, 2002 while golfing</u>
"But the **intelligence and facts** were being **fixed around the policy**" [and don't forget...] "Bush wanted to remove Saddam, through **military action**, justified by the conjunction of **terrorism and WMD**"	"Intelligence gathered by this and other governments leaves **no doubt that the Iraq regime continues to possess and conceal some of the most lethal weapons ever devised.** This regime has already used weapons of mass destruction against Iraq's neighbors and against Iraq's people. The regime has a history of reckless aggression in the Middle East. It has a deep hatred of America and our friends. And it has **aided, trained and harbored terrorists, including operatives of al Qaeda.**" —George W. Bush, <u>Mar. 17, 2003, the War begins</u> "I want you to keep focused on what you are doing here," [...] **"This war came to us, not the other way around."** —Condoleeza Rice <u>May 15, 2005, Rice makes surprise visit to Iraq</u>

"The NSC had **no patience with the UN route**, and no enthusiasm for publishing material on the Iraqi regime's record"	"America tried to **work with the United Nations** to address this threat because we wanted to resolve the issue peacefully. We **believe in the mission of the United Nations.**" —George W. Bush, <u>Mar. 17, 2003, the War begins</u>
"There was **little discussion** in Washington of the **aftermath after military action.**"	**1,600+ US Soldiers Dead** **12,300+ Wounded** Iraqi casualties 20,000 – ????? —CBC, <u>May 9, 2005, Casualties in Iraq War</u> "**Any military presence, should it be necessary, will be temporary** and intended to promote security and elimination of weapons of mass destruction; the delivery of humanitarian aid; and the conditions for the reconstruction of Iraq." —The White House, <u>March 16, 2003, Statement of the Atlantic Summit</u> "Liberated people don't misbehave." —Former Secretary of Army Thomas White, (on Cheney and Rumsfeld's post-war views leading up to the war) <u>July 7, 2003, War in Iraq's aftermath hits troops hard</u>
"**Bush had made up his mind to take military action**, even if the timing was not yet decided. But **the case was thin**. Saddam was not threatening his neighbours, and **his WMD capability was less than that of Libya, North Korea or Iran.**"	"**The President has made no decisions** about what the next step will be. Clearly, we will continue to talk to the United Nations about the inspection process." —Ari Fleischer, <u>Oct. 10, 2002, White House press briefing</u> "This is about disarmament and this is a final opportunity for Saddam Hussein to disarm. If he chooses not to do so peacefully, then the United

States is prepared to act, with our friends, to do so by force. And we will do so forcefully and swiftly and decisively, as the President has outlined. **But the President continues to seek a peaceful resolution. War is a last resort."**

—Scott McClellan,
<u>Nov. 12, 2002, White House
press briefing</u>

"The larger point is, and the fundamental question is, **did Saddam Hussein have a weapons program? And the answer is, absolutely.** And we gave him a chance to allow the inspectors in, and he wouldn't let them in. **And, therefore, after a reasonable request, we decided to remove him from power,** along with other nations, so as to make sure he was not a threat to the United States and our friends and allies in the region..."

—George W. Bush,
<u>Jul. 14, 2003, White House
press briefing</u>

"He cautioned that **many in the US did not think it worth going down the ultimatum route."**

"And now they must demonstrate that commitment to peace and security is the only effective way, by supporting the **immediate and unconditional disarmament** of Saddam Hussein.

The dictator of Iraq and **his weapons of mass destruction** are a threat to the security of free nations. He is a **danger to his neighbors.** He's a **sponsor of terrorism.** He's an obstacle to progress in the Middle East."

—George W. Bush,
<u>Mar. 16, 2003, in the Azores</u>

The intentional use of faulty intelligence to substantiate a war

British political theoriest, Glen Rangwala and journalist Raymond Whitaker of the *UK Independent* Newspaper have compiled a list of twenty lies regarding the invasion and occupation of Iraq which may be viewed at:
The URL of this article is: http://globalresearch.ca/articles/RAN307A.html

As if the duplicitous use of intelligence to substantiate the U.S. invasion and occupation of Iraq were not egregious enough, it appears that the Central Intelligence Agency has actually been provoking the terrorist insurgents of Iraq. In a *New York Times Magazine* article, "The Salvadorization Of Iraq", May, 2005, Peter Maas, author of the book *Serpico*, argues that two of the top U.S. military advisers to Iraqi paramilitary commandos fighting the insurgents are veterans of U.S. counterinsurgency operations in Latin America during the Iran-Contra era and that these advisers are actually fanning the fires of insurgency in Iraq as they did in El Salvador in the 1980s.[136] If true, the end result would be a prolonged war which would produce endless casualties and require infinite expenditure of resources.

And who would benefit from such a strategy? Would it not be the same individuals who benefitted from the Vietnam War in which the United States was funding both sides of the conflict? Is this scenario not reminiscent of Smedley Butler's assessment that "war is a racket"?

In October, 2005, the *New York Times* reported that Robert Hanyok, former historian for the National Security Agency had researched the Gulf of Tonkin incident during the Vietnam Era and confirmed that the intelligence on which the U.S. response to a supposed North Vietnamese attack on American naval ships in the Gulf of Tonkin was falsified. Matthew Aid, an independent historian who worked with Hanyok, released the findings in 2005 because he believed that "This material is relevant to debates we as Americans are having about a war in Iraq and intelligence reform." American ships were not attacked in the Gulf of Tonkin, but the Lyndon Johnson administration dishonestly manufactured the incident in 1964 to justify a massive expansion of the Vietnam War.[137]

On March 27, 2006, the *New York Times* published an explosive story, "Bush Was Set On Path To War," which revealed a January 31, 2003 memo in which President Bush, during a White House meeting with British Prime Minister, Tony Blair, made clear to Blair that he was determined to go to war even if the United Nations did not produce a second resolution condemning Iraq and even if weapons of mass destruction were not found in Iraq. *The Times* article also states that, "The memo also shows that the president and the prime minister acknowledged that no unconventional weapons had been found inside Iraq. Faced with the possibility of not finding any before the planned invasion, Mr. Bush talked about several ways to provoke a confrontation, including a proposal to paint a United States surveillance plane in the colors of the United Nations in hopes of drawing fire, or assassinating Mr. Hussein."[138] Does this sound familiar? It should. Is this not reminiscent of the Operation Northwoods ruse discussed above?

While it is true that the United States military and the plethora of of corporations with which it has contracts profit handsomely from the wars in Iraq and Afghanistan, and while the empire that the United States has become intends to dominate the world militarily, politically, and economically, the ultimate motivation for the Administration's intractable foreign policy is not merely insatiable greed and a voracious appetite for power. The ultimate underpinning of U.S. foreign policy at the beginning of the twenty-first century is an unprecedented historical reality and a frightening survival connundrum which in the geostrategy of the current administration "necessitates" global domination. That reality was forecast in the 1950s by a petroleum geologist named M. King Hubbert and has more recently come to be known as Peak Oil.

---

[136] "The Salvadorization of Iraq", Peter Maas, *New York Times Magazine*, May 1, 2005
  (http://www.petermaass.com/core.cfm?p=1&mag=123&magtype=1)
[137] Vietnam Study, Casting Doubts, Remains Secret, http://www.nytimes.com/2005/10/31/politics/31war.html
[138] "Bush Was Set On Path To War," *New York Times*, March 27, 2006.

29

PEAK OIL AND GLOBAL RESOURCE WARS

In order to answer the question of *cui bono*, or "who benefits?", we must address another reality—a reality with which we began this abstract: The end of the age of oil.

What is extremely important to understand about Peak Oil is that due to the neglect of developing nations to address the issue in the twentieth century, the problem has exacerbated to a level of severity that means that:

- No combination of alternative energies can be implemented in time to avoid a global energy crisis.
- Peak Oil will result ultimately in enormous loss of life, skyrocketing food prices, astronomical energy prices, societal chaos and violence.
- Peak Oil cannot, I repeat, cannot be ameliorated until developing nations, particularly the United States, are willing to drastically reduce consumption of all goods and services, not just energy.
- The longer the problem is ignored, the more dire will be its consequences.

Following is an article by author and activst, James Howard Kunstler from his book *The Long Emergency*:

The Long Emergency
By James Howard Kunstler

28 March, 2005

Rolling Stone

A few weeks ago, the price of oil ratcheted above fifty-five dollars a barrel, which is about twenty dollars a barrel more than a year ago. The next day, the oil story was buried on page six of the New York Times business section. Apparently, the price of oil is not considered significant news, even when it goes up five bucks a barrel in the span of ten days. That same day, the stock market shot up more than a hundred points because, CNN said, government data showed no signs of inflation. Note to clueless nation: Call planet Earth.

Carl Jung, one of the fathers of psychology, famously remarked that "people cannot stand too much reality." What you're about to read may challenge your assumptions about the kind of world we live in, and especially the kind of world into which events are propelling us. We are in for a rough ride through uncharted territory.

It has been very hard for Americans—lost in dark raptures of nonstop infotainment, recreational shopping and compulsive motoring—to make sense of the gathering forces that will fundamentally alter the terms of everyday life in our technological society. Even after the terrorist attacks of 9/11, America is still sleepwalking into the future. I call this coming time the Long Emergency.

Most immediately we face the end of the cheap-fossil-fuel era. It is no exaggeration to state that reliable supplies of cheap oil and natural gas underlie everything we identify as the necessities of modern life—not to mention all of its comforts and luxuries: central heating, air conditioning, cars, airplanes, electric lights, inexpensive clothing, recorded music, movies, hip-replacement surgery, national defense—you name it.

The few Americans who are even aware that there is a gathering global-energy predicament usually misunderstand the core of the argument. That argument states that we don't have to run out of oil to start having severe problems with industrial civilization and its dependent systems. We only have to slip over the all-time production peak and begin a slide down the arc of steady depletion.

The term "global oil-production peak" means that a turning point will come when the world produces the most oil it will ever produce in a given year and, after that, yearly production will inexorably decline. It is usually represented graphically in a bell curve. The peak is the top of the curve, the halfway point of the world's all-time total endowment, meaning half the world's oil will be left. That seems like a lot of oil, and it is, but there's a big catch: It's the half that is much more difficult to extract, far more costly to get, of much poorer quality and located mostly in places where the people hate us. A substantial amount of it will never be extracted.

The United States passed its own oil peak—about 11 million barrels a day—in 1970, and since then production has dropped steadily. In 2004 it ran just above 5 million barrels a day (we get a tad more from natural-gas condensates). Yet we consume roughly 20 million barrels a day now. That means we have to import about two-thirds of our oil, and the ratio will continue to worsen.

The U.S. peak in 1970 brought on a portentous change in geoeconomic power. Within a few years, foreign producers, chiefly OPEC, were setting the price of oil, and this in turn led to the oil crises of the 1970s. In response, frantic development of non-OPEC oil, especially the North Sea fields of England and Norway, essentially saved the West's ass for about two decades. Since 1999, these fields have entered depletion. Meanwhile, worldwide discovery of new oil has steadily declined to insignificant levels in 2003 and 2004.

Some "cornucopians" claim that the Earth has something like a creamy nougat center of "abiotic" oil that will naturally replenish the great oil fields of the world. The facts speak differently. There has been no replacement whatsoever of oil already extracted from the fields of America or any other place.

Now we are faced with the global oil-production peak. The best estimates of when this will actually happen have been somewhere between now and 2010. In 2004, however, after demand from burgeoning China and India shot up, and revelations that Shell Oil wildly misstated its reserves, and Saudi Arabia proved incapable of goosing up its production despite promises to do so, the most knowledgeable experts revised their predictions and now concur that 2005 is apt to be the year of all-time global peak production.

It will change everything about how we live.

To aggravate matters, American natural-gas production is also declining, at five percent a year, despite frenetic new drilling, and with the potential of much steeper declines ahead. Because of the oil crises of the 1970s, the nuclear-plant disasters at Three Mile Island and Chernobyl and the acid-rain problem, the U.S. chose to make gas its first choice for electric-power generation. The result was that just about every power plant built after 1980 has to run on gas. Half the homes in America are heated with gas. To further complicate matters, gas isn't easy to import. Here in North America, it is distributed through a vast pipeline network. Gas imported from overseas would have to be compressed at minus-260 degrees Fahrenheit in pressurized tanker ships and unloaded (re-gasified) at special terminals, of which few exist in America. Moreover, the first attempts to site new terminals have met furious opposition because they are such ripe targets for terrorism.

Some other things about the global energy predicament are poorly understood by the public and even our leaders. This is going to be a permanent energy crisis, and these energy problems will synergize with the disruptions of climate change, epidemic disease and population overshoot to produce higher orders of trouble.

We will have to accommodate ourselves to fundamentally changed conditions.

No combination of alternative fuels will allow us to run American life the way we have been used to running it, or even a substantial fraction of it. The wonders of steady technological progress achieved through the reign of cheap oil have lulled us into a kind of Jiminy Cricket syndrome, leading many Americans to believe that anything we wish for hard enough will come true. These days, even people who ought to know better are wishing ardently for a seamless transition from fossil fuels to their putative replacements.

The widely touted "hydrogen economy" is a particularly cruel hoax. We are not going to replace the U.S. automobile and truck fleet with vehicles run on fuel cells. For one thing, the current generation of fuel cells is largely designed to run on hydrogen obtained from natural gas. The other way to get hydrogen in the quantities wished for would be electrolysis of water using power from hundreds of nuclear plants. Apart from the dim prospect of our building that many nuclear plants soon enough, there are also numerous severe problems with hydrogen's nature as an element that present forbidding obstacles to its use as a replacement for oil and gas, especially in storage and transport.

Wishful notions about rescuing our way of life with "renewables" are also unrealistic. Solar-electric systems and wind turbines face not only the enormous problem of scale but the fact that the components require substantial amounts of energy to manufacture and the probability that they can't be manufactured at all without the underlying support platform of a fossil-fuel economy. We will surely use solar and wind technology to generate some electricity for a period ahead but probably at a very local and small scale.

Virtually all "biomass" schemes for using plants to create liquid fuels cannot be scaled up to even a fraction of the level at which things are currently run. What's more, these schemes are predicated on using oil and gas "inputs" (fertilizers, weed-killers) to grow the biomass crops that would be converted into ethanol or bio-diesel fuels. This is a net energy loser—you might as well just burn the inputs and not bother with the biomass products. Proposals to distill trash and waste into oil by means of thermal depolymerization depend on the huge waste stream produced by a cheap oil and gas economy in the first place.

Coal is far less versatile than oil and gas, extant in less abundant supplies than many people assume and fraught with huge ecological drawbacks—as a contributor to greenhouse "global warming" gases and many health and toxicity issues ranging from widespread mercury poisoning to acid rain. You can make synthetic oil from coal, but the only time this was tried on a large scale was by the Nazis under wartime conditions, using impressive amounts of slave labor.

If we wish to keep the lights on in America after 2020, we may indeed have to resort to nuclear power, with all its practical problems and eco-conundrums. Under optimal conditions, it could take ten years to get a new generation of nuclear power plants into operation, and the price may be beyond our means. Uranium is also a resource in finite supply. We are no closer to the more difficult project of atomic fusion, by the way, than we were in the 1970s.

The upshot of all this is that we are entering a historical period of potentially great instability, turbulence and hardship. Obviously, geopolitical maneuvering around the world's richest energy regions has already led to war and promises more international military conflict. Since the Middle East contains two-thirds of the world's remaining oil supplies, the U.S. has attempted desperately to stabilize the region by, in effect, opening a big police station in Iraq. The intent was not just to secure Iraq's oil but to modify and influence the behavior of neighboring states around the Persian Gulf, especially Iran and Saudi Arabia. The results have been far from entirely positive, and our future prospects in that part of the world are not something we can feel altogether confident about.

And then there is the issue of China, which, in 2004, became the world's second-greatest consumer of oil, surpassing Japan. China's surging industrial growth has made it increasingly dependent on the imports we are counting on. If China wanted to, it could easily walk into some of these places—the Middle East, former Soviet republics in central Asia—and extend its hegemony by force. Is America prepared to contest for this oil in an Asian land war with the Chinese army? I doubt it. Nor can the U.S. military occupy regions of the Eastern Hemisphere indefinitely, or hope to secure either the terrain or the oil infrastructure of one distant, unfriendly country after another. A likely scenario is that the U.S. could exhaust and bankrupt itself trying to do this, and be forced to withdraw back into our own hemisphere, having lost access to most of the world's remaining oil in the process.

We know that our national leaders are hardly uninformed about this predicament. President George W. Bush has been briefed on the dangers of the oil-peak situation as long ago as before the 2000 election and repeatedly since then. In March, the Department of Energy released a report that officially acknowledges for the first time that peak oil is for real and states plainly that "the world has never faced a problem like this. Without massive mitigation more than a decade before the fact, the problem will be pervasive and will not be temporary."

Most of all, the Long Emergency will require us to make other arrangements for the way we live in the United States. America is in a special predicament due to a set of unfortunate choices we made as a society in the twentieth century. Perhaps the worst was to let our towns and cities rot away and to replace them with suburbia, which had the additional side effect of trashing a lot of the best farmland in America. Suburbia will come to be regarded as the greatest misallocation of resources in the history of the world. It has a tragic destiny. The psychology of previous investment suggests that we will defend our drive-in utopia long after it has become a terrible liability.

Before long, the suburbs will fail us in practical terms. We made the ongoing development of housing subdivisions, highway strips, fried-food shacks and shopping malls the basis of our economy, and when we have to stop making more of those things, the bottom will fall out.

The circumstances of the Long Emergency will require us to downscale and re-scale virtually everything we do and how we do it, from the kind of communities we physically inhabit to the way we grow our food to the way we work and trade the products of our work. Our lives will become profoundly and intensely local. Daily life will be far less about mobility and much more about staying where you are. Anything organized on the large scale, whether it is government or a corporate business enterprise such as Wal-Mart, will wither as the cheap energy props that support bigness fall away. The turbulence of the Long Emergency will produce a lot of economic losers, and many of these will be members of an angry and aggrieved former middle class.

Food production is going to be an enormous problem in the Long Emergency. As industrial agriculture fails due to a scarcity of oil-and gas-based inputs, we will certainly have to grow more of our food closer to where we live, and do it on a smaller scale. The American economy of the mid-twenty-first century may actually center on agriculture, not information, not high tech, not "services" like real estate sales or hawking cheeseburgers to tourists. Farming. This is no doubt a startling, radical idea, and it raises extremely difficult questions about the reallocation of land and the nature of work. The relentless subdividing of land in the late twentieth century has destroyed the contiguity and integrity of the rural landscape in most places. The process of readjustment is apt to be disorderly and improvisational. Food production will necessarily be much more labor-intensive than it has been for decades. We can anticipate the re-formation of a native-born American farm-laboring class. It will be composed largely of the aforementioned economic losers who had to relinquish their grip on the American dream. These masses of disentitled people may enter into quasi-feudal social relations with those who own land in exchange for food and physical security. But their sense of grievance will remain fresh, and if mistreated they may simply seize that land.

The way that commerce is currently organized in America will not survive far into the Long Emergency. Wal-Mart's "warehouse on wheels" won't be such a bargain in a non-cheap-oil economy. The national chain stores' 12,000-mile manufacturing supply lines could easily be interrupted by military contests over oil and by internal conflict in the nations that have been supplying us with ultra-cheap manufactured goods, because they, too, will be struggling with similar issues of energy famine and all the disorders that go with it.

As these things occur, America will have to make other arrangements for the manufacture, distribution and sale of ordinary goods. They will probably be made on a "cottage industry" basis rather than the factory system we once had, since the scale of available energy will be much lower—and we are not going to replay the twentieth century. Tens of thousands of the common products we enjoy today, from paints to pharmaceuticals, are made out of oil. They will become increasingly scarce or unavailable. The selling of things will have to be reorganized at the local scale. It will have to be based on moving merchandise shorter distances. It is almost certain to result in higher costs for the things we buy and far fewer choices.

The automobile will be a diminished presence in our lives, to say the least. With gasoline in short supply, not to mention tax revenue, our roads will surely suffer. The interstate highway system is more delicate than the public realizes. If the "level of service" (as traffic engineers call it) is not maintained to the highest degree, problems multiply and escalate quickly. The system does not tolerate partial failure. The interstates are either in excellent condition, or they quickly fall apart.

America today has a railroad system that the Bulgarians would be ashamed of. Neither of the two major presidential candidates in 2004 mentioned railroads, but if we don't refurbish our rail system, then there may be no long-range travel or transport of goods at all a few decades from now. The commercial aviation industry, already on its knees financially, is likely to vanish. The sheer cost of maintaining gigantic airports may not justify the operation of a much-reduced air-travel fleet. Railroads are far more energy efficient than cars, trucks or airplanes, and they can be run on anything from wood to electricity. The rail-bed infrastructure is also far more economical to maintain than our highway network.

The successful regions in the twenty-first century will be the ones surrounded by viable farming hinterlands that can reconstitute locally sustainable economies on an armature of civic cohesion. Small towns and smaller cities have better prospects than the big cities, which will probably have to contract substantially. The process will be painful and tumultuous. In many American cities, such as Cleveland, Detroit and St. Louis, that process is already well advanced. Others have further to fall. New York and Chicago face extraordinary difficulties, being oversupplied with gigantic buildings out of scale with the reality of declining energy supplies. Their former agricultural hinterlands have long been paved over. They will be encysted in a surrounding fabric of necrotic suburbia that will only amplify and reinforce the cities' problems. Still, our cities occupy important sites. Some kind of urban entities will exist where they are in the future, but probably not the colossi of twentieth-century industrialism.

Some regions of the country will do better than others in the Long Emergency. The Southwest will suffer in proportion to the degree that it prospered during the cheap-oil blowout of the late twentieth century. I predict that Sunbelt states like Arizona and Nevada will become significantly depopulated, since the region will be short of water as well as gasoline and natural gas. Imagine Phoenix without cheap air conditioning.

I'm not optimistic about the Southeast, either, for different reasons. I think it will be subject to substantial levels of violence as the grievances of the formerly middle class boil over and collide with the delusions of Pentecostal Christian extremism. The latent encoded behavior of Southern culture includes an outsized notion of individualism and the belief that firearms ought to be used in the defense of it. This is a poor recipe for civic cohesion.

The Mountain States and Great Plains will face an array of problems, from poor farming potential to water shortages to population loss. The Pacific Northwest, New England and the Upper Midwest have somewhat better prospects. I regard them as less likely to fall into lawlessness, anarchy or despotism and more likely to salvage the bits and pieces of our best social traditions and keep them in operation at some level.

These are daunting and even dreadful prospects. The Long Emergency is going to be a tremendous trauma for the human race. We will not believe that this is happening to us, that 200 years of modernity can be brought to its knees by a world-wide power shortage. The survivors will have to cultivate a religion of hope—that is, a deep and comprehensive belief that humanity is worth carrying on. If there is any positive side to stark changes coming our way, it may be in the benefits of close communal relations, of having to really work intimately (and physically) with our neighbors, to be part of an enterprise that really matters and to be fully engaged in meaningful social enactments instead of being merely entertained to avoid boredom. Years from now, when we hear singing at all, we will hear ourselves, and we will sing with our whole hearts.

Adapted from The Long Emergency, 2005, by James Howard Kunstler, and reprinted with permission of the publisher, Grove/Atlantic, Inc.

©Copyright Grove/Atlantic, Inc.

FOR ADDITIONAL INFORMATION ON PEAK OIL:
- Matt Savinar Website: http://www.lifeaftertheoilcrash.net
- The Coming Global Oil Crisis: http://www.oilcrisis.com/
- Oil.com: http://www.oil.com/
- From The Wilderness: http://www.fromthewilderness.com
- End Of Suburbia: http://www.endofsuburbia.com/
- Peak Oil: http://peakoil.com/
- Surviving Peak Oil: http://www.survivingpeakoil.com/
- Peak Oil and 9-11: http://www.oilempire.us
- The Post-Carbon Institute: http://www.postcarbon.org/
- PeakOil.org: http://www.peakoil.org/

PEAK OIL AND THE CURRENT ADMINISTRATION

A natural response to "The Long Emergency" article above is to ask whether this current administration is aware of Peak Oil and if so, to find out what it is doing about it. The best answer to this question is the following article by Richard Heinberg from the March 22, 2006 issue of the Energy Bulletin:[139]

Energy Bulletin

George W. Bush and Peak Oil: Beyond Incompetence
By Richard Heinberg

While it would be difficult to create an airtight legal case for impeaching George W. Bush based on his ignoring the very real threat posed by Peak Oil, nevertheless I believe that his actions—and inaction—in this regard constitute dereliction of duty on an unprecedented scale.

It is part of the job of leaders to foresee problems and either steer around them or prepare for them. A head of state is analogous to the captain of a ship, who is responsible not only for keeping his vessel on course but also for avoiding hazards such as storms and icebergs. Some problems are not foreseeable; others are. A ship's captain who loses his vessel to a freak "perfect storm" may be blameless, but one who steers his passenger liner directly into a foggy ice field, having no sonar or radar, is worse than a fool: he is criminally negligent.

The argument I will make, in brief, is this:
- Peak Oil is foreseeable.
- The consequences are also foreseeable and are likely to be ruinous.
- The Bush administration has been repeatedly warned.
- Actions could be taken to reduce the impact, but the longer those actions are delayed, the worse the impact will be.
- The administration, rather than taking steps to mitigate these looming catastrophic impacts, has instead done things that can only worsen them.

Let us go through these points one by one.

I. Is Peak Oil Foreseeable?

Peak Oil—the point at which the rate of global production of petroleum begins its inevitable historic decline—is a subject of growing public interest. The basic concept is derived from experience: during the past century-and-a-half all older oil wells have been observed to peak and decline in output. The same has been noted with entire oilfields, and with the collective oil endowment of whole nations. Indeed, most oil-producing nations have already seen their output enter terminal decline. Few informed observers doubt that the rate of oil production for the world in total will reach a maximum at some point and then slowly wane.

The science of Peak Oil was worked out in the 1950s by veteran geophysicist M. King Hubbert, who successfully used his method to predict the U.S. peak (1970). Declassified CIA documents show that by the late 1970s the Agency was using similar methods to forecast the Soviet Union's oil peak.[1]

We do not know exactly when the global peak will occur, but it will almost certainly happen within the period between now and 2035.

Considering the importance of the peaking event, the range of uncertainty regarding its timing is disturbing. If the peak were to occur within the next five years, our national economy would be unable to adjust quickly enough to avert calamity (as we will discuss below), while a peak 30 years from now would present a much greater opportunity for adaptation.

---

[139] George W. Bush And Peak Oil: Beyond Incompetence, (http://www.energybulletin.net/14102.html)

Though there is continuing controversy over the question of when the peak will happen, there is strong evidence for concluding that it may come sooner rather than later, and that the world may already have entered the peaking period. Signs of a near-term peak include the fact that global rates of oil discovery have been falling since the early 1960s—as has been confirmed by ExxonMobil. Declining discovery rates represent a well-established trend and cannot be said to be the result merely of transient factors. In 2005, according to IHS Energy Inc., a total of 4.5 billion barrels of oil were discovered in new fields, while 30 billion barrels of oil were extracted and used worldwide. Thus, currently only about one barrel of oil is being discovered for every six extracted.[2]

Until now, the global oil industry has been able to replace depleted reserves on a yearly basis, mostly by re-estimating the size of existing fields. The Royal Swedish Academy of Sciences, in a recent publication, "Statements on Energy," describes the situation this way:
> In the last 10—15 years, two-thirds of the increases in reserves of conventional oil have been based on increased estimates of recovery from existing fields and only one-third on discovery of new fields. In this way, a balance has been achieved between growth in reserves and production. This can't continue. 50% of the present oil production comes from giant fields and very few such fields have been found in recent years.[3]

The 100 or so giant and super-giant fields that are collectively responsible for about half of current world production were all discovered in the 1940s, '50s, '60s, and '70s and most are now going into decline. These days, exploration turns up only much smaller fields that deplete relatively quickly.

Chris Skrebowski, editor of *Petroleum Review* and author of the study "Oil Field Megaprojects," notes that "90% of known reserves are in production," and that "as much as 70% of the world's producing oil fields are now in decline" with decline rates averaging between four and six percent per year.[4]

Thus, while the US Department of Energy predicts that world oil production will increase over the next 20 years from 85 million barrels per day (Mb/d) to 120 Mb/d in order to meet anticipated demand, a growing chorus of petroleum geologists and other energy analysts warns that such levels of production will never be seen.

A French report from the Economics, Industry & Finance Ministry, "The Oil Industry 2004," took a careful look at future supply issues, forecasting a possible peak in world production as early as 2013.[5]

Ford Motor Company Executive Vice President Mark Fields, in his keynote address in October, 2005 at the Society of Automotive Engineers' "Global Leadership Conference at the Greenbrier," noted the seven most serious challenges to his industry, one of which was that "oil production is peaking."[6] Volvo motor company has for several years acknowledged in its company literature that a global oil production peak is likely by 2015.[7]

Legendary petroleum geologist T. Boone Pickens, who started his career in the early 1950s as a roughneck in oilfields in Oklahoma and Texas and went on to co-found Mesa Petroleum and Petroleum Exploration, told the 11th National Clean Cities conference in May, 2005 that "Global oil [production] is 84 million barrels [a day]. I don't believe you can get it any more than 84 million barrels....I think they are on decline in the biggest oil fields in the world today and I know what it's like once you turn the corner and start declining, it's a treadmill that you just can't keep up with."[8]

Royal Dutch Shell Chief Executive Jeroen Van Der Veer has said, "My view is that 'easy' oil has probably passed its peak."[9]

J. Robinson West, founder and chairman of PFC Energy, one of Washington's most influential international energy consulting firms, and a former Assistant Secretary of the Interior in the Reagan Administration, predicts that the "tipping point" when global supply of oil ceases to grow could arrive in 2015.[10]

Veteran petroleum geologist Henry Groppe, a Houston-based independent analyst who began his career in 1945 and who is today a consultant to global corporations as well as to nations, said in 2005 that "Total crude oil production may have peaked this year, or perhaps will peak next year."[11]

Matthew Simmons, founder of Simmons & Company International energy investment bank, has been perhaps the most outspoken of oil analysts and investors regarding Peak Oil. A consultant to the Cheney Energy Policy Development Group that met in secret in 2001, he is the author if *Twilight in the Desert: The Coming Saudi Oil Shock and the World Economy* (Wiley, 2005). Simmons has concluded, on the basis of his study of technical papers from the Society of Petroleum Engineers, that Saudi Arabian oil production is close to its maximum, and that world oil production is also therefore close to its peak.

On March 1, 2006 the New York *Times* published an editorial by Robert Semple, Associate Editor of the Editorial Page for the *Times* since 1998, in which he wrote, "The concept of peak oil has not been widely written about. But people are talking about it now. It deserves a careful look—largely because it is almost certainly correct."[12]

In short, the science behind Peak Oil is well established, and, while there is some disagreement about exactly when the global peak will arrive, there can be no excuse at this stage for ignoring the problem.

II. Does the Administration Know About Peak Oil?

The New York *Times* knows about Peak Oil, but does the president? On this point the evidence is conclusive.

First of all, agencies within the government clearly understand the problem, and therefore relevant information must be readily available to the chief executive if he wishes to have it.

Explicit warnings of Peak Oil have started to turn up in official U.S. government literature. For example, a paper prepared for the U.S. Army Corps of Engineers titled "Energy Trends and Implications for U.S. Army Installations" (Sept., 2005) includes the following tidbit:

> The supply of oil will remain fairly stable in the very near term, but oil prices will steadily increase as world production approaches its peak. The doubling of oil prices in the past couple of years is not an anomaly, but a picture of the future. Peak oil is at hand....[13]

Then there is the following from the U.S. Department of Energy, Office of Deputy Assistant Secretary for Petroleum Reserves, Office of Naval Petroleum and Oil Shale Reserves, dated March 2004:

> The disparity between increasing production and declining reserves can have only one outcome: a practical supply limit will be reached and future supply to meet conventional oil demand will not be available. The question is when peak production will occur and what will be its ramifications. Whether the peak occurs sooner or later is a matter of relative urgency....In spite of projections for growth of non-OPEC supply, it appears that non-OPEC and non-Former Soviet Union countries have peaked and are currently declining. The production cycle of countries...and the cumulative quantities produced reasonably follow Hubbert's model....The Nation must start now to respond to peaking global oil production to offset adverse economic and national security impacts.[14]

And then there is the 2005 Report, "Peaking of World Oil Production: Impacts, Mitigation and Risk Management," commissioned by the U.S. Department of Energy, about which we will have more to say below.[15]

If none of this is specific enough (in fairness, we cannot expect George W. Bush to spend his evenings poring over obscure Army Corps of Engineers studies), we have the fact that Representative Roscoe Bartlett, Republican from Maryland's sixth district—who has made many speeches about Peak Oil on the floor of Congress—has spent thirty minutes in private conversation with the president explaining the science of Peak Oil and seeking to convey the enormity of the problem.[16]

But what if Bush wasn't able to understand what Bartlett was telling him? After all, Bartlett has a Ph.D. in physics; perhaps he was using words that were too big, or concepts too abstruse for our president to grasp.

Even if that were the case, we have evidence that Bush's second-in-command, vice president Cheney, understands Peak Oil; given time, Cheney could surely make the concept comprehensible to his superior. In a speech in 1999 (while he was still CEO of Halliburton Corporation, the giant oil services company) to the Petroleum Institute in London, Cheney pointed out that

> By some estimates there will be an average of two per cent annual growth in global oil demand over the years ahead along with conservatively a three per cent natural decline in production from existing reserves. That means by 2010 we will need on the order of an additional fifty million barrels a day.[17]

This is a fair statement of the depletion dilemma: 50 million barrels per day is almost five times the current output of Saudi Arabia.

Finally there is the fact that is that Bush and Cheney are themselves former oilmen: their inside knowledge of the industry should give them enhanced insight into the problem of Peak Oil. Some would say that these officials' former ties to the petroleum industry imply a conflict of interest (they have been accused of giving perks to oil companies, even to Halliburton—perish the thought!). However, some of the most outspoken authorities on Peak Oil are retired petroleum geologists or engineers who have spent decades working for oil companies. Having former industry insiders in public office today could be good, if they used their technical knowledge to benefit the country by warning of the consequences of continued oil dependency. But, as we will see below, there is no evidence that the particular former oilmen currently occupying the highest offices in the land are doing any such thing—at least not genuinely or effectively.

In sum, while it is impossible to say whether Mr. Bush understands Peak Oil, no one could credibly argue that that he simply hasn't heard about it.

III. How Serious Is the Threat?

Addressing this question requires some speculation: the peaking of global oil production is an event that has never occurred before. However, we need not speculate baselessly; for guidance we have a U.S. government-funded study that could hardly be more relevant—"The Peaking of World Oil Production: Impacts, Mitigation and Risk Management," prepared by Science Applications International (SAIC) for the U.S. Department of Energy, released in February 2005. The project leader for the study was Robert L. Hirsch, who has had a distinguished career in formulating energy policy. The report on the study will hereinafter be referred to as "The Hirsch Report."

The first paragraph of the Hirsch Report's Executive Summary states:

> The peaking of world oil production presents the U.S. and the world with an unprecedented risk management problem. As peaking is approached, liquid fuel prices and price volatility will increase dramatically, and, without timely mitigation, the economic, social, and political costs will be unprecedented. Viable mitigation options exist on both the supply and demand sides, but to have substantial impact, they must be initiated more than a decade in advance of peaking.[18]

As the Hirsch Report explains in detail, due to our systemic dependence on oil for transportation, agriculture, and the production of plastics and chemicals, every sector of society will be impacted.

The Hirsch Report effectively undermines the standard free-market argument that oil depletion poses no serious problem, now or later, because as oil becomes scarcer the price will rise until demand is reduced commensurate with supply; meanwhile, higher prices will stimulate more exploration, the development of alternative fuels, and the more efficient use of remaining quantities. While it is true that rising prices will do all of these things, we have no assurance that the effects will be sufficient to avert severe, protracted economic, social, and political disruptions.

First, price increases may or may not stimulate more exploration, or do so sufficiently or productively. During the early 20th century, more exploration resulted in more oil being discovered. However, in recent decades, expanded exploration efforts have turned up fewer and fewer finds. It is difficult to avoid the obvious conclusion that there simply isn't much oil left to discover.

Higher prices for oil will also no doubt spur new investment in alternative fuels. But the time required to produce substantial quantities of alternative fuels will be considerable, given the volume of our national transportation fuel consumption. Moreover the amount of investment required will be immense. And it would be unrealistic to expect most alternatives to fully or even substantially replace oil at any level of investment, and even with decades of effort, given practical, physical constraints to their development.

Higher prices will also no doubt spur efficiency measures, but the most productive of these will likewise require time and investment. For example, raising the fuel efficiency of the U.S. auto fleet would require years for industry retooling and more years for consumers to trade in their current vehicles for more-efficient replacements.

James Schlesinger, who served as CIA director in the Nixon administration, defense secretary in the Nixon and Ford administrations, and energy secretary in the Carter administration, in November, 2005 testimony before the Senate Foreign Relations Committee urged lawmakers to begin preparing for declining oil supplies and increasing prices in the coming decades. "We are faced with the possibility of a major economic shock and the political unrest that would ensue," he said.[19]

Schlesinger was far from overstating the threat. In fact, it would be no exaggeration to view Peak Oil as potentially representing the economic, social, and political impact of a hundred Katrinas. And that impact will not subside in a few days' or years' time: once global oil production has peaked, the energy shortfalls for transportation and agriculture will be ongoing, relentless, and cumulative.

IV. What Should the Administration Be Doing?

Responsible and competent people who have studied the problem of Peak Oil, (including Robert Hirsch and his colleagues) agree that efforts will be needed to create alternative sources of energy, to reduce demand for oil through heightened energy efficiency, and to redesign entire systems (including both cities and the rural agricultural economy) to operate with less petroleum.

The Hirsch Report's methodology involved the examination of three scenarios:

- Scenario I assumed that action is not initiated until peaking occurs.
- Scenario II assumed that action is initiated 10 years before peaking.
- Scenario III assumed action is initiated 20 years before peaking.

In all three scenarios, the Hirsch study assumed a "crash program" scale of effort (that is, all the resources of government and industry are marshalled to the tasks of creating supplies of alternative fuels and reducing demand through efficiency measures). The study found that, due to the time required to start efforts and the scale of mitigation required, Scenario I will result in at least 20 years of fuel shortfalls. With 10 years of preparation, a 10-year shortfall is likely. And with 20 years of advance mitigation effort, there is "the possibility" of averting fuel shortages altogether. The Report also concludes that "Early mitigation will almost certainly be less expensive than delayed mitigation."[20]

In other words, if global Peak Oil is 20 years away or fewer, *or we believe it might be*, then we must begin immediately with a full-scale effort to address the problem.

Most Americans would understandably prefer to solve the dilemma simply by switching to alternative fuels, thus enabling them to maintain their current habits. But, as we have already noted, there are problems with that strategy.

Biofuels (ethanol, wood methanol, and biodiesel) require land area for production and are plagued by the problem of low net-energy yields. According to the calculations of Jeffrey Dukes of the University of Massachusetts, over a hundred tons of ancient plant matter are concentrated in every gallon of gasoline we use today.[21] Granted, modern methods of biofuels production are more efficient than nature's slow means of producing crude oil, but still this analysis should give us pause: trying to replace a substantial fraction of our 20 million barrels per day of national oil consumption with biofuels could potentially overwhelm an agricultural system already destroying topsoil and drawing down ancient aquifers unsustainably.

It is possible to produce liquid transportation fuels from coal and natural gas. However, natural gas is itself a problematic fuel in North America (domestic production peaked in 2001), and coal—a low-quality hydrocarbon—would present a host of environmental and practical quandaries if we tried to increase mining sufficiently to replace a significant proportion of our oil budget. In the end, coal is likewise a depleting fossil fuel: while it is often said that we have hundreds of years' worth of the stuff, that assumes current rates of consumption and ignores variable quality;

assuming dramatic *increases* in consumption (for oil replacement) and taking into account the fact that much coal offers a low energy yield, those centuries shrink to a very few decades.[22]

Which brings us to the strategies of conservation, efficiency, and curtailment. These clearly present the best opportunities, though efforts along these lines will eventually require significant changes in Americans' habits and expectations.

Our automobiles could be made much more fuel-efficient, though this will require government leadership via higher CAFE standards. But over the long term automobiles and trucks simply aren't good options for transportation, given their inherent energy inefficiency. Thus the nation will need a much-expanded freight and passenger rail system. Our cities, most of which have been designed for the automobile, need to be made more neighborhood-oriented and walkable, and provided with light-rail transit systems. Meanwhile agricultural production must be freed, as quickly and completely as possible, from fossil-fuel inputs. All of these efforts will require substantial investment and many years of work.

If, as the Hirsch Report tells us, the market will be incapable of shifting investment incentives quickly enough away from the old oil-based, energy-guzzling energy infrastructure and toward the new alternatives-based, super-efficient one, then government will have to lead the way through a sustained commitment of effort on a wartime scale. The estimated one to three trillion dollars consumed so far in the invasions and occupations of Afghanistan and Iraq, had they been spent instead on domestic energy security, would probably have represented an appropriate level and rate of funds allocation.

V.   What Has the Administration Done?

Before examining what Bush and Cheney have done (and not done), we should in fairness note that previous administrations are far from blameless. During the Clinton—Gore years, imports of oil increased while CAFE standards languished. However, in a court of law the incompetence or even criminality of others is seldom a viable defense for one's own culpable actions.

That said, in light of the threat and the needed effort, what has the current president actually accomplished?

First of all, the administration effectively buried the Hirsch Report. For many months it was available only on a high school web site, then on the Project Censored site; only toward the end of 2005 did it appear on a Department of Energy site. There has been no public mention whatever of the Report by any official in the Executive Branch. Thus the administration has sought not to respond to warnings of approaching crisis, but simply to muffle the warnings.

During the past six years, funding for renewable energy programs and for energy efficiency has not increased substantially. Meanwhile the administration has consistently sought to remove subsidies for the nation's passenger rail system, Amtrak, while continuing to support immense subsidies for highways.

To be sure, Bush has occasionally spoken about the need for an energy policy, as in a speech to the nation in April 2005:

> First, we must better use technology to become better conservers of energy. And secondly, we must find innovative and environmentally sensitive ways to make the most of our existing energy resources, including oil, natural gas, coal and safe, clean nuclear power. Third, we must develop promising new sources of energy, such as hydrogen, ethanol or bio-diesel. Fourth, we must help growing energy consumers overseas, like China and India, apply new technologies to use energy more efficiently and reduce global demand of fossil fuels.[23]

I would disagree with a few of these suggestions, but over all this is not a bad summary of what actually needs to happen. But talk is cheap, and talk that accomplishes next to nothing is, in this situation, a criminally negligent diversion and waste of time. The words just quoted were spoken in the context of the president's promotion of an energy bill that actually did very little except to increase tax breaks to the fossil fuel industry.

In his 2006 State of the Union address, Bush said that the U.S. is "addicted to oil," and put forward the goal of reducing oil imports from the Middle East. The next day his staff backpedaled, saying that this goal was only an "example."[24]

Five years into the Bush administration, the nation is more dependent on imported oil than ever before. It is facing an impending energy crisis that a government-funded study says will be "unprecedented" in scope and consequences. And needed preparation efforts are nowhere to be seen.

* * *

Given all this, how will impeachment help? While it would be justified as a punishment for ineptitude or criminality, impeachment will not materially assist the nation to deal with Peak Oil unless current officials are replaced with ones who understand the problem and who are prepared to implement policies that radically shift America's priorities in terms of energy, transportation, urban infrastructure, and agriculture. Looking out over the current political landscape in Washington, it is difficult to identify who those new officials might be. Nevertheless, it would help the nation to start now with a clean slate, and with a popular mandate for the new team of leaders to move rapidly to achieve energy security.

Notes

1. See discussion of this topic in my book *Powerdown: Options and Actions for a Post Carbon World* (New Society, 2004), pp. 40—41.

2. IHS discovery numbers are proprietary and costly, and so cannot be referenced directly; however this 4.5 billion-barrel figure was confirmed in personal correspondence by Chris Skrebowski, editor of *Petroleum Review*.

3. "Statements on Oil" Royal Swedish Academy of Sciences Energy Committee. (17 Oct. 2005) www.energybulletin.net/9824.html (accessed 17 Jan., 2006)

4. Chris Skrebowski, "Prices Set Firm, Despite Massive New Capacity," *Petroleum Review*, October 2005.

5. news.bbc.co.uk/1/hi/business/4077802.stm (accessed 13 March, 2006)

6. www.greencarcongress.com/2005/10/ford_exec_oil_p.html (accessed 13 March, 2006)

7. www.volvo.com/NR/rdonlyres/A9A59F6A-AA6F-F48E-A048-BF9D6DE505DB/0/future_fuels_large.pdf (accessed 13 March, 2006)

8. Michael DesLauriers, "Famed Oil Tycoon Sounds Off on Peak Oil, *Resource Investor*, 23 June, 2005 www.resourceinvestor.com/pebble.asp?relid=10766 (accessed 13 March, 2006)

9. Jeroen Van Der Veer, "Vision for Meeting Energy Needs Beyond Oil," *Financial Times*, 24 January 2006 news.ft.com/cms/s/fb775ee8-8d0e-11da-9daf-0000779e2340.html (accessed 13 March, 2006)

10. www.nixoncenter.org/Program%2520Briefs/PB2005/Vol11no12GlobalEnergyMarkets.pdf (accessed 13 March, 2006)

11. Michael DesLauriers, "Oil Forecasting Legend Discusses Peak Oil, Share Prices," *Resource Investor*, 19 October, 2005 www.resourceinvestor.com/pebble.asp?relid=13837 (accessed 13 March, 2006)

12. Robert B. Semple, Jr., *The End of Oil*, New York *Times*, 1 March, 2006 select.nytimes.com/2006/03/01/opinion/01talkingpoints.html (accessed 13 March, 2006)

13. Adam Fenderson and Bart Anderson, "US Army: Peak Oil and the Army's Future," *Energy Bulletin* 13 March, 2006 www.energybulletin.net/13737.html (accessed 13 March, 2006)

14. "Strategic Significance of America's Shale Oil Resource," Vol. 1, "Assessment of Strategic Issues," Office of Deputy Assistant Secretary for Petroleum Reserves, Office of Naval Petroleum and Oil Shale Reserves, U.S. Department of Energy, March 2004.

15. Robert L. Hirsch, *et al.*, "The Peaking of World Oil Produciton: Impacts, Mitigation and Risk Management," February 2005. www.projectcensored.org/newsflash/the_hirsch_report.pdf (accessed 13 March, 2006)

16. "Congressman Bartlett Discusses Peak Oil with President Bush," staff, *Energy Bulletin*, 29 June, 2005 www.energybulletin.net/7024.html (accessed 13, March, 2006)

17. www.energybulletin.net/559.html (accessed 13 March, 2006)

18. Hirsch, *op. cit.*

19. www.senate.gov/~foreign/testimony/2005/SchlesingerTestimony051116.pdf (accessed 13 March, 2006)

20. Hirsch, *op. cit.*

21. "Price of Gas," *ScienCentral News,* 28 July, 2005, www.sciencentral.com/articles/view.php3?article_id=218392605&cat=all (accessed 13 March, 2006)

22. Gregson Vaux, "The Peak in US Coal Production," *From the Wilderness,* 27 May, 2004 www.fromthewilderness.com/free/ww3/052504_coal_peak.html (accessed 13 March, 2006)

23. www.whitehouse.gov/news/releases/2005/04/20050428-9.html (accessed 13 March, 2006)

24. www.whitehouse.gov/stateoftheunion/2006/index.html (accessed 13 March, 2006)

---------------- *Editorial Notes* --------------------

This article is the April 2006 edition (#168) of Richard Heinberg's MuseLetter series. For regular editions of the MuseLetter, subscribe at www.museletter.com/subscription.html

Heinberg is the author of two of the most essential books in the Peak Oil canon, The Party's Over and Powerdown as well as a forthcoming small book to introduce the Depletion Protocol to a wide audience.

The Invasion and Occupation of Iraq

The invasion and occupation of Iraq cannot be understood apart from an analysis of Zbigniew Brzezinski's *Grand Chessboard* and the Project For A New American Century's "Rebuilding America's Defenses" document. Furthermore, one must be informed by the reality of Peak Oil in order to fully appreciate the urgency, duplicitousness, and recklessness with which the Bush Administration bulldozed its way into the nation of Iraq in March, 2003. When these pieces of evidence are configured, and when one adds to the equation the enormous profits that the U.S. occupation of Iraq have brought a multitude of American corporations since the invasion, it becomes obvious that a regime that refuses to acknowledge the existence of Peak Oil could not have acted otherwise.

Pratap Chatterjee is program director and managing editor of CorpWatch.org. His 2004 book *Iraq, Inc.: A Profitable Occupation* superbly documents the government contracts made with transnational corporations such as Halliburton, Bechtel, Dyncorp, and Blackwater for their services in Iraq and the enormous profits they are reaping as a result. A www.corpwatch.org review of the book states:

> Chatterjee reveals the systemic failings of Bechtel, DynCorp, Halliburton and other war profiteers to make good to either their paymasters, the American public, or their "clients," the Iraqi public. He describes the insidious daily instances of incompetence, waste, and Iraqi humiliation that have become both the Achilles' heel of U.S. occupation architects and their contractors, as well as the key recruiting tool of the Iraqi resistance. Drawing on insights gained during his time in Washington, DC and Iraq, the author reveals the conflicting strategies of Pentagon and the State Department planners that have drawn thousands of civilians employed by these companies into a bloody no-exit scenario.[140]

Canadian author and UK *Guardian Unlimited* columnist, Naomi Klein, has written extensively about government contractors and the profits they reap in rebuilding the world's war zones. In an April, 2005 *Nation Magazine* article bearing the same title as her recently-published book, "The Rise Of Disaster Capitalism", Klein writes:

> And there is no doubt that there are profits to be made in the reconstruction business. There are massive engineering and supplies contracts ($10 billion to Halliburton in Iraq and Afghanistan alone); "democracy building" has exploded into a $2 billion industry; and times have never been better for public-sector consultants—the private firms that advise governments on selling off their assets, often running government services themselves as subcontractors. (Bearing Point, the favored of these firms in the United

---

[140] Iraq Inc.:A Profitable Occupation, Pratap Chatterjee, (http://corpwatch.org/article.php?id=11583)

States, reported that the revenues for its "public services" division "had quadrupled in just five years," and the profits are huge: $342 million in 2002—a profit margin of 35 percent.)[141]

As Chatterjee and Klein both document, the United States has for decades adhered to a policy of bringing about the decimation of infrastructures of other nations through war and then swiftly sent its government contactors to those very places of devastation to repair and reconstruct them.

Who benefits? Everyone in the United States who has taken for granted the availability of cheap and abundant energy; the oil companies who profit handsomely from having unlimited access to Iraqi oil; government contractors who not only rebuild a devastated Iraq, but provide an infinite variety of services to U.S. and coalition troops in Iraq and will ultimately reap the benefits of the privatization of Iraq's water and electricity; and finally, the neocons who seek to cement the primacy of Israel in the Middle East for generations to come. Moreover, a significant number of the PNAC members and authors of "Rebuilding America's Defenses" themselves have strong ties with Israel, and their involvement with Zionist causes is a matter of public record.

The PNAC document has listed a number of nations considered menacing by its authors. Included in this list are Iraq, Iran, and Syria. Not surprisingly, Iran sits between an occupied Iraq and an occupied Afghanistan with the nation of Syria to the west of Iraq. With the occupations of Iran and Syria, the regional dominance by Israel and the United States would be guaranteed.

War—The "Health" Of the State

As we have discussed above, the United States has a long history of using pretexts for entering wars, financing its own enemies, and employing its intelligence community to ferment existing conflicts in order to perpetuate them.

In *JFK, The CIA, Vietnam, And The Plot To Assassinate John F. Kennedy*, Fletcher Prouty argues that wars will not stop "as long as warfare remains synonymous with nationhood. The elimination of war, in our structured society that is so much dependent upon superstition, implies the inevitable elimination of national sovereignty and the traditional nation-state."[142]

In 1967 the war in Vietnam was escalating, and race riots were breaking out in many major U.S. cities. Popular distrust of the federal government was growing. It was in this context that on October 16 a book appeared titled *Report From Iron Mountain on the Possibility and Desirability of Peace*. It was published by Dial Press, a division of Simon & Schuster. The *Report* has been written off by many individuals as "fiction". I do not consider it so for a number of reasons, not the least of which is that when we examine the rationale and machinations behind much of recent American history, it eerily coincides with the theories expressed in the *Report*.

Leonard C. Lewin, a New York freelance writer, wrote the introduction to the book. He explained that the report had been compiled by 15 experts known as the Special Study Group (SSG) who had been brought together by the U.S. government. The SSG had first met in 1963 at a secret "underground nuclear hideout" called Iron Mountain. They had then held periodic meetings during the next two and a half years to discuss the problems that would confront the United States if it entered into a period of permanent peace. According to Lewin, one of the experts ("John Doe") who was identified as a professor of social science at a 'large Middle Western University,' had decided to release the report to the public.

The report, which is very difficult to obtain, having been out-of-print for several years, states that:

---

[141] "The Rise Of Disaster Capitalism", Naomi Klein, (http://www.thenation.com/doc.mhtml?i=20050502&s=klein)
[142] Prouty, JFK, The CIA, Vietnam, And the Plot To Assassinate John F. Kennedy, pp. 40-41.

> War has provided both ancient and modern societies with a dependable system for stabilizing and controlling national economies. No alternate method of control has yet been tested in a complex modern economy that has shown itself remotely comparable in scope or effectiveness.[143]

Following World War I, journalist and social critic, Randolph Bourne wrote an article entitled, "War Is The Health Of The State." In it, he postulates the notion that modern states utilize war not only to gain territory and resources, but also to galvanize support from their citizens and manipulate them to rally round their nation and flag. Through war, Bourne argues, nations come into their own or rediscover themselves:

> War is the health of the state. It automatically sets in motion throughout society those irresistible forces for uniformity, for passionate cooperation with the Government in coercing into obedience the minority groups and individuals which lack the larger herd sense.[144]

U.S. And Possibly Global Economic Collapse

In a stunning speech before the U.S. House of Representatives in February, 2006, Republican Congressman Ron Paul, of Texas, addressed the issues of: The end of U.S. dollar hegemony or domination of world markets, America's military industrial complex whose sustenance requires perpetual war, and the likelihood of global economic collapse.

Energy Bulletin

Before the U.S. House of Representatives, February, 2006
The End of Dollar Hegemony[145]
By Hon. Ron Paul of Texas

A hundred years ago it was called "dollar diplomacy." After World War II, and especially after the fall of the Soviet Union in 1989, that policy evolved into "dollar hegemony." But after all these many years of great success, our dollar dominance is coming to an end.

It has been said, rightly, that he who holds the gold makes the rules. In earlier times it was readily accepted that fair and honest trade required an exchange for something of real value.

First it was simply barter of goods. Then it was discovered that gold held a universal attraction, and was a convenient substitute for more cumbersome barter transactions. Not only did gold facilitate exchange of goods and services, it served as a store of value for those who wanted to save for a rainy day.

Though money developed naturally in the marketplace, as governments grew in power they assumed monopoly control over money. Sometimes governments succeeded in guaranteeing the quality and purity of gold, but in time governments learned to outspend their revenues. New or higher taxes always incurred the disapproval of the people, so it wasn't long before Kings and Caesars learned how to inflate their currencies by reducing the amount of gold in each coin—always hoping their subjects wouldn't discover the fraud. But the people always did, and they strenuously objected.

---

[143] *Report From Iron Mountain*, Ed. Leonard C. Lewin (http://www.museumofhoaxes.com/iron.html)
[144] "War Is The Health Of The State", Randolph Bourne, 1918 (http://struggle.ws/hist_texts/warhealthstate1918.html)
[145] The End Of Dollar Hegemony, (http://www.house.gov/paul/congrec/congrec2006/cr021506.htm)

This helped pressure leaders to seek more gold by conquering other nations. The people became accustomed to living beyond their means, and enjoyed the circuses and bread. Financing extravagances by conquering foreign lands seemed a logical alternative to working harder and producing more. Besides, conquering nations not only brought home gold, they brought home slaves as well. Taxing the people in conquered territories also provided an incentive to build empires. This system of government worked well for a while, but the moral decline of the people led to an unwillingness to produce for themselves. There was a limit to the number of countries that could be sacked for their wealth, and this always brought empires to an end. When gold no longer could be obtained, their military might crumbled. In those days those who held the gold truly wrote the rules and lived well.

That general rule has held fast throughout the ages. When gold was used, and the rules protected honest commerce, productive nations thrived. Whenever wealthy nations—those with powerful armies and gold—strived only for empire and easy fortunes to support welfare at home, those nations failed.

Today the principles are the same, but the process is quite different. Gold no longer is the currency of the realm; paper is. The truth now is: "He who prints the money makes the rules"—at least for the time being. Although gold is not used, the goals are the same: compel foreign countries to produce and subsidize the country with military superiority and control over the monetary printing presses.

Since printing paper money is nothing short of counterfeiting, the issuer of the international currency must always be the country with the military might to guarantee control over the system. This magnificent scheme seems the perfect system for obtaining perpetual wealth for the country that issues the de facto world currency. The one problem, however, is that such a system destroys the character of the counterfeiting nation's people—just as was the case when gold was the currency and it was obtained by conquering other nations. And this destroys the incentive to save and produce, while encouraging debt and runaway welfare.

The pressure at home to inflate the currency comes from the corporate welfare recipients, as well as those who demand handouts as compensation for their needs and perceived injuries by others. In both cases personal responsibility for one's actions is rejected.

When paper money is rejected, or when gold runs out, wealth and political stability are lost. The country then must go from living beyond its means to living beneath its means, until the economic and political systems adjust to the new rules—rules no longer written by those who ran the now defunct printing press.

"Dollar Diplomacy," a policy instituted by William Howard Taft and his Secretary of State Philander C. Knox, was designed to enhance U.S. commercial investments in Latin America and the Far East. McKinley concocted a war against Spain in 1898, and (Teddy) Roosevelt's corollary to the Monroe Doctrine preceded Taft's aggressive approach to using the U.S. dollar and diplomatic influence to secure U.S. investments abroad. This earned the popular title of "Dollar Diplomacy." The significance of Roosevelt's change was that our intervention now could be justified by the mere "appearance" that a country of interest to us was politically or fiscally vulnerable to European control. Not only did we claim a right, but even an official U.S. government "obligation" to protect our commercial interests from Europeans.

This new policy came on the heels of the "gunboat" diplomacy of the late 19th century, and it meant we could buy influence before resorting to the threat of force. By the time the "dollar diplomacy" of William Howard Taft was clearly articulated, the seeds of American empire were planted. And they were destined to grow in the fertile political soil of a country that lost its love and respect for the republic bequeathed to us by the authors of the Constitution. And indeed they did. It wasn't too long before dollar "diplomacy" became dollar "hegemony" in the second half of the 20th century.

This transition only could have occurred with a dramatic change in monetary policy and the nature of the dollar itself.

Congress created the Federal Reserve System in 1913. Between then and 1971 the principle of sound money was systematically undermined. Between 1913 and 1971, the Federal Reserve found it much easier to expand the money supply at will for financing war or manipulating the economy with little resistance from Congress—while benefiting the special interests that influence government.

Dollar dominance got a huge boost after World War II. We were spared the destruction that so many other nations suffered, and our coffers were filled with the world's gold. But the world chose not to return to the discipline of the gold standard, and the politicians applauded. Printing money to pay the bills was a lot more popular than taxing or restraining unnecessary spending. In spite of the short-term benefits, imbalances were institutionalized for decades to come.

The 1944 Bretton Woods agreement solidified the dollar as the preeminent world reserve currency, replacing the British pound. Due to our political and military muscle, and because we had a huge amount of physical gold, the world readily accepted our dollar (defined as 1/35th of an ounce of gold) as the world's reserve currency. The dollar was said to be "as good as gold," and convertible to all foreign central banks at that rate. For American citizens, however, it remained illegal to own. This was a gold-exchange standard that from inception was doomed to fail.

The U.S. did exactly what many predicted she would do. She printed more dollars for which there was no gold backing. But the world was content to accept those dollars for more than 25 years with little question—until the French and others in the late 1960s demanded we fulfill our promise to pay one ounce of gold for each $35 they delivered to the U.S. Treasury. This resulted in a huge gold drain that brought an end to a very poorly devised pseudo-gold standard.

It all ended on August 15, 1971, when Nixon closed the gold window and refused to pay out any of our remaining 280 million ounces of gold. In essence, we declared our insolvency and everyone recognized some other monetary system had to be devised in order to bring stability to the markets.

Amazingly, a new system was devised which allowed the U.S. to operate the printing presses for the world reserve currency with no restraints placed on it—not even a pretense of gold convertibility, none whatsoever! Though the new policy was even more deeply flawed, it nevertheless opened the door for dollar hegemony to spread.

Realizing the world was embarking on something new and mind boggling, elite money managers, with especially strong support from U.S. authorities, struck an agreement with OPEC to price oil in U.S. dollars exclusively for all worldwide transactions. This gave the dollar a special place among world currencies and in essence "backed" the dollar with oil. In return, the U.S. promised to protect the various oil-rich kingdoms in the Persian Gulf against threat of invasion or domestic coup. This arrangement helped ignite the radical Islamic movement among those who resented our influence in the region. The arrangement gave the dollar artificial strength, with tremendous financial benefits for the United States. It allowed us to export our monetary inflation by buying oil and other goods at a great discount as dollar influence flourished.

This post-Bretton Woods system was much more fragile than the system that existed between 1945 and 1971. Though the dollar/oil arrangement was helpful, it was not nearly as stable as the pseudo gold standard under Bretton Woods. It certainly was less stable than the gold standard of the late 19th century.

During the 1970s the dollar nearly collapsed, as oil prices surged and gold skyrocketed to $800 an ounce. By 1979 interest rates of 21% were required to rescue the system. The pressure on the dollar in the 1970s, in spite of the benefits accrued to it, reflected reckless budget deficits and monetary inflation during the 1960s. The markets were not fooled by LBJ's claim that we could afford both "guns and butter."

Once again the dollar was rescued, and this ushered in the age of true dollar hegemony lasting from the early 1980s to the present. With tremendous cooperation coming from the central banks and international commercial banks, the dollar was accepted as if it were gold.

Fed Chair Alan Greenspan, on several occasions before the House Banking Committee, answered my challenges to him about his previously held favorable views on gold by claiming that he and other central bankers had gotten paper money—i.e. the dollar system—to respond as if it were gold. Each time I strongly disagreed, and pointed out that if they had achieved such a feat they would have defied centuries of economic history regarding the need for money to be something of real value. He smugly and confidently concurred with this.

In recent years central banks and various financial institutions, all with vested interests in maintaining a workable fiat dollar standard, were not secretive about selling and loaning large amounts of gold to the market even while decreasing gold prices raised serious questions about the wisdom of such a policy. They never admitted to gold price fixing, but the evidence is abundant that they believed if the gold price fell it would convey a sense of confidence to the market, confidence that they indeed had achieved amazing success in turning paper into gold.

Increasing gold prices historically are viewed as an indicator of distrust in paper currency. This recent effort was not a whole lot different than the U.S. Treasury selling gold at $35 an ounce in the 1960s, in an attempt to convince the world the dollar was sound and as good as gold. Even during the Depression, one of Roosevelt's first acts was to remove free market gold pricing as an indication of a flawed monetary system by making it illegal for American citizens to own gold. Economic law eventually limited that effort, as it did in the early 1970s when our Treasury and the IMF tried to fix the price of gold by dumping tons into the market to dampen the enthusiasm of those seeking a safe haven for a falling dollar after gold ownership was re-legalized.

Once again the effort between 1980 and 2000 to fool the market as to the true value of the dollar proved unsuccessful. In the past 5 years the dollar has been devalued in terms of gold by more than 50%. You just can't fool all the people all the time, even with the power of the mighty printing press and money creating system of the Federal Reserve.

Even with all the shortcomings of the fiat monetary system, dollar influence thrived. The results seemed beneficial, but gross distortions built into the system remained. And true to form, Washington politicians are only too anxious to solve the problems cropping up with window dressing, while failing to understand and deal with the underlying flawed policy. Protectionism, fixing exchange rates, punitive tariffs, politically motivated sanctions, corporate subsidies, international trade management, price controls, interest rate and wage controls, super-nationalist sentiments, threats of force, and even war are resorted to—all to solve the problems artificially created by deeply flawed monetary and economic systems.

In the short run, the issuer of a fiat reserve currency can accrue great economic benefits. In the long run, it poses a threat to the country issuing the world currency. In this case that's the United States. As long as foreign countries take our dollars in return for real goods, we come out ahead. This is a benefit many in Congress fail to recognize, as they bash China for maintaining a positive trade balance with us. But this leads to a loss of manufacturing jobs to overseas markets, as we become more dependent on others and less self-sufficient. Foreign countries accumulate our dollars due to their high savings rates, and graciously loan them back to us at low interest rates to finance our excessive consumption.

It sounds like a great deal for everyone, except the time will come when our dollars—due to their depreciation—will be received less enthusiastically or even be rejected by foreign countries. That could create a whole new ballgame and force us to pay a price for living beyond our means and our production. The shift in sentiment regarding the dollar has already started, but the worst is yet to come.

The agreement with OPEC in the 1970s to price oil in dollars has provided tremendous artificial strength to the dollar as the preeminent reserve currency. This has created a universal demand for the dollar, and soaks up the huge number of new dollars generated each year. Last year alone M3 increased over $700 billion.

The artificial demand for our dollar, along with our military might, places us in the unique position to "rule" the world without productive work or savings, and without limits on consumer spending or deficits. The problem is, it can't last.

Price inflation is raising its ugly head, and the NASDAQ bubble—generated by easy money—has burst. The housing bubble likewise created is deflating. Gold prices have doubled, and federal spending is out of sight with zero political will to rein it in. The trade deficit last year was over $728 billion. A $2 trillion war is raging, and plans are being laid to expand the war into Iran and possibly Syria. The only restraining force will be the world's rejection of the dollar. It's bound to come and create conditions worse than 1979-1980, which required 21% interest rates to correct. But everything possible will be done to protect the dollar in the meantime. We have a shared interest with those who hold our dollars to keep the whole charade going.

Greenspan, in his first speech after leaving the Fed, said that gold prices were up because of concern about terrorism, and not because of monetary concerns or because he created too many dollars during his tenure. Gold has to be discredited and the dollar propped up. Even when the dollar comes under serious attack by market forces, the central banks and the IMF surely will do everything conceivable to soak up the dollars in hope of restoring stability. Eventually they will fail.

Most importantly, the dollar/oil relationship has to be maintained to keep the dollar as a preeminent currency. Any attack on this relationship will be forcefully challenged—as it already has been.

In November 2000 Saddam Hussein demanded Euros for his oil. His arrogance was a threat to the dollar; his lack of any military might was never a threat. At the first cabinet meeting with the new administration in 2001, as reported by Treasury Secretary Paul O'Neill, the major topic was how we would get rid of Saddam Hussein—though there was no evidence whatsoever he posed a threat to us. This deep concern for Saddam Hussein surprised and shocked O'Neill.

It now is common knowledge that the immediate reaction of the administration after 9/11 revolved around how they could connect Saddam Hussein to the attacks, to justify an invasion and overthrow of his government. Even with no evidence of any connection to 9/11, or evidence of weapons of mass destruction, public and congressional support was generated through distortions and flat out misrepresentation of the facts to justify overthrowing Saddam Hussein.

There was no public talk of removing Saddam Hussein because of his attack on the integrity of the dollar as a reserve currency by selling oil in Euros. Many believe this was the real reason for our obsession with Iraq. I doubt it was the only reason, but it may well have played a significant role in our motivation to wage war. Within a very short period after the military victory, all Iraqi oil sales were carried out in dollars. The Euro was abandoned.

In 2001, Venezuela's ambassador to Russia spoke of Venezuela switching to the Euro for all their oil sales. Within a year there was a coup attempt against Chavez, reportedly with assistance from our CIA.

After these attempts to nudge the Euro toward replacing the dollar as the world's reserve currency were met with resistance, the sharp fall of the dollar against the Euro was reversed. These events may well have played a significant role in maintaining dollar dominance.

It's become clear the U.S. administration was sympathetic to those who plotted the overthrow of Chavez, and was embarrassed by its failure. The fact that Chavez was democratically elected had little influence on which side we supported.

Now, a new attempt is being made against the petrodollar system. Iran, another member of the "axis of evil," has announced her plans to initiate an oil bourse in March of this year. Guess what, the oil sales will be priced Euros, not dollars.

Most Americans forget how our policies have systematically and needlessly antagonized the Iranians over the years. In 1953 the CIA helped overthrow a democratically elected president, Mohammed Mossadeqh, and install the authoritarian Shah, who was friendly to the U.S. The Iranians were still fuming over this when the hostages were seized in 1979. Our alliance with Saddam Hussein in his invasion of Iran in the early 1980s did not help matters, and obviously did not do much for our relationship with Saddam Hussein. The administration announcement in 2001 that Iran was part of the axis of evil didn't do much to improve the diplomatic relationship between our two countries. Recent threats over nuclear power, while ignoring the fact that they are surrounded by countries with nuclear weapons, doesn't seem to register with those who continue to provoke Iran. With what most Muslims perceive as our war against Islam, and this recent history, there's little wonder why Iran might choose to harm America by undermining the dollar. Iran, like Iraq, has zero capability to attack us. But that didn't stop us from turning Saddam Hussein into a modern day Hitler ready to take over the world. Now Iran, especially since she's made plans for pricing oil in Euros, has been on the receiving end of a propaganda war not unlike that waged against Iraq before our invasion.

It's not likely that maintaining dollar supremacy was the only motivating factor for the war against Iraq, nor for agitating against Iran. Though the real reasons for going to war are complex, we now know the reasons given before the war started, like the presence of weapons of mass destruction and Saddam Hussein's connection to 9/11, were false. The dollar's importance is obvious, but this does not diminish the influence of the distinct plans laid out years ago by the neo-conservatives to remake the Middle East. Israel's influence, as well as that of the Christian Zionists, likewise played a role in prosecuting this war. Protecting "our" oil supplies has influenced our Middle East policy for decades.

But the truth is that paying the bills for this aggressive intervention is impossible the old fashioned way, with more taxes, more savings, and more production by the American people. Much of the expense of the Persian Gulf War in 1991 was shouldered by many of our willing allies. That's not so today. Now, more than ever, the dollar hegemony—it's dominance as the world reserve currency—is required to finance our huge war expenditures. This $2 trillion never-ending war must be paid for, one way or another. Dollar hegemony provides the vehicle to do just that.

For the most part the true victims aren't aware of how they pay the bills. The license to create money out of thin air allows the bills to be paid through price inflation. American citizens, as well as average citizens of Japan, China, and other countries suffer from price inflation, which represents the "tax" that pays the bills for our military adventures. That is until the fraud is discovered, and the foreign producers decide not to take dollars nor hold them very long in payment for their goods. Everything possible is done to prevent the fraud of the monetary system from being exposed to the masses who suffer from it. If oil markets replace dollars with Euros, it would in time curtail our ability to continue to print, without restraint, the world's reserve currency.

It is an unbelievable benefit to us to import valuable goods and export depreciating dollars. The exporting countries have become addicted to our purchases for their economic growth. This dependency makes them allies in continuing the fraud, and their participation keeps the dollar's value artificially high. If this system were workable long term, American citizens would never have to work again. We too could enjoy "bread and circuses" just as the Romans did, but their gold finally ran out and the inability of Rome to continue to plunder conquered nations brought an end to her empire.

The same thing will happen to us if we don't change our ways. Though we don't occupy foreign countries to directly plunder, we nevertheless have spread our troops across 130 nations of the world. Our intense effort to spread our power in the oil-rich Middle East is not a coincidence. But unlike the old days, we don't declare direct ownership of the natural resources—we just insist that we can buy what we want and pay for it with our paper money. Any country that challenges our authority does so at great risk.

Once again Congress has bought into the war propaganda against Iran, just as it did against Iraq. Arguments are now made for attacking Iran economically, and militarily if necessary. These arguments are all based on the same false reasons given for the ill-fated and costly occupation of Iraq.

Our whole economic system depends on continuing the current monetary arrangement, which means recycling the dollar is crucial. Currently, we borrow over $700 billion every year from our gracious benefactors, who work hard and take our paper for their goods. Then we borrow all the money we need to secure the empire (DOD budget $450 billion) plus more. The military might we enjoy becomes the "backing" of our currency. There are no other countries that can challenge our military superiority, and therefore they have little choice but to accept the dollars we declare are today's "gold." This is why countries that challenge the system—like Iraq, Iran and Venezuela—become targets of our plans for regime change.

Ironically, dollar superiority depends on our strong military, and our strong military depends on the dollar. As long as foreign recipients take our dollars for real goods and are willing to finance our extravagant consumption and militarism, the status quo will continue regardless of how huge our foreign debt and current account deficit become.

But real threats come from our political adversaries who are incapable of confronting us militarily, yet are not bashful about confronting us economically. That's why we see the new challenge from Iran being taken so seriously. The urgent arguments about Iran posing a military threat to the security of the United States are no more plausible than the false charges levied against Iraq. Yet there is no effort to resist this march to confrontation by those who grandstand for political reasons against the Iraq war.

It seems that the people and Congress are easily persuaded by the jingoism of the preemptive war promoters. It's only after the cost in human life and dollars are tallied up that the people object to unwise militarism.

The strange thing is that the failure in Iraq is now apparent to a large majority of American people, yet they and Congress are acquiescing to the call for a needless and dangerous confrontation with Iran.

But then again, our failure to find Osama bin Laden and destroy his network did not dissuade us from taking on the Iraqis in a war totally unrelated to 9/11.

Concern for pricing oil only in dollars helps explain our willingness to drop everything and teach Saddam Hussein a lesson for his defiance in demanding Euros for oil.

And once again there's this urgent call for sanctions and threats of force against Iran at the precise time Iran is opening a new oil exchange with all transactions in Euros.

Using force to compel people to accept money without real value can only work in the short run. It ultimately leads to economic dislocation, both domestic and international, and always ends with a price to be paid.

The economic law that honest exchange demands only things of real value as currency cannot be repealed. The chaos that one day will ensue from our 35-year experiment with worldwide fiat money will require a return to money of real value. We will know that day is approaching when oil-producing countries demand gold, or its equivalent, for their oil rather than dollars or Euros. The sooner, the better.

CATHERINE AUSTIN FITTS AND OTHERS HAVE WRITTEN EXTENSIVELY OF THE VAST SUMS ($4 TRILLION AT PRESENT) THAT HAVE COME MISSING FROM THE U.S. TREASURY IN THE PAST TWO DECADES. IN THE LIGHT OF THIS ENORMOUS SUM OF VANISHED ASSETS, WE ARE FORCED TO WONDER IF WE ARE WITNESSING ANOTHER MASSIVE TRANSFER OF WEALTH SUCH AS OCCURRED DURING THE GREAT DEPRESSION.

30

ELECTIONS IN THE UNITED STATES

Many Americans who have not researched the 2000 and 2004 elections continue to hold hope that the electoral process in the United States is legitimate, uncorrputed, and functioning effectively enough to offer viable options to the empire that has been constructed by the neo-conservative administration currently in power.

In addition to the compelling evidence for fraud in the 2000 elections, there is even more substantiation for charges of massive fraud in the elections of 2004.
A superb collection of research on the subject can be found at:
 http://www.nov2truth.org/ http://www.tompaine.com/articles/best_of_2004_election_irregularities.php.
http://www.ecotalk.org/VotingSecurity.htm
http://www.blackboxvoting.org/
http://www.freepress.org/departments/display/19/2005/1070

In researching both the 2000 and 2004 elections, I have come to believe that the use of electronic voting machines, with or without paper trails, has eviscerated the integrity of the voting process in America. As long as the three manufacturers of voting machines in the nation, Diebold, Election Systems and Software, and Sequoia are closely linked with any presidential candidate, contributing to that candidate's campaign financially or otherwise; as long as the Secretary of State of any state, such as Katherine Harris in Florida in 2000, is also allowed to be the both the Secretary of State, charged with overseeing the electoral process of that state, and at the same time, chief executive of a presidential campaign, the electoral process will grow increasingly dysfunctional and corrupt.

If this is so, and the preponderance of evidence suggests that it is, then the notion that the United States is a democratic republic, its government abiding by its Constitution and the laws of the Congress and Supreme Court, is now a vaccuous fantasy. In fact, if we return to the political continuum above, it appears that the United States has drifted, and continues to drift, to the right of the continuum, displaying increasingly fascist-like characteristics.

In June, 2006, my article "Godfather Government: The Sopranos Aren't Leaving", was published on the *From The Wilderness* website[146]:

---

[146] (http://www.fromthewilderness.com/members/061206_godfather_government_P.shtml)

GODFATHER GOVERNMENT: THE SOPRANOS AREN'T LEAVING

Don't you get the idea I'm one of those goddam radicals.
Don't get the idea I'm knocking the American system.

Al Capone

Behind every great fortune, there is a crime.

Lucky Luciano

Historians study not only the past but using their analysis of the past, speculate about how the future might unfold. However, historians are not psychics; we can't predict the exact occurrence of events with specificity, but we can analyze past and current events and conjecture likely future scenarios based on those events. In 1937, during the German Third Reich, historian Robert Brady wrote *The Spirit And Structure Of German Fascism*, one of the most incisive books of the twentieth century, now out of print and deemed "irrelevant" to contemporary events by most traditional historians. In his last chapter, "The Looming Shadow Of Fascism Over The World," Brady hypothesized that corporatist influences would ultimately come to dominate many of the governments of the modern world, including and especially, the United States.

Certainly, America's triumphant emergence from World War II and the subsequent institutionalization of the military industrial complex established significant components of incipient fascism, as throughout the Cold War, the Central Intelligence Agency fomented anti-Communist hysteria and right-wing coup d'etats around the world. Meanwhile, at home, McCarthyism gave way to consumerism on steroids and the triumph of the American corporation on all fronts— a feat that had its roots in an obscure Supreme Court technicality in the decision, *Santa Clara vs. Union Pacific Railroad* in 1886, which declared that corporations were "persons" who had the same "civil rights" guaranteed freed slaves under the Fourteenth Amendment.

While most presidential administrations of the twentieth century gave lip service to government regulation of corporations, a new era dawned in the eighties with Reagan's "war on government." It was the beginning of the dismantling of government regulation of industry in America, and it was further exacerbated by a momentous Executive Order signed by Reagan. Executive Order 12615 required departments and agencies to "establish full and ambitious privatization goals." It also created the Office of Privatization within the Office of Management And Budget to oversee the program and established an independent Commission on Privatization to study and recommend opportunities for privatization within the federal government.

According to Chapter 17 of Webster Tarpley's *The Unauthorized Biography of George Bush, Sr.* and the research of Catherine Austin Fitts, Reagan's Executive Order meant that private corporate contractors would no longer have to be accountable for the work they did nor how they used the money allocated to them. As a result, an opportunity for a black budget was created in which government money would be spent without the oversight of Congress and the American people. Clearly, this was a disastrous recipe for fraud and corruption to become standard operating procedure in the federal government.

Concurrently, the CIA was secretly financing the illegal Contra War in Nicaragua with cocaine trafficking, and the Department of Housing and Urban Development (HUD) was operating, a member of Senator Kit Bond's staff told Catherine Austin Fitts, as a criminal enterprise. More recently art has imitated life in a Sopranos episode[147] which mirrored HUD's corrupt activities in South Central Los Angeles—the illumination of which by Fitts contributed to the dirty

---

[147] (http://www.solari.com/learn/articles_risk.htm)

tricks unleashed against her long before the Sopranos became an HBO series. Enter the Democratic Clinton Administration which gave us NAFTA and made U.S. corporations sovereign (See above article on "Sovereign Corporations" by William Greider) domestically and internationally as globalism was born and its proponents championed the demise of nations and the supremacy of corporations. It was during that administration, not a Republican one, that the criminal enterprise we call the federal government came down on Fitts and nearly destroyed her.

But can anyone find a more stellar symbol of corporate dominance than that infamous glass skyscraper in Houston, formerly occupied by the Enron Corporation? Catherine Austin Fitts has superbly connected the dots between the egregious criminality of Enron, the Harvard Endowment, and one of the federal government's principal contractors, Dyncorps[148]. More recently, with the conviction of former Enron golden boys, Jeff Skillings and Ken Lay, investigative journalist, Greg Palast, has unleashed a scathing expose of Enron throughout alternative media[149]. However, I must add one caveat. Palast has recently attempted to debunk Peak Oil and demonstrate the unsoundness of M. King Hubbert's theory—a tangent which has drawn heavy fire from the most hardcore Peak Oil researchers. Hopefully, Palast will stop chasing these windmills and stick with his real forte and claim to fame, racketeering investigations and government corruption.

With the convictions of Lay and Skillings, Palast has seized the opportunity to muckrake enough dirt on Enron to fill its former Houston headquarters from basement to rooftop. So too have Peter Elkind and Bethany Mc Lean in their fabulous 2006 documentary, "The Smartest Guys In The Room"; however, what Palast and the filmmakers both failed to address and what Mike Ruppert covered astutely in *CROSSING THE RUBICON*, was Enron's involvement in moving and laundering massive quantities of drug money through its Enron Online trading company. From the research of Palast, Elkind, and Mc Lean, it is obvious that Enron cooked its books and used the smoke and mirrors of Mark To Market accounting to book profits out of thin air, but none of them can explain where Enron acquired the money to actually run its corporation while selling worthless stock and paving the way to financial oblivion for its investors and employees. The missing link in the Enron story is drug profits, but Mike Ruppert caught that link, as did Catherine Austin Fitts in her many articles revealing the Enron-Harvard-Citibank-Dyncorps connection[150].

To his credit, Palast has also recently nailed Choice Point, an enormous data-gathering empire which helped rig the 2000 election and has more recently been deeply involved in assisting the National Security Agency in spying on innocent American citizens. Calling Choice Point a "private KGB", Palast writes: By 'private KGB,' I mean ChoicePoint, Inc., the Atlanta company that keeps over 16 billion records on Americans which it sells to the FBI, Homeland Security and, through a bit of a slip-up, identity thieves. They are watching you because George and Dick don't have time to track everyone in America (and that would be illegal, to boot), so Choice Point does it. Then turns over the electronic you—cross-matched profiles of voting registration, your DNA info and who knows what else—for a price."[151]

When one thoroughly digests the machinations of corporations like Dyncorps, Enron, and Choice Point, it is axiomatic that whatever we have come to call "the government" is now virtually indistinguishable from private corporations—entities which are in themselves criminal syndicates. As Catherine Austin Fitts for years has taken great pains to point out, when local communities of individuals do not control government databases, mind boggling corruption and exploitation of innocent citizens is inevitable. This is one of the principal arguments for local, not national, solutions; the more centralized systems become, the greater the potential for abuse. Conversely, the more de-centralized systems are, the more illumined and amenable to local monitoring they are likely to be.

---

[148] (http://www.scoop.co.nz/stories/HL0202/S00030.htm)
[149] (http://www.gregpalast.com)
[150] (http://www.solari.com/learn/articles_risk.htm)
[151] (http://www.gregpalast.com/printerfriendly.cfm?artid=503)

From hindsight we now know that 9-11 was not only orchestrated by the U.S. government for the purpose of capturing the last remaining drops of oil on earth, but also as a pretext for sanctioning a pandemic of corruption within the federal government and corporations in the name of "national security." (Below, I will offer a recent, glaring example.) Subsequently, the invasions of Afghanistan and Iraq corporatized those countries to such an extent that it would be more appropriate for them to fly the flags of Halliburton and Bechtel than the colors of their respective nations. Add to this the Bush Administration's admission that billions of dollars designated for the Iraq War cannot be accounted for. Why are we not surprised?

At home in the U.S. the Bush regime muscled through Congress its Medicare Reform Bill and firmly placed American healthcare in the hands of its cronies and lobbyist friends from the pharmaceutical and insurance industries, spiking the costs of prescription medications and health insurance. At the same time, millions of working and middle class individuals who had no health insurance and who were being squeezed to death by the costs of mortgage payments, childcare, and simply putting food on the table in their households, found themselves decimated by medical bills, losing their jobs, or simply getting in over their heads financially with the credit cards they frantically used to "rob Peter and pay Paul." But the Godfather Government saw this coming and found the "losses" incurred by Citibank, Chase, and other cronies of the banking industry intolerable, thereby making certain that the Bankruptcy Reform Act of 2005[152] would sail through Congress with only a whisper of opposition.

The consequences of this legislation will savage the lives of countless middle and working class Americans. In fact, *From The Wilderness* has conjectured that the grinding albatross of personal debt may engender a massive pool of slave laborers in America who see no alternative to "working off their debt", and economist Paul Krugman articulates a similar perspective in his 2005 article, "Debt Peonage"[153]. In any event, the gargantuan amounts of personal and collective debt in the United States will be a pivotal ingredient in the collapse of the nation's economy—a phenomenon impeccably documented by Kevin Phillips in his latest book, *American Theocracy: The Peril And Politics Of Radical Religion, Oil, And Borrowed Money In The Twenty-First Century*.

As I write this article, *Business Week Online* has just reported that George W. Bush on May 5 signed a memo entitled "Assignment Of Function Relating To Granting Of Authority For Issuance Of Certain Directives: Memorandum For The Director Of National Intelligence." In the document, Bush assigned intelligence czar, John Negroponte, the task of waiving Securities and Exchange Commission rules, established in 1934, pertaining to accounting disclosures by publicly-traded companies.[154] As a result of no longer needing to reveal financial information in the name of national security, the cloning of Enron, having been in process for several years, is now complete. Instead of being required to disclose valid accounting *ledgers*, U.S. corporations have now been given *carte blanche* to maintain fiduciary *legerdemain*. I must now ask: How can any sane human being persist in believing that a legitimate government exists in the United States?

But we have a Congress, you may argue. Really? Is that the Congress that passed the Medicare Reform Bill, that passed the Bankruptcy Reform Bill, that rolled over during the confirmation hearings of John Roberts and Samuel Alito? Is that the Congress that just this past week confirmed Spymaster, General Michael Hayden to be the new Director of the Central Intelligence Agency?

And what about all those so-called "liberals" in Congress such as Carl Levin who in a letter to one of his constituents in May, 2006 stated: "One major question I will seek to answer as I consider General Hayden's nomination is whether he will restore analytical independence and objectivity at the CIA and *speak truth to power* [don't ya love it?], or whether he will shape intelligence to support Administration policy and mislead Congress and the American people, as former Director of Central Intelligence Tenet did. Another major question is General Hayden's view on the electronic surveillance of American citizens."

---

152 (http://www.opensecrets.org/payback/issue.asp?issueid=BA3&CongNo=109)
153 (http://www.nytimes.com/2005/03/08/opinion/08krugman.html?ex=1268024400 &en=6d6569e77840a01d&ei=5088)
154 (http://www.businessweek.com/bwdaily/dnflash/may2006/nf20060523_2210.htm?campaign_id=rss_daily.)

Good job, Carl!! So how is it that you assumed the lapdog position on May 26 and voted to confirm Hayden?

How many times has Congress cratered since September 11, 2001? Many more times than I have hours in the day to spend documenting it. In the past six years, we've all asked why. Post-9-11, we attributed Congressional loss of spine to the fear of the administration and political pressure to placate it. What is now being revealed almost daily, however, is the extent to which the tentacles of mobsters like Jack Abramoff and the K Street crowd reach into the halls of Congress. Kit Bond's staffer was wrong only about one thing when he said that HUD was being run as a criminal enterprise: What is left of the entire former government of the United States has been and is still being run as a criminal enterprise.

Perhaps even after all I have written here, you still believe you have a government. Whether you do or not, I'm fairly certain that when you read Catherine Austin Fitts' most recent expose on government-corporate corruption[155], you will no longer entertain the delusion that your so-called government is anything but institutionalized organized crime ensconsed in an empire now teetering on the precipice of collapse. If you can digest that reality and still vote in federal elections, God help you, because you still haven't gotten that what you are voting for are hired liars, mobsters, and murderers.

If you think your "government" is going to do anything to protect and support its citizens in the wake of Peak Oil, economic collapse, global warming, global pandemics, natural disasters, massive food shortages, unprecedented outbreaks of violence and unrest, rates of unemployment that will dwarf those of the Great Depression, debt peonage, rapidly diminishing water supplies and a rotting infrastructure, as well as trainloads of worthless U.S. dollars, then the price you will pay for your ignorance and denial will be horrific. If you want to see what your "government" can do for you, think Katrina. Think the AIDS epidemic of the 1980s in this country when tens of thousands of human beings died while your government stood by and did nothing—and still is.

The only thing the members of your government care about is the colossal transfer of wealth—the financial coup d' etat that is in progress that will devastate you and your family economically and produce unparalleled profits for the gangsters you vote for.

In 1937 Robert Brady called the corporate world view "organized piracy" and asked:

> Is there any fundamental difference in appreciation of human values or in general outlook on life between a stockbroker and a pirate?...What on the open seas is thought of as an outlaw and 'piratical' raid of group on group is in another setting played as a legitimate game in which each man is pitted against every other man for all he can 'get by with' short of a snarl with criminal law.

This is fascism, and your "government" is already there. They tell me that the Sopranos are going away and that the HBO series has bitten the dust. My response is that they *aren't* going away; they're just getting warmed up. Tony, Carmela, Silvio Dante, Bobby Bacala, Uncle Junior, Feech La Manna, Paulie Walnuts, and Dr. Melfi—a cast of thugs and enablers such as these, is the only government you have now or ever will have in the United States of America.

Political scientist, Lawrence Britt, describes fourteen characteristics of fascism, as enumerated below:

---

155 (http://www.dunwalke.com)

The 14 Characteristics of Fascism
by Lawrence Britt
Spring 2003
Free Inquiry magazine[156]

Political scientist Dr. Lawrence Britt recently wrote an article about fascism ("Fascism Anyone?," *Free Inquiry*, Spring 2003, page 20). Studying the fascist regimes of Hitler (Germany), Mussolini (Italy), Franco (Spain), Suharto (Indonesia), and Pinochet (Chile), Dr. Britt found they all had 14 elements in common. He calls these the identifying characteristics of fascism. The excerpt is in accordance with the magazine's policy. (Copyright © 2003 *Free Inquiry magazine*.Reprinted for Fair Use Only)

The 14 characteristics are:

1. **Powerful and Continuing Nationalism**
   Fascist regimes tend to make constant use of patriotic mottos, slogans, symbols, songs, and other paraphernalia. Flags are seen everywhere, as are flag symbols on clothing and in public displays.

2. **Disdain for the Recognition of Human Rights**
   Because of fear of enemies and the need for security, the people in fascist regimes are persuaded that human rights can be ignored in certain cases because of "need." The people tend to look the other way or even approve of torture, summary executions, assassinations, long incarcerations of prisoners, etc.

3. **Identification of Enemies/Scapegoats as a Unifying Cause**
   The people are rallied into a unifying patriotic frenzy over the need to eliminate a perceived common threat or foe: racial, ethnic or religious minorities; liberals; communists; socialists, terrorists, etc.

4. **Supremacy of the Military**
   Even when there are widespread domestic problems, the military is given a disproportionate amount of government funding, and the domestic agenda is neglected. Soldiers and military service are glamorized.

5. **Rampant Sexism**
   The governments of fascist nations tend to be almost exclusively male-dominated. Under fascist regimes, traditional gender roles are made more rigid. Opposition to abortion is high, as is homophobia and anti-gay legislation and national policy.

6. **Controlled Mass Media**
   Sometimes to media is directly controlled by the government, but in other cases, the media is indirectly controlled by government regulation, or sympathetic media spokespeople and executives. Censorship, especially in war time, is very common.

7. **Obsession with National Security**
   Fear is used as a motivational tool by the government over the masses.

---

[156] (http://www.secularhumanism.org/index.php?section=library&page=britt_23_2

8. **Religion and Government are Intertwined**
   Governments in fascist nations tend to use the most common religion in the nation as a tool to manipulate public opinion. Religious rhetoric and terminology is common from government leaders, even when the major tenets of the religion are diametrically opposed to the government's policies or actions.

9. **Corporate Power is Protected**
   The industrial and business aristocracy of a fascist nation often are the ones who put the government leaders into power, creating a mutually beneficial business/government relationship and power elite.

10. **Labor Power is Suppressed**
    Because the organizing power of labor is the only real threat to a fascist government, labor unions are either eliminated entirely, or are severely suppressed.

11. **Disdain for Intellectuals and the Arts**
    Fascist nations tend to promote and tolerate open hostility to higher education, and academia. It is not uncommon for professors and other academics to be censored or even arrested. Free expression in the arts is openly attacked, and governments often refuse to fund the arts.

12. **Obsession with Crime and Punishment**
    Under fascist regimes, the police are given almost limitless power to enforce laws. The people are often willing to overlook police abuses and even forego civil liberties in the name of patriotism. There is often a national police force with virtually unlimited power in fascist nations.

13. **Rampant Cronyism and Corruption**
    Fascist regimes almost always are governed by groups of friends and associates who appoint each other to government positions and use governmental power and authority to protect their friends from accountability. It is not uncommon in fascist regimes for national resources and even treasures to be appropriated or even outright stolen by government leaders.

14. **Fraudulent Elections**
    Sometimes elections in fascist nations are a complete sham. Other times elections are manipulated by smear campaigns against or even assassination of opposition candidates, use of legislation to control voting numbers or political district boundaries, and manipulation of the media. Fascist nations also typically use their judiciaries to manipulate or control elections.

31

DISSENT IN THE UNITED STATES

Dissent is the highest form of patriotism.

-Thomas Jefferson-

Based on the tyrannical behavior of their colonizer, England, our Founding Fathers constructed a Constitution which contained a Bill of Rights guaranteeing that Americans would have the right to speak and write freely their disagreements with the government of the United States. At the outset, the Fathers did not think such a Bill of Rights necessary but were pressured and ultimately convinced by citizens of the colonies to include it.

In the early days of our nation, shortly after the nation's Constitution had been written, the Alien and Sedition Acts were passed which were supposed to protect the nation from "dangerous aliens", but ultimately, they were used by the Federalist party to suppress other political parties.

In this abstract, we have seen that in the late-nineteenth and early twentieth centuries, individuals who expressed dissent were fired from jobs, arrested, deported, beaten, and sometimes killed as a result. In 1917, during World War I, the Espionage Act made it a crime, punishable by a $10,000 fine and 20 years in jail, for a person to convey false reports or false statements with intent to interfere with the operation or success of the military or naval forces of the United States or to promote the success of its enemies. The Sedition Act of 1918 was an amendment to the Espionage Act of 1917 which forbade an American to use "disloyal, profane, scurrilous, or abusive language" about the United States government, flag, or armed forces. The act also allowed the Postmaster General to deny mail delivery to dissenters. This legislation was a forerunner to the repression of the Red-Scare 1920s.

Never in American history, however, have we seen a piece of legislation so antagonistic to the Bill of Rights as the Patriot Act of 2001. Passed in the middle of the night six weeks after September 11, this legislation enervates the Bill of Rights and American civil liberties. Every American should be aware of the law's contents and the fact that the act was signed permanently into law in 2006.

An excellent series of articles on the Patriot Act by attorney Jennifer Van Bergen may be read at: http://www.truthout.org/docs_02/04.02A.JVB.Patriot.htm

What appears most dangerous to American civil liberties is the assumption on which the Patriot Act was formulated and passed, namely, that the government provides human rights. When I ask my students where they received the freedoms they enjoy in the United States, they tend to respond with "from the government" or "from all the wars America has fought." The majority of Americans are ignorant of the position of the Founding Fathers, based on the tradition of English civil liberties argued for during the Enlightenment by thinkers such as Thomas Hobbes, John Locke, and later the French philosopher, Jean Jacques Rousseau, which adamantly proclaimed that human rights are *inalienable*, meaning that they are the birthright of every human being by virtue of simply being alive. The Founding Fathers passionately opposed the notion that any rights could be given to humans by any government.

Alexander Hamilton stated in 1775 that "the sacred rights of mankind are not to be rummaged for among old parchments or musty records. They are written, as with a sunbeam, in the whole volume of human nature, by the hand of the divinity itself, and can never be erased or obscured by mortal power."[157] Yet another Constitutional framer, John Dickinson of Pennsylvania, speaking of "the rights essential to happiness" asserted:

> We claim them from a higher source—from the King of kings, and the Lord of all the earth. They are not annexed to us by parchments and seals. They are created in us by the decrees of Providence, which establish the laws of our nature. They are born with us; exist with us; and cannot be taken from us by any human power without taking our lives. In short, they are founded on the immutable maxims of reason and justice.[158]

However, in the twenty-first century, a "bizarre re-writing of American history", as historian Thom Hartmann names it, adhered to by none other than the Chief Justice of the Supreme Court, Antonin Scalia, proposes a new conservative doctrine called "originalism" which holds that the government gives us rights, and that if rights are not explicitly written into the Constitution, they do not exist.[159] The proponents of this doctrine believe that if citizens want rights such as the right to chose to end a pregnancy, the right to marry someone of the same gender, or the right to die, these rights are invalid unless a law is passed granting such rights. While originalists would theoretically agree that the Bill of Rights is law and guarantees freedoms of speech, religion, press, assembly, and other human rights, their position is an extraordinarily dangerous one for civil liberties because if one asserts that these rights are "given" by the government via the Constitution, then one can also assert that in a time of national emergency, or for some other reason, these rights can be revoked by government. The position of the Constitutional framers, however, is that fundamental human rights can neither be given nor taken away.

In addition to the destruction of individual civil liberties as a result of the Patriot Act, the Supreme Court, on June 24, 2005, ruled on the issue of *eminent domain* which, as stated in the Constitution, gives federal, state, and local governments the right to confiscate private property in order to construct *public* works such as roads, bridges, or power plants. The 2005 ruling, however, states that private corporations can utilize *eminent domain* in order to build big-box stores such as Walmart, Target, shopping malls, or offices complexes.[160] In other words, the rights of those "artificial persons" called corporations patently have precedence over the rights of real persons, not for public good, but for personal profit.

As a result of the Patriot Act and the militarizing of urban police forces, it is now becoming extremely dangerous to engage in public protest in the streets of America. In addition, technology is now available to law enforcement that can severely wound, deafen, and disable protestors.

Diane Cecelia Weber, a Virginia-based writer on law enforcement states that:

---

[157] Levy, Leonard W, Origins Of The Bill Of Rights, New Haven: Yale University Press, 1999, p.250.
[158] Ibid., p. 250.
[159] "Bush & Scalia: You Want Privacy Rights? Pass A Law", Thom Hartmann, *Scoop Media* of New Zealand, (http://www.scoop.co.nz/stories/HL0410/S00154.htm)
[160] "Eminent Domain: A Big-Box Bonanza"? (http://money.cnn.com/2005/06/23/news/fortune500/retail_eminentdomain/index.htm?cnn=yes

> The militarization of law enforcement in America is a deeply disturbing development. Police officers are not supposed to be warriors. The job of a police officer is to keep the peace while adhering to constitutional procedures. Soldiers, on the other hand, consider enemy personnel human targets. Confusing the police function with the military function can lead to dangerous and unintended consequences—such as unnecessary shootings and killings. The proliferation of SWAT teams is particularly worrisome because such units are rarely needed. SWAT teams are created to deal with emergency situations that are beyond the capacity of the ordinary street cop. But, as time passes, inactive SWAT units tend to jettison their original, limited mission for more routine policing activities.[161]

With the cooperation of a corporate-owned news media in America, the prevailing attitude toward dissent equates it with terrorism. But always in critically thinking any issue, we must ask: "Cui bono?" Who benefits? Like the Alien and Sedition Acts of 1789, repression of dissent is being used to champion imperialism, militarism, endless resource wars, and the slightest shred of analysis of or variance with the ideology of the ruling elite in America.

I believe that historians will look back at September 11, 2001 and conclude that on that day, the United States embarked decisively on a path toward fascism that it had begun to follow in the late-nineteenth century when corporations became "persons" and in the 1920s when the permanent symbiosis of government and corporations was sealed.

---

[161] Cato Institute: "The Ominous Growth Of Paramilitarism In American Police Departments" (http://www.tysknews.com/Depts/The_Law/paramilitarism_in_police2.htm)

32

OF NATURE'S WRATH, RACISM, AND RESOURCE WARS

Scientists from around the world are telling us that we have very little time left to address the ecosystem emergency of climate change and that, in fact, we may have passed the point of no return. In a 2005 news story, British journalist, Geoffrey Lean warns of the dire climatic situation facing our planet: (http://www.countercurrents.org/cc-lean240105.htm).

On August 29, 2005, a Category Five hurricane slammed the southern United States, obliterating parts of Southern Mississipi, Alabama, and Louisiana, with the most severe devastation occuring in New Orleans. It was the worst natural disaster in American history, and it came amid the worst hurricane season on record.

Katrina revealed three monumentally important realities. 1) The likelihood that global warming is creating dramatic climate changes around the globe and exacerbating bizarre weather patterns;[162] 2) That oil supply in the Gulf of Mexico region is incredibly fragile and vulnerable to severe weather events;[163] 3) that in the wake of a natural disaster, the United States government and infrastructure are in many cases pathetically unprepared, *and* in coping with such events, people of color are more likely than others to perish, suffer enormous losses to person and property, or be endlessly exploited on a variety of levels.[164] Or as the subtitle of Mike Ruppert's article on the blocking of the Gretna Bridge in New Orleans states, "Racism and Resource Scarcity May Be Siamese Twins in a Post-Petroleum World." In his article, "Hurricane Katrina And Holocaust", author Larry Chin asserts that the behavior of the Bush Administration during the Katrina crisis constituted "criminal negligence at the very least and perhaps much more."[165]

---

[162] Hurricane Katrina And Climate Justice, (http://www.corpwatch.org/article.php?id=12629)
[163] Damaged Gulf Oil Rigs, (http://www.fromthewilderness.com/free/ww3/032006_world_stories.shtml)
[164] Blocking The Gretna Bridge, (http://www.fromthewilderness.com/free/ww3/091505_blocking_gretna.shtml)
[165] Hurricane Katrina And Holocaust, (http://www.onlinejournal.org/Special_Reports/090505Chin/090505chin.html)

33

IS THERE HOPE?

Students and readers of my articles are often exasperated with me because I do not immediately offer "solutions" to the disturbing historical account I have presented in this abstract. I'm fond of reminding them that wanting magic bullet solutions is very American and that life doesn't lend itself to quick fixes, particularly when coping with the gargantuan issues human beings face at the beginning of the twenty-first century.

THE TERMINAL TRIANGLE

As we have seen from the information above, human beings of this century are very likely to encounter a Terminal Triangle of Peak Oil, Climate Change, and Global Economic Collapse. The juxtaposition and convergence of these phenomena are Inexplicably ominous for our planet and its inhabitants—and absolutely unprecedented.

I prefer to address the issue of "solutions" with the following article by me recently published exclusively in *From The Wilderness*:

KILLING HOPE, ENLIVENING OPTIONS

As George W. Bush's poll ratings continue plummeting, as the stench of Washington's cesspool of corruption wafts across the nation, and as one courageous Senator, Russ Feingold, introduced censure of the President, I continue witnessing the clueless political left clutching teddy bears of hope that somehow, some way, the 2008 elections offer the promise of "taking back America", a phrase that I have come to loathe in the last five years, as the nations sinks more blatantly and precariously into the quicksand of fascism. Although I have long ago said my good-byes to "hope", I cautiously embrace options, and in the following essay, I intend to clarify the difference between the two and enumerate a few of the options I have come to believe are available to those who clearly recognize that we are living in a fascist empire locked into the Terminal Triangle of Peak Oil, global climate change, and planetary economic meltdown.

For a number of reasons I perceive hope as detrimental to our sanity and survival. First, I have no interest in "taking back America" because the America to which most left-liberals refer when mouthing this empty slogan is not an America that I want back. I want no part of "lesser evils" and political parties that collude in the demise of the nation, the planet, and its inhabitants. As long as any of us "hopes" for the return of that America, we delude and infantalize ourselves, waiting like toddlers for the appearance of Santa Claus. Tragically, the plump, jolly St. Nicholas the left longs to have back is not a pal, but a predator who delivers economic, environmental, social, and spiritual devastation in packages with more appealing gift-wrap.

Living as I do near the U.S.-Mexican border, I was privileged for some years to teach in Mexico where I learned far more from my students who were university-educated professionals than they could have ever learned from me. They taught me much about their culture and their country's politics. In those days I believed in "lesser-evils" and found it difficult to understand the complete absence of hope among educated Mexicans for political change in their country. While I learned much about the depth of corruption in Mexico, its abject, merciless poverty, and the barbaric lengths to which its corrupt underworld of politicians and narcotraffickers were willing to go to maintain their power, what was most valuable was finally comprehending the attitude of my students toward all this—an attitude which was virtually devoid of hope. While their perspective may be labeled by some as "passive", I witnessed in awe their determination to create options in their personal worlds because they had fully come to understand the futility of trying to alter the big picture. Because they had no illusions, they had no hope, but they did have options.

The ruling elite of the United States and its corporate media in giddy complicity, have created an almost impenetrable illusion that this nation is a polar opposite of Mexico. When I cross the border, get stopped by a Mexican police officer making $300 a month and slip him $10 not to arrest me, confiscate my license, and impound my car, then return to the U.S. and tell my friends about it, heads shake and distressed expressions appear on faces, almost always followed by the words, "Those poor Mexican people; their nation is so corrupt." These days, when trying to explain the depths of corruption in the United States, I'm fond of saying that America is quite simply, Mexico with makeup. When American citizens thoroughly understand that, they will stop "hoping" and have more energy available for creating options. As Catherine Austin Fitts is fond of saying, we spent two years of time and energy trying to get a lesser-evil elected in 2004 when we could have been creating sustainable solutions instead of supporting yet another rigged election.

So when we've "gotten it", what options do we have? Bear with me if some of these suggestions sound too elementary. I'm laying out a process here:

1. First and most fundamental is the willingness to look at how ugly the situation really is. This is not unlike being willing to look at the extent of dysfunction in a family. In the family system, this may begin with feelings of discomfort, followed by thoughts that someone in the family may have a dirty little secret, followed by the awareness that that someone is an addict or alcoholic, followed by the realization that that someone was a child molester, followed by the awareness that that person may have molested many children. The journey from "feelings of discomfort" to the realization that one may have been sexually abused to the realization that it happened many times to oneself and one's siblings is a daunting, painful odyssey of hurt, rage, shame, and a plethora of

other negative emotions. At any time in the process, one may choose to go "thus far and no farther", but then one is confronted with the reality that "thus far" is not the whole truth.

So it has been as I have discussed September 11, 2001 with hundreds of people. Quite often the response is, "I don't *want* to know the whole truth." That is always a prerogative to which one has every right, *and* it must be remembered that if one stops there, the remainder of reality always awaits revelation. Like the full disclosure of ugly secrets in dysfunctional families, owning and assimilating the abhorrent realities of our government is a process that requires a willingness to invest time and energy in developing one's learning curve, not to mention extraordinary courage.

2. One of the most important things that awakened progressives can do is stop fearing and dreading talking about and dealing with money. For decades, I walked around quite pleased with myself because I only had what I needed and recoiled at words like "investment", "abundance", "wealth". More recently, especially through the work of Catherine Austin Fitts. I have come to understand that money, like a hammer, is simply a tool. The tool can be used to drive a nail, or it can be used to bludgeon someone to death.

One of the most important concepts activists need to understand is that money is not the enemy and that people who know a lot about money are not necessarily rich, greedy extortioners. In fact, they are natural allies for economic transformation.

An enormously important piece of this, of course, is eliminating personal debt, particularly in the light of the 2005 Bankruptcy Reform Laws[166]

3. Not only must we move through our fear of the topic of money, we must come to understand how it works in our communities. Until that is changed, the election of politicians to national office is a waste of time and energy because it is nothing more than the re-arrangement of deck chairs on a sinking ship. Again, thanks to the work of Catherine Austin Fitts, this reality has changed my focus and functioning as an activist. All genuine solutions are local. All others are props in the scenario of a crumbling empire.

4. We can continue to research and prepare for the realities of Peak Oil. We know that there is no combination of alternative energies that can be implemented on a national or planetary scale in time to avert a global energy crisis, but there is much we can do locally. Gaining much popularity across the nation is the Local First[167] movement which focuses on purchasing from local businesses first, banking only with local banks, networking with local farmers and food co-ops to create a sustainable food supply as Peak Oil impacts the price of food and other products. A stellar example of this trend is Willits, California whose population is overwhelmingly united in creating a sustainable future for its community. In addition, we can experiment locally with alternative energies and address other resource issues such as water and creating non-genetically modified seed banks.

5. We can invest in precious metals. Not everyone can afford to invest in gold, but almost everyone can invest in silver, and the sooner the better! An excellent source for silver is The Money Changer[168] and for gold, Goldline[169]. During the Great Depression, there were over 200 local currencies in the U.S. Groups working locally on sustainability may also want to explore possible alternative currencies that would be feasible in their places.

---

[166] Bankruptcy Reform, 2005, (http://www.opensecrets.org/payback/issue.asp?issueid=BA3&CongNo=109)
[167] Business Alliance For Local Living Economies, (http://www.livingeconomies.org/)
[168] Franklin Sanders Website, (http://www.the-moneychanger.com/entry.phtml)
[169] Goldline (http://www.goldline.com)

6. Many individuals and families are relocating to areas of the country that are more amenable to building sustainability. There are no ironclad rules about this. Arable land, available firewood and water supply are important, as well as other factors such as severity of seasons and the presence of kindred spirits with whom to build community. In his article and book *The Long Emergency*, James Howard Kuntsler offers some suggestions.

7. Sustainability cannot be created in isolation. Crucial in one's "options portfolio" is a sense of community. In my opinion, having the ideal location is less important than establishing a network of support with others who are journeying on the path of sustainable options.[170] We must also prepare spiritually for the demise of Western civilization as we have known it. Whether or not one has a spiritual path, it is important to be able to make sense of and give meaning to the unprecedented and dizzying changes that the Terminal Triangle will present in the coming years. (Please see my article "Navigating The Collapse Of Civilization: A Spiritual Map"[171]

Paralleling the transformation of the community is the re-making of one's inner world. In fact, one will impact the other as Catherine Austin Fitts explains in her wonderful article "Coming Clean".[172]

Recently a friend remarked that I seem more relaxed and less stressed. I replied that one reason might be that I have stopped trying to change the world and the country and am focusing more on changing myself and my community. Without thinking, the words, "I feel more hopeful than I have felt in years," came out of my mouth. Later as I reflected on my comment I realized that, for me, genuine hope is a byproduct of channeling my energy into sustainability on the local level—a cellular awareness that no government, politician, or political party can or will reverse the unprecedented, catastrophic challenges that human beings have created in the past five hundred years. Only we can do that, place by place, as, in community with each other, we enliven and expand our options.

---

[170] Surviving Peak Oil, (http://www.survivingpeakoil.com/article.php?id=community_survival)
[171] Navigating The Collapse Of Civilization, (http://adaptationzine.com/)
[172] Coming Clean, (www.solari.com)

AMERICA'S BLINDERS AND THE PRICE OF IGNORING HISTORY

Throughout this abstract I have frequently quoted Howard Zinn. I feel it is more than appropriate to conclude with a timely, hard-hitting article by him which exquisitely articulates the most recent example of America's collective disregard of history.

Published on Tuesday, March 21, 2006[173]

America's Blinders

by Howard Zinn

Now that most Americans no longer believe in the war, now that they no longer trust Bush and his Administration, now that the evidence of deception has become overwhelming (so overwhelming that even the major media, always late, have begun to register indignation), we might ask: How come so many people were so easily fooled?

The question is important because it might help us understand why Americans—members of the media as well as the ordinary citizen—rushed to declare their support as the President was sending troops halfway around the world to Iraq.

A small example of the innocence (or obsequiousness, to be more exact) of the press is the way it reacted to Colin Powell's presentation in February 2003 to the Security Council, a month before the invasion, a speech which may have set a record for the number of falsehoods told in one talk. In it, Powell confidently rattled off his "evidence": satellite photographs, audio records, reports from informants, with precise statistics on how many gallons of this and that existed for chemical warfare. The New York Times was breathless with admiration. The Washington Post editorial was titled "Irrefutable" and declared that after Powell's talk "it is hard to imagine how anyone could doubt that Iraq possesses weapons of mass destruction."

It seems to me there are two reasons, which go deep into our national culture, and which help explain the vulnerability of the press and of the citizenry to outrageous lies whose consequences bring death to tens of thousands of people. If we can understand those reasons, we can guard ourselves better against being deceived.

One is in the dimension of time, that is, an absence of historical perspective. The other is in the dimension of space, that is, an inability to think outside the boundaries of nationalism. We are penned in by the arrogant idea that this country is the center of the universe, exceptionally virtuous, admirable, superior.

If we don't know history, then we are ready meat for carnivorous politicians and the intellectuals and journalists who supply the carving knives. I am not speaking of the history we learned in school, a history subservient to our political leaders, from the much-admired Founding Fathers to the Presidents of recent years. I mean a history which is honest about the past. If we don't know that history, then any President can stand up to the battery of microphones, declare that we must go to war, and we will have no basis for challenging him. He will say that the nation is in danger, that democracy and liberty are at stake, and that we must therefore send ships and planes to destroy our new enemy, and we will have no reason to disbelieve him.

But if we know some history, if we know how many times Presidents have made similar declarations to the country, and how they turned out to be lies, we will not be fooled. Although some of us may pride ourselves that we were never fooled, we still might accept as our civic duty the responsibility to buttress our fellow citizens against the mendacity of our high officials.

We would remind whoever we can that President Polk lied to the nation about the reason for going to war with Mexico in 1846. It wasn't that Mexico "shed American blood upon the American soil," but that Polk, and the slave-owning aristocracy, coveted half of Mexico.

---

[173] America's Blinders, (http://progressive.org/mag_zinn0406)

We would point out that President McKinley lied in 1898 about the reason for invading Cuba, saying we wanted to liberate the Cubans from Spanish control, but the truth is that we really wanted Spain out of Cuba so that the island could be open to United Fruit and other American corporations. He also lied about the reasons for our war in the Philippines, claiming we only wanted to "civilize" the Filipinos, while the real reason was to own a valuable piece of real estate in the far Pacific, even if we had to kill hundreds of thousands of Filipinos to accomplish that.

President Woodrow Wilson—so often characterized in our history books as an "idealist"—lied about the reasons for entering the First World War, saying it was a war to "make the world safe for democracy," when it was really a war to make the world safe for the Western imperial powers.

Harry Truman lied when he said the atomic bomb was dropped on Hiroshima because it was "a military target."

Everyone lied about Vietnam—Kennedy about the extent of our involvement, Johnson about the Gulf of Tonkin, Nixon about the secret bombing of Cambodia, all of them claiming it was to keep South Vietnam free of communism, but really wanting to keep South Vietnam as an American outpost at the edge of the Asian continent.

Reagan lied about the invasion of Grenada, claiming falsely that it was a threat to the United States.

The elder Bush lied about the invasion of Panama, leading to the death of thousands of ordinary citizens in that country.

And he lied again about the reason for attacking Iraq in 1991—hardly to defend the integrity of Kuwait (can one imagine Bush heartstricken over Iraq's taking of Kuwait?), rather to assert U.S. power in the oil-rich Middle East.

Given the overwhelming record of lies told to justify wars, how could anyone listening to the younger Bush believe him as he laid out the reasons for invading Iraq? Would we not instinctively rebel against the sacrifice of lives for oil?

A careful reading of history might give us another safeguard against being deceived. It would make clear that there has always been, and is today, a profound conflict of interest between the government and the people of the United States. This thought startles most people, because it goes against everything we have been taught.

We have been led to believe that, from the beginning, as our Founding Fathers put it in the Preamble to the Constitution, it was "we the people" who established the new government after the Revolution. When the eminent historian Charles Beard suggested, a hundred years ago, that the Constitution represented not the working people, not the slaves, but the slaveholders, the merchants, the bondholders, he became the object of an indignant editorial in The New York Times.

Our culture demands, in its very language, that we accept a commonality of interest binding all of us to one another. We mustn't talk about classes. Only Marxists do that, although James Madison, "Father of the Constitution," said, thirty years before Marx was born that there was an inevitable conflict in society between those who had property and those who did not.

Our present leaders are not so candid. They bombard us with phrases like "national interest," "national security," and "national defense" as if all of these concepts applied equally to all of us, colored or white, rich or poor, as if General Motors and Halliburton have the same interests as the rest of us, as if George Bush has the same interest as the young man or woman he sends to war.

Surely, in the history of lies told to the population, this is the biggest lie. In the history of secrets, withheld from the American people, this is the biggest secret: that there are classes with different interests in this country. To ignore that—not to know that the history of our country is a history of slaveowner against slave, landlord against tenant, corporation against worker, rich against poor—is to render us helpless before all the lesser lies told to us by people in power.

If we as citizens start out with an understanding that these people up there—the President, the Congress, the Supreme Court, all those institutions pretending to be "checks and balances"—do not have our interests at heart, we are on a course towards the truth. Not to know that is to make us helpless before determined liars.

The deeply ingrained belief—no, not from birth but from the educational system and from our culture in general—that the United States is an especially virtuous nation makes us especially vulnerable to government deception. It starts early, in the first grade, when we are compelled to "pledge allegiance" (before we even know what that means), forced to proclaim that we are a nation with "liberty and justice for all."

And then come the countless ceremonies, whether at the ballpark or elsewhere, where we are expected to stand and bow our heads during the singing of the "Star-Spangled Banner," announcing that we are "the land of the free and the home of the brave." There is also the unofficial national anthem "God Bless America," and you are looked on with suspicion if you ask why we would expect God to single out this one nation—just 5 percent of the world's population—for his or her blessing.

If your starting point for evaluating the world around you is the firm belief that this nation is somehow endowed by Providence with unique qualities that make it morally superior to every other nation on Earth, then you are not likely to question the President when he says we are sending our troops here or there, or bombing this or that, in order to spread our values—democracy, liberty, and let's not forget free enterprise—to some God-forsaken (literally) place in the world.

It becomes necessary then, if we are going to protect ourselves and our fellow citizens against policies that will be disastrous not only for other people but for Americans too, that we face some facts that disturb the idea of a uniquely virtuous nation.

These facts are embarrassing, but must be faced if we are to be honest. We must face our long history of ethnic cleansing, in which millions of Indians were driven off their land by means of massacres and forced evacuations. And our long history, still not behind us, of slavery, segregation, and racism. We must face our record of imperial conquest, in the Caribbean and in the Pacific, our shameful wars against small countries a tenth our size: Vietnam, Grenada, Panama, Afghanistan, Iraq. And the lingering memory of Hiroshima and Nagasaki. It is not a history of which we can be proud.

Our leaders have taken it for granted, and planted that belief in the minds of many people, that we are entitled, because of our moral superiority, to dominate the world. At the end of World War II, Henry Luce, with an arrogance appropriate to the owner of Time, Life, and Fortune, pronounced this "the American century," saying that victory in the war gave the United States the right "to exert upon the world the full impact of our influence, for such purposes as we see fit and by such means as we see fit."

Both the Republican and Democratic parties have embraced this notion. George Bush, in his Inaugural Address on January 20, 2005, said that spreading liberty around the world was "the calling of our time." Years before that, in 1993, President Bill Clinton, speaking at a West Point commencement, declared: "The values you learned here…will be able to spread throughout this country and throughout the world and give other people the opportunity to live as you have lived, to fulfill your God-given capacities."

What is the idea of our moral superiority based on? Surely not on our behavior toward people in other parts of the world. Is it based on how well people in the United States live? The World Health Organization in 2000 ranked countries in terms of overall health performance, and the United States was thirty-seventh on the list, though it spends more per capita for health care than any other nation. One of five children in this, the richest country in the world, is born in poverty. There are more than forty countries that have better records on infant mortality. Cuba does better. And there is a sure sign of sickness in society when we lead the world in the number of people in prison—more than two million.

A more honest estimate of ourselves as a nation would prepare us all for the next barrage of lies that will accompany the next proposal to inflict our power on some other part of the world. It might also inspire us to create a different history for ourselves, by taking our country away from the liars and killers who govern it, and by rejecting nationalist arrogance, so that we can join the rest of the human race in the common cause of peace and justice.

CONCLUSION

I invite the reader to reflect back to the beginning of the abstract when I suggested viewing "The End of Suburbia" (or "Oil Crash"), and when I stated that the purpose of viewing a documentary on the twenty-first-century issue of Peak Oil was to begin from the current moment and journey back in time, beginning with 1865 America, in order to understand how we have arrived where we now are.

The journey we have taken from 1865 to the present has revealed much human suffering, injustice, and violence. It is difficult to face it honestly and without, in the words of Howard Zinn, "airbrushing history" which, in my opinion, is exactly what many traditional history textbooks and the historians who write them do.

Yet we stand at another crossroads in American history, facing on a variety of levels, the loss of our very way of life, but even more formidably, the likelihood that the human race will destroy the ecosystems, if not its own species. This horrendous possibility compels students to demand that in addition to this dismal scenario, I also provide possible solutions. As mentioned above, I should expect this; it is very American. The way of our culture and our history has been to overcome, invent, improvise, and above all, succeed. Yet, I firmly believe that until we are thoroughly familiar with the problems, we cannot even begin to construct solutions. Although few Americans recognize it, we are at the end of our "this is America, we can do anything" saga. We now face insurmountable challenges to our global survival, and unless we jettison our denial systems and face the consequences of the history we have created, survival will not be possible.

I offer these words from Mike Ruppert at the end of his marvelous book *Crossing The Rubicon: The Decline Of The American Empire At The End Of The Age Of Oil*:

> IF THERE IS ANYTHING THAT I WANT YOU TO UNDERSTAND, IT IS THAT AS A SPECIES AND AS A PLANET WE HAVE REACHED A POINT OF SELF-IMPOSED CRISIS THAT CAN NEITHER BE POSTPONED NOR EVADED. THAT CRISIS AND THE VALUES WITH WHICH IT IS ADDRESSED ARE MATTERS OF LIFE AND DEATH.

One of the salient features of this abstract is that it has not focused on the Founding Fathers or presidents, but on common people, heroes and s/heroes of social justice and human dignity. Throughout the twentieth century, in particular, we have looked to politicians to save us, and sadly, U.S. history as it is traditionally taught, only reinforces this illusion. Again, in the words of Howard Zinn from *The Twentieth Century:*

> All those histories of this country centered on the Founding
> Fathers and the Presidents weigh oppressively on the capacity of the ordinary citizen to act. They suggest that in times of crisis we must look to someone to save us: in the Revolutionary crisis, the Founding Fathers; in the slavery crisis, Lincoln; in the Depression, Roosevelt; in the Vietnam-Watergate crisis, Carter. And that between occasional crises, everything is all right, and it is sufficient for us to be restored to that normal state. They teach us that the supreme act of citizenship is to choose among saviors, by going into a voting booth every four years to choose between two white and well-off Anglo-Saxon males of inoffensive personality and orthodox opinions.

Like the Populists of the late-nineteenth century, like the courageous men and women at Haymarket and Pullman, Scott Nearing, Ida Tarbell, Jane Addams, W.E.B. Dubois, Smedley Butler, Fletcher Prouty, Martin Luther King, Rosa Parks, Robert Kennedy, Daniel Ellsberg, Alfred McCoy, Gary Webb, Peter Brewton, Mike Ruppert, Catherine Austin Fitts, Karen Kwiatkowski, and others whose achievements have or have not been considered in this abstract, we must see our country and our world with new eyes, no longer mindlessly chanting "this is the greatest country in the world", but rather, facing the dark side of our history both past and present, with a firm conviction that no one can save us but ourselves.

Here is my prediction for the New World Order. I don't know when. I don't know where. I don't know how many satellite systems, electromagnetic weapons, subliminal programming broadcasters, computer hackers, bio weapons labs, cocaine plantations and how much environmental destruction they will enlist along the way. I don't know how many patents on fundamental life process that Monsanto will claim sufficient to not let me cough without paying them a fee. I don't know how many people the New World Order will reduce to poverty, assassinate and torture before they fail. I just know that they will fail. Because ultimately large complex systems cannot be held together by greed, technology and fear alone. Suspicion, lawlessness and smallness of mind ultimately cause implosion from within. The thing that will ultimately accelerate their failure is the creation of investment alternatives to govern our global resources on a responsible, wealth creating basis. That is why we can gather significant power for change when we vote with our social affirmation, our time and attention, the currency we use, our bank deposits, our investments and our donations for authentic people and solutions.

~~Catherine Austin Fitts~~

TAKE-HOME EXAM OR ORAL PRESENTATION

At the end of this course, I offer students the opportunity to either write a take-home final exam or give an oral presentation which will require them to synthesize course material and connect the dots from the past to the present. I do not allow some students to give oral presentations and others to write take-home exams, but rather require the entire class to do one or the other depending on the writing levels of students I have in class. My general preference, however, is an oral presentation, which obviously, is easier for the instructor to evaluate.

This assignment allows the student to do his/her own research and: 1) Discover details about particular issues that may not have been covered in class, and 2) Discover for him/herself that what has been presented in class is well-documented and is not mere hearsay. I have found this assignment to be one of the most profound I have ever given. Frequently, it is nothing short of life-changing for the student. Moreover, it is an aspect of the course over which the student has total control.

I divide the class into small groups of 4 or 5 students who will work together on one topic. Each student in the group will decide which aspect of the topic he/she will present, but each student must make his/her own oral presentation. I also allow students to use Power Point presentations if they choose.

If the assignment is in oral presentation form, I require the student to present a detailed outline of the presentation to me before giving the presentation to the class, and I provide students with an outline template since some students may not be familiar with outlining.

**I have done my own research on each of these topics. Some of it is contained in this abstract, and some is not. I have acquired a list of internet links on each topic where in-depth information can be acquired. I encourage the instructor to research each topic for him/herself in order to: 1) Further educate oneself on the issue, and 2) Be able to offer students the best links for their research.

The following topics are the options I offer for oral presentations:

RESEARCH TOPICS

Students are required to use alternative media websites, and may use mainstream websites. The difference between these two are explained clearly in class. The purpose of using alternative sites is to discover information that the student may not be aware of and may never hear from mainstream websites.

Following are the research topics we will cover in the presentations:

- DID THE UNITED STATES GOVERNMENT HAVE FOREKNOWLEDGE OF THE ATTACKS OF SEPTEMBER 11, 2001? MANY PEOPLE WHO HAVE RESEARCHED THE TOPIC BELIEVE THAT THE U.S. GOVERNMENT NOT ONLY HAD ADVANCE KNOWLEDGE OF THE ATTACKS BUT ALSO FACILITATED THEM. IF THE U.S. GOVERNMENT DID FACILITATE THE ATTACKS, WHAT DIFFERENCE DOES THAT MAKE IN TERMS OF U.S. FOREIGN POLICY? WHAT DIFFERENCE WOULD U.S. GOVERNMENT FACILITATION OF THE ATTACKS MAKE IN DOMESTIC POLICY, FOR EXAMPLE, THE CIVIL LIBERTIES OF AMERICAN CITIZENS? WHO MIGHT HAVE BENEFITED FROM THE ATTACKS AND HOW?

- WHAT IS PEAK OIL? HOW IS IT CONNECTED WITH THE SEPTEMBER 11 ATTACKS? HOW IS IT CONNECTED WITH THE INCREASED IMPERIALISM OF THE UNITED STATES SINCE THE YEAR 2000? HOW MIGHT IT AFFECT U.S. FOREIGN POLICY IN THE FUTURE? WHERE IN RECENT U.S. HISTORY (SINCE WORLD WAR II) DID THE UNITED STATES HAVE THE OPPORTUNITY TO ADDRESS PEAK OIL? WHAT DID IT DO INSTEAD? WHY DO YOU THINK IT CHOSE THAT OPTION?

- HAS THE U.S. GOVERNMENT EVER BEEN INVOLVED IN DRUG TRAFFICKING AND MONEY LAUNDERING? IF SO, WHY? WHAT PURPOSE WOULD THAT SERVE? FOR WHAT MIGHT THE PROFITS OF DRUG TRAFFICKING BE USED?

- DO CORPORATIONS RULE THE WORLD? WHAT IS THEIR RELATIONSHIP WITH THE U.S. GOVERNMENT? HOW DO THEY ARM AND PROVIDE SERVICES FOR THE U.S GOVERNMENT? WHAT IS PRIVATIZATION? WHAT EFFECT WILL IT HAVE ON BASIC SERVICES FOR AMERICAN CITIZENS IN THE AREAS OF HEALTH CARE, POVERTY PROGRAMS, NATIONAL PARKS, EDUCATION, BUILDING ROADS AND INFRASTRUCTURE, ETC.?

- WHO CONTROLS THE U.S. MEDIA? IS NEWS MANIPULATED BY POLITICAL AND CORPORATE INTERESTS? WHAT ARE SOME SPECIFIC EXAMPLES? ON THIS QUESTION, ONE COULD EXPLORE SIMILARITIES AND DIFFERENCES BETWEEN THIS PHENOMENON AND "YELLOW JOURNALISM" BEFORE THE SPANISH-AMERICAN WAR.

- MOST AMERICANS BELIEVE THAT THE U.S. GOVERNMENT, UNLIKE THE GOVERNMENT OF MEXICO, IS NOT CORRUPT. DO YOU AGREE OR DISAGREE? WHY? EXPLORE THE REALITY OF $59 MILLION MISSING FROM THE DEPARTMENT OF HOUSING AND URBAN DEVELOPMENT (H.U.D.) AND $1.3 TRILLION MISSING FROM THE PENTAGON.

- DO LEGITIMATE NATIONAL ELECTIONS ANY LONGER EXIST IN AMERICA? ARE CLEAN ELECTIONS POSSIBLE IN THE U.S. IN THE TWENTY-FIRST CENTURY? WHY OR WHY NOT?

GLOSSARY OF TERMS

ANARCHY: Anarchism is a philosophy with many variations, but the central belief is that hierarchy and imposed authority are harmful to human society. It is an anti-capitalist, anti-state movement struggling to maximize true freedom for all people and rejecting all forms of domination. It does not necessarily mean the absence of government or laws since some anarchists favor laws and structure if agreed to by consensus.

CAPITALISM: An economic system in which the means of production and distribution are privately owned. In small business capitalism, a sole proprietor or small group of proprietors invest in and manage a business entity. Generally, that entity serves the interest of the local community and makes a profit at the same time. In corporate capitalism a group of shareholders invest in a corporation and hire a board of directors to manage it. Their highest priority is increasing the value of the corporation's stock and making a profit. Unless regulated, the corporation will ultimately sacrifice the quality of life of its community and its employees in order to increase profits. Unregulated corporate capitalism overwhelmingly gravitates to the right of the political and economic spectrum, behaving in an increasingly fascist manner.

CONSERVATIVISM: A general preference for the existing order of society and an opposition to all efforts to bring about rapid or fundamental change in that order. Conservative ideologies characteristically strive to show that existing economic and political inequalities are well justified and that the existing order is about as close as is practically attainable to an ideal order. Favoring traditional views and values; tending to oppose change.

DEMOCRACY: Government by the people, exercised either directly or through elected representatives; a political or social unit that has such a government; the common people, considered as the primary source of political power; majority rule; the principles of social equality and respect for the individual within a community.

EMPIRE: A political unit having an extensive territory or comprising a number of territories or nations and ruled by a single supreme authority; the territory included in such a unit; imperial or imperialistic sovereignty, domination, or control. An empire always makes war on other nations—*and* on its own citizens.

FASCISM: A system of government marked by centralization of authority under a dictator, stringent socio-economic controls, suppression of the opposition through terror and censorship, and typically a policy of belligerent nationalism and racism. It is an economic system in which private industry controls the means of production, but where the federal government controls who produces what merchandise, what quantities will be produced, and to whom it will be distributed. In general, government and corporations cooperate in their endeavors for the mutual benefit of each. Fascist societies are almost always tightly-controlled dictatorships characterized by racism, sexism, and homophobia.

LIBERALISM: Classical liberalism is a political and economic philosophy, originally founded on the Enlightenment tradition, that tries to circumscribe the limits of political power and to define and support individual rights. Liberals tend to value change and progress over the conservative status quo.

OLIGARCHY/PLUTOCRACY: Any system of government in which virtually all political power is held by a very small number of wealthy but otherwise unmeritorious people who shape public policy primarily to benefit themselves financially through direct subsidies to their agricultural estates or business firms, lucrative government contracts, and protectionist measures aimed at damaging their economic competitors—while displaying little or no concern for the broader interests of the rest of the citizenry. Plutocracy is literally rule by the very wealthy. This author strongly believes that the United States of America in the twenty-first century is indeed a plutocracy.

REPUBLIC: A political system in which the supreme power lies in a body of citizens who can elect people to represent them. The United States is theoretically a democratic (rule by the people) republic (the people elect officials to represent them in government). In general, a republic differs from a democracy in that while a democracy is theoretically based on government by the people, it often does not distinguish *which* people. A republic seeks to guard and protect the rights of individuals and insure that all individuals have equal rights and opportunities.

SOCIALISM: An economic system in which the government owns all means of production and does not allow capitalism or the making of profit from business. Under socialism, the government returns to the manufacturer what he/she needs in order to continue to produce a product. Production, however, is for the benefit of the entire society, and not for the benefit of the individual manufacturer. Corporations do not exist, and business is strictly regulated. In addition, the government provides benefits for citizens such as food supply, health care, housing, education, and sometimes a guaranteed annual income. Typically in a socialist system, tax rates are much higher than in capitalist economies. Proponents of socialism argue that in return for paying much higher taxes, services and resources are also dramatically increased. Some socialist societies have been or are tightly-controlled dictatorships. Most modern socialist societies are not.

POSSIBLE OPPORTUNITIES FOR RE-MAKING OUR WORLD

As I conclude this abstract of U.S. History, 1865 to the present, I notice that throughout the nation and the world, a number of locally-based movements for sustainability and social justice are working hard to transform the madness created by the human race in the past five centuries. What the majority of these movements seem to have in common are:

- An awareness that solutions will not come from the top down, but from the ground up as local neighborhoods (73,000 in the United States) and communities join together to re-make the economic, environmental, political, and spiritual landscape by becoming self-sufficiently sustainable.

- A commitment to consume less and decrease their individual and collective energy footprints on the planet.

- A willingness to develop financial and resource literacy in their communities and to demand financial transparency and sane resource allocation and usage in their places.

- Avoidance of patronizing, being employed by, or supporting corporations or institutions that exploit people or the environment and that are not financially and environmentally accountable.

- A commitment to energize their communities by patronizing local businesses first, entrusting local banks and credit unions, not large corporate branch banks, with their deposits, and a commitment to invest in local endeavors as opposed to publicly-traded transnational corporations.

- A long-term commitment to increasing their individual learning curves by boycotting mainstream media and engaging only with credible, well-documented alternative media. (A list of such resources follows this summary.)

- Unwavering commitment to personal transformation and building community with others. Understanding that navigating the daunting challenges of our planet and our local places cannot be done alone or in isolation.

A FEW ALTERNATIVE MEDIA LINKS

NEWS
From The Wilderness: www.fromthewilderness.com
Antiwar: www.antiwar.com
Center For Research On Globalization: www.globalresearch.ca
Information Clearing House: www.informationclearinghouse.info
Truthout: www.truthout.org
Sam Smith's Progressive Review: www.prorev.com
Raw Story: www.rawstory.com
What Really Happened: www.whatreallyhappened.com
Project For The Old American Century: www.oldamericancentury.org
Arianna Huffington: www.huffingtonpost.com
Op Ed News: www.opednews.com

GOVERNMENT THEFT AND CORRUPTION
Catherine Austin Fitts, Solari: www.solari.com (Click on "Articles")
Dillon Read And The Aristocracy Of Prison Profits: www.dunwalke.com
Where Is The Money?: www.whereisthemoney.org

PEAK OIL
Matt Savinar: www.lifeaftertheoilcrash.net (Best overall site on Peak Oil)
Association For The Study Of Peak Oil: www.peakoil.net
General Website On Peak Oil: www.peakoil.org
The Energy Bulletin: www.energybulletin.net
Surviving Peak Oil: www.survivingpeakoil.com
The Community Solution To Peak Oil: www.communitysolution.org

SUSTAINABILITY
Business Alliance For Local Living Economies: www.livingeconomies.org
New Rules Project: http://www.newrules.org/
E.F. Schumacher Society On Sustainability: http://www.schumachersociety.org/
Adaptationzine: www.adaptationzine.com
Biocycle, Organics And Recycling: http://www.jgpress.com
Organic Consumers Association: http://www.organicconsumers.org/
Global Exchange: (Economic And Environmental Justice):
http://www.globalexchange.org/

Carolyn Baker grew up in the Midwest and resided in Colorado and California for most of her adult life. She holds a Ph.D. in Health and Human Services and a Masters in History. She has worked extensively in non-profit administration and was a psychotherapist in private practice for nearly two decades. In addition, she is the author of *Reclaiming The Dark Feminine: The Price Of Desire* and *The Journey Of Forgiveness: Fulfilling The Healing Process*. For the past eight years, she has been an adjunct professor of history and is currently Managing Editor for From The Wilderness Publications.

978-0-595-39586-6
0-595-39586-4